Embodying Democracy

First published 2002 by
PALGRAVE MACMILLAN
Houndmills, Basingstoke, Hampshire RG21 6XS and
175 Fifth Avenue, New York, N.Y. 10010
Companies and representatives throughout the world

PALGRAVE MACMILLAN is the global academic imprint of the Palgrave Macmillan division of St. Martin's Press, LLC and of Palgrave Macmillan Ltd. Macmillan® is a registered trademark in the United States, United Kingdom and other countries. Palgrave is a registered trademark in the European Union and other countries.

ISBN 0–333–99360–8

This book is printed on paper suitable for recycling and made from fully managed and sustained forest sources.

A catalogue record for this book is available from the British Library.

Library of Congress Cataloging-in-Publication Data

Embodying democracy : electoral system design in post-Communist Europe / Sarah Birch ... [et al.].
        p. cm. — (One Europe or several?)
        Includes bibliographical references and index.
        ISBN 0–333–99360–8 (cloth)
        1. Elections—Europe, Eastern—Case studies. 2. Europe, Eastern—Politics and government—1989—Case studies. 3. Representative government and representation—Europe, Eastern—Case studies. I. Birch, Sarah, 1963– II. Series.
JN96.A95 E5453 2002
324.6'3'0943—dc21   2002074843

10   9   8   7   6   5   4   3   2   1
11   10   09   08   07   06   05   04   03   02

Printed and bound in Great Britain by
Antony Rowe Ltd, Chippenham and Eastbourne

Contents

List of Tables   vii

List of Party Acronyms   viii

Preface   xi

1 Explaining the Design and Redesign of Electoral Systems   1
Elections under communism   3
The distinguishing characteristics of
   post-communist electoral reform   7
How electoral systems are shaped   9
Expectations and chapter plan   22

2 Poland: Experimenting with the Electoral System   25
The impetus to electoral reform   26
The process of change   34
Conclusion   45

3 Hungary: the Politics of Negotiated Design   48
The origins of the origins   49
The negotiating parties   51
The Round Table negotiations   54
The law   60
The aftermath   61
Assessing the outcome   63
The incentive system of the Hungarian law   64
Conclusion   65

**4 The Czech and Slovak Republics: the Surprising
Resilience of Proportional Representation**   67
Initial choice of electoral regime   68
The unintended consequences of the pursuit of
   stable government   75
Explaining electoral reform in the successor states   86
Conclusions   88

5 Romania: Stability without Consensus   90
Provisional institutions and the first
   post-communist electoral law   91

The 1992 electoral legislation and the 1992 elections   96
Reform proposals after 1996   101
Conclusion   105

**6   Bulgaria: Engineering Legitimacy through
Electoral System Design**   109
Bulgaria's electoral history   111
The Round Table talks and the electoral law for
  the Grand National (Constituent) Assembly, 1990   113
The parliamentary electoral law of 1991   119
Post-1991 changes to the electoral law   123
Conclusion   125

7   Russia: the Limits of Electoral Engineering   128
Late Soviet electoral liberalization: 1989–90   128
The 1993 electoral decree   132
The 1995 electoral law   137
The electoral law in the context of 'managed democracy'   140
Conclusion   141

8   Ukraine: the Struggle for Democratic Change   143
The pre-independence period: elections before
  multi-party competition   145
Electoral reform in the wake of independence,
  1992–3: parties versus the 'party of power'   146
  1994–8: the drive to institutionalize political parties 152
  1998–2001: parties versus the president   158
Conclusion   162

9   Conclusion: Embodying Democracy   164
Characterizing the process of post-communist
  electoral reform   166
Explaining reform outcomes   178
Accounting for variations   182
Conclusion   187

Notes   189

Bibliography   221

Glossary   234

Index   237

List of Tables

2.1 Main changes in the law on elections to the Polish Sejm   27
2.2 Party representation in the Sejm, 1993   31
2.3 Successful contenders in elections to the Sejm,
     25 September 1997   32
2.4 Major party positions in March 1993   40
2.5 Selected votes on third reading amendments, 1993   41
2.6 Proposals for electoral system change in Poland, 1999   42
4.1 Summary of Czechoslovak electoral laws   72
4.2 Wasted votes and deviation from proportionality in the
     Czechoslovak 1990 and 1992 elections   74
4.3 Summary of Slovak electoral laws   79
4.4 Allocations of seats according to formula,
     using the 1998 vote   82
4.5 How poll ratings would have translated into seats
     under the new Czech electoral system had an
     election been held in June 2000   83
4.6 Summary of Czech electoral laws   85
5.1 Main changes in the rules on elections to the
     Romanian Chamber of Deputies   90
6.1 Main changes in the laws on elections to
     Bulgarian legislative assemblies   110
8.1 Main changes in the law on elections to the
     Verkhovna Rada   144
9.1 Electoral laws in post-communist Europe:
     patterns in variation among regions and over time   165
9.2 Nomination requirements: variations over time   179
9.3 Constituency design and seat allocation formulae:
     variations over time   181

List of Party Acronyms

AWS	Solidarity Election Action (*Akcja Wyborcza Solidarność*)
AWS-RS	Solidarity Election Action – Social Movement (*Akcja Wyborcza Solidarność – Ruch Społeczny*)
BBWR	Non-Party Reform Bloc (*Bezpartyjny Blok Wspierania Rządem*)
BCP	Bulgarian Communist Party (*Bulgarska Komunisticheska Partiya*)
BSP	Bulgarian Socialist Party (*Bulgarska Sotsialisticheska Partiya*)
CD	Christian Democracy (*Chrześcijańska Demokracja*)
CDR	Romanian Democratic Convention (*Convenţia Democrată Română*)
CFSN	Council of the National Salvation Front (*Consiliul Frontului Salvării Naţionale*)
DPS	Movement for Rights and Freedoms (*Dvizhenie za Prava i Svobodi*)
FDSN	Democratic Front of National Salvation (*Frontul Democrat al Salvării Naţionale*), renamed PDSR in July 1993
FIDESZ	Federation of Young Democrats (*Fiatal Demokraták Szövetsége*)
Fidesz-MPP [ex-FIDESZ]	Fidesz-Hungarian Civic Party (*Fidesz – Magyar Polgári Párt*)
FKgP	Independent Smallholders Party (*Független Kisgazda-, Földmunkás-és Polgári Párt*)
FSN	National Salvation Front (*Frontul Salvării Naţionale*)
HZDS	Movement for a Democratic Slovakia (*Hnutie za demokratické Slovensko*)
KDNP	Christian Democratic Party (*Kereszténydemokrata Néppárt*)
KLD	Liberal Democratic Congress (*Kongres Liberalno-Demokratyczny*)
KP	Polish Convention (*Konwencja Polska*)
KPN	Confederation for Independent Poland (*Konfederacja Polski Niepodległej*)
KPRF	Communist Party of the Russian Federation (*Kommunisticheskaya partiya Rossiiskoi Federatsii*)
MDF	Hungarian Democratic Forum (*Magyar Demokrata Fórum*)

MN	German Minority (*Mniejszość Niemiecka*)
MSzMP	Hungarian Socialist Workers' Party (*Mágyar Szocialista Munkáspárt*)
MSzP	Hungarian Socialist Party (*Magyar Szocialista Párt*)
NDP	Popular Democratic Party (*Narodno-demokratychna partiya Ukraïny*)
ODS	Civic Democratic Party – Christian Democratic Party (*Občanská demokratická strana*)
OKP	Citizens' Parliamentary Club (*Obywatelski Klub Parlamentarny*)
PC	Centre Alliance (*Porozumienie Centrum*)
PChD	Christian Democracy (*Partia Chrześcijańskiej Demokracji*)
PD	Democratic Party (formerly FSN, FSN-Roman) (*Partidul Democrat*)
PDAR	Democratic Agrarian Party of Romania (*Partidul Democrat Agrar din Romania*)
PDSR	Party of Social Democracy of Romania (*Partidul Democratiei Sociale din Romania*), formerly FDSN, since 2001 PSD
PDVU	Party of Democratic Rebirth of Ukraine (*Partiya demokratych-noho vidrodzhennya Ukraïny*)
PKLD	Parliamentary Club of the Democratic Left (*Parlamentarny Klub Lewicy Demokratycznej*)
PL	Peasant Alliance (*Porozumienie Ludowe*)
PNL	National Liberal Party (*Partidul Naţional Liberal*)
PNŢCD	National Peasant Party – Christian Democrat (*Partidul Naţional Ţărănesc-Creştin Democrat*)
PO	Civic Platform (*Platforma Obywatelska*)
PSD	Social Democratic Party (*Partidul Social Democrat*), formerly PDSR
PSL	Polish Peasant Party (*Polskie Stronnictwo Ludowe*)
PUNR	Party of Romanian National Unity (*Partidul Unităţii Naţionale Române*)
PZPR	Polish United Workers' Party (the Communist Party) (*Polska Zjednoczona Partia Robotnicza*)
RdR	Movement for the Republic (*Ruch Odbudowy Polski*)
Rukh	Popular Movement of Ukraine (*Narodnyi Rukh Ukraïny*)
SDK	Slovak Democratic Coalition (*Slovenská demokratická koalícia*)
SdRP	Social Democracy of the Republic of Poland (*Socjalno-demokracja Rzeczypospolitej Polskiej*)
SDS	Union of Democratic Forces (*Suyuz na Demokratichniti Sili*)
SKL	Conservative-People's Party (*Stronnictwo Konserwatywno-Ludowe*)

SKL (AWS)	Conservative-People's Party – Solidarity Election Action (*Stronnictwo Konserwatywno-Ludowe – Akcja Wyborcza Solidarność*)
SLD	Alliance of the Democratic Left (*Sojusz Lewicy Demokratycznej*)
SNS	The Slovak National Party (*Slovenská národná strana*)
SO	Self-Defence (*Samo-Obrona*)
SP	Labour Solidarity (*Solidarność Pracy*)
SzDSz	Alliance of Free Democrats (*Szabad Demokraták Szövetsége*)
UD	Democratic Union (*Unia Demokratyczna*)
UDMR	Democratic Union of Hungarians in Romania (*Uniunea Democrata Maghiară din Romania*)
UPR	Union of Political Realism (*Unia Polityki Realnej*)
UW	Freedom Union (*Unia Wolności*)
ZChN	Christian National Union (*Zjednoczenie Chrześcijańsko-Narodowe*)
ZRS	Association of Workers of Slovakia (*Združenie robotníkov Slovenska*)

Preface

The embodiment of democratic principles in practical rules for choosing representatives was a key aspect of the transitions that remodelled Europe in the last years of the twentieth century. The mechanism through which representatives are elected is an important determinant of any state's political system. But the significance of this factor was magnified during the collapse of communism due to the prominent lack of effective representation in the old regime. Thus while opposition to communism focused first on dismantling the old governing institutions, it was not long before the urgent need for their replacement became apparent, requiring the advocates of democracy to consider just how the will of the people was to be captured and translated into functioning decision-making bodies. There followed a complex process of institutional design and redesign which resulted in a variety of different electoral laws.

The study of electoral systems was long dominated by efforts to trace their effects, to the detriment of their causes. There were few general theories of electoral system design. Recently, however, attention has increasingly focused on the topic. This can be traced to three factors: firstly, an increase in the concern of political scientists with explaining institutional design in general; secondly, interest sparked by the spate of recent reforms in established democracies as diverse as New Zealand, Japan and Italy; and thirdly, the extensive electoral system change accompanying the post-1989 wave of democratization in Central and Eastern Europe and sub-Saharan Africa. Though this study does not aim to elaborate a general theory of either the process of designing electoral institutions or of the outcome of that process, it does seek to provide an explanation of electoral system design in eight post-communist states during the first decade of transition, in the hopes that such explanation will contribute to more general understandings of institutional choice in transition societies.

In particular, the aim of this volume is to explore the multiple factors that shaped the parliamentary electoral laws adopted in the first decade of post-communist transition. A companion volume will analyse the effects of these electoral systems.* The present study seeks to answer two questions. The first is a descriptive question about the modality of electoral system change: under what circumstances and through what

* Sarah Birch, *Electoral Systems and Political Transformation in Post-Communist Europe*, to be published by Palgrave Macmillan in 2003.

processes did reform take place and how was it embedded in the larger process of post-communist institutional change? The second question, explanatory in nature, concerns the factors that determined the choices ultimately made about each aspect of the electoral system and the theoretical frameworks best able to account for these choices. These questions constitute two interlocking dimensions of analysis that will guide the chapters that follow.

The focus of the analysis is on eight post-communist states spanning Central Europe and the former Soviet Union: Poland, Hungary, the Czech Republic, Slovakia, Romania, Bulgaria, Russia and Ukraine. These states all experienced similar political institutions under communism (which distinguished them from those of the former Yugoslavia). And though they have demonstrated varying degrees of success in realizing democratic principles, they can all be described as democracies in the loose sense that they approach this model more than any other (which cannot be said of Belarus or many of the Caucasian and Central Asian states during the period under consideration). Finally, they can all trace their main cultural roots to European historical traditions, with all the value assumptions this implies as regards human worth and potential. The similarities among these eight cases enable a degree of acuity of comparative insight not possible with a more disparate set of countries.

At the same time, the eight cases exhibit enough variation on the key process and outcome parameters of interest to allow meaningful distinctions to be made and contrasts to be drawn among them. These include differences in the timing and pace of reform; Hungary and Bulgaria engaged in electoral system overhauls at the very start of the transition process, whereas Ukraine did not fundamentally alter its electoral institutions until nine years after the first experiments with electoral competition. On the outcome side, five of the eight states adopted proportional representation for their main or sole houses of parliament (Poland, the Czech Republic, Slovakia, Hungary and Romania), two opted for mixed systems (Russia and Bulgaria), and Ukraine initially retained its single-member electoral law. The systems in two of the eight states subsequently underwent radical changes – Bulgaria moved to PR and Ukraine switched to a mixed system. The other states contented themselves with reforms of the newly adopted mode, though Poland and the Czech Republic significantly amended their proportional systems. Finally, Poland, Russia, the Czech Republic and Romania have bicameral legislatures (the first three use different types of electoral system for the two chambers), while the remaining four states are unicameral. The eight cases thus afford sufficient variety to enable us to probe important differences among them.

The analysis employs a variety of types of data, including transcripts of parliamentary debates, interviews with relevant actors, analyses of press reports and secondary literature. The laws themselves and the electoral results on which the analysis draws can be found in the database of the Project on Political Transformation and the Electoral Process in Post-Communist Europe at <www.essex.ac.uk/elections>. All electoral results and references to legislation are taken from this database.

Though the monograph is a collective effort on which the authors have collaborated closely and for which they assume joint responsibility, the country studies were initially drafted to exploit the particular expertise of each author. Frances Millard drafted the chapters on Poland and Hungary; Kieran Williams was responsible for the Czech Republic and Slovakia; Marina Popescu wrote the Romania chapter, Sarah Birch authored the chapters on Bulgaria and Ukraine, and the Russia chapter was the joint effort of Sarah Birch and Kieran Williams. The introductory chapter and the conclusion were fully collaborative undertakings.

The resulting study is the product of wide-ranging research to which numerous individuals and organizations gave their support. We are first and foremost grateful to the Economic and Social Research Council's 'One Europe or Several?' Programme which funded the project of which this investigation is a part (through grant L213252021). Our thanks are due also to the International Foundation for Electoral Systems and to the Association of Central and Eastern European Electoral Officials who helped to construct the database to which we refer at numerous points in the analysis. Sarah Birch would like to acknowledge the support of the Department of Government at the University of Essex for valuable leave time in which to complete the necessary work. We also acknowledge a particular debt of gratitude to Gábor Tóka and Laura Belin. In addition, thanks are also due to Wojciech Czaplicki and Henryk Bielski of the National Election Office in Warsaw, to Jiři Hoppe and Jiři Suk for supplying unpublished materials from the Civic Forum archive at the Institute of Contemporary History in Prague, and to Tim Haughton, Karen Henderson, Petr Kopecký, Tomasz Mickiewicz, Milada Vachudová, and Sándor Gallai for useful and constructive comments. Gabriela and Grigore Popescu and Alin Ciocârlie facilitated the often difficult task of collecting data on Romanian developments. Tatiana Kostatinova, Dimitar Dimitrov and Marcus Harper provided help with the Bulgaria chapter, and Laura Belin gave invaluable help with Russia. Of course, the authors remain collectively responsible for any errors of fact or interpretation.

SARAH BIRCH, FRANCES MILLARD,
MARINA POPESCU, KIERAN WILLIAMS

1
Explaining the Design and Redesign of Electoral Systems

Electoral institutions are often regarded as 'sticky' in the sense that they are difficult to change. However, relatively little attention has been given to the factors that shape them in the early stages of their development or the ways in which they evolve. A number of democratic countries made changes to their electoral laws in the 1990s, belying the view that 'fundamental changes are rare and arise only in extraordinary situations'.[1] Yet the large-scale rewriting of electoral laws in post-communist Europe between 1989 and 1991 was certainly a phenomenon not witnessed since the adoption of proportional representation across most of Western Europe from the late nineteenth century. Moreover, most countries in the post-communist region altered their electoral laws to some degree after the initial 'founding' elections had given the population a political choice for the first time in decades. Even where it failed, electoral reform was on the political agenda of new elites. Political actors generally found it 'worthwhile to take the risk of launching a new process of bargaining and political change'.[2]

There are thus two distinct stages of electoral design in post-communist countries. The first coincides with the initial impetus to democratization, with free elections as the centrepiece and hallmark of new commitments to democracy. The second involves changes instituted by the newly legitimized elites following free elections once the effects of the new systems had become apparent to all affected. It is far from clear that the same factors should drive both stages of this process, or that the same factors influence the degree of 'lock-in' of electoral institutions.

The post-communist regimes were unusual in that the timing of the first free elections generated a wave of near-simultaneous electoral reform. It is not difficult to explain the impetus to reform in a general sense. It clearly resulted from the collapse of the old regimes;

the universal commitment in rhetoric – if not always in practice – to democracy; and the recognition by elites of the need to adapt to popular pressures or to the demands of aspiring counter-elites. In the former Soviet Union changes in electoral law were a central element of General Secretary Gorbachev's urge to 'democratize'. The shift from uncompetitive to fully competitive elections was slower there than in much of Central Europe, where regimes either adapted to dramatically changing circumstances or imploded under the weight of their own inertia. Throughout the region free elections were both cause and consequence of the 'transition to democracy'.

However, the identity of the new electoral 'designers' varied considerably. Sometimes elites negotiated with their challengers, sometimes the challengers themselves took over the process. In some cases existing parliamentarians played a considerable role, in others their role was negligible. Given the variations among actors at this stage as well as their different experiences and objectives, we might well expect diversity in the factors involved in choosing an electoral system, and in the nature of the initial electoral choices. Yet in all cases perceptions of electoral institutions were inflected with attitudes toward the systems associated with the communist regime.

Once free elections had been held, electoral reform became the province of those democratically elected parliamentarians who had benefited from the initial definition of the new rules of the game. Electoral rules have the unique characteristic that their subject and their object are the same, for under normal democratic conditions they are rules made by rule-makers about their own fitness to continue making rules. In voting electoral systems into law, parliamentarians determine the mechanism through which they as individuals may or may not be chosen at the next election. It should not surprise us if they tend to be biased in favour of the systems that elected them. Thus the question of why subsequent change transpired is also crucial to understanding the content of new post-communist electoral legislation.

In this chapter we begin with an analysis of the communist approach to elections. This reveals much of the conceptual baggage carried forward by actors involved in electoral system design, but it also shows how electoral reform could not be painted on a blank sheet of paper. In all cases actors were shaped by and reacted to previous developments. The second section places our topic in a wider context. It identifies the distinguishing features of post-communist electoral reform and the crucial ways in which it differs from the reforms that took place at the time of the 'first wave' of democratization in Western Europe. The third section deals with the general factors shaping electoral systems. It argues for the need to distinguish the first stage of reform, when multiparty elections had yet to take place, from the second stage of change, following the first fully competitive elections. We present different scholarly explanations of electoral system design and change, with a preliminary assessment of their utility and appropriateness for our analysis. Finally, we outline the focus of our subsequent chapters.

Elections under communism

The theory underlying communist electoral-system design grew in part from Marx's analysis of the representative institutions of the Paris Commune.

> The Commune was formed of municipal councillors chosen by universal suffrage in the various wards of the town, responsible and revocable at short notice. The majority of its members were naturally working men, or acknowledged representatives of the working class. The Commune was to be a working, not a parliamentary, body, executive and legislative at the same time.[3]

Two aspects of this description had a direct bearing on the development of representative assemblies under twentieth-century communism. Firstly, the Commune was a truly popular institution: its members were mostly workers, and they were chosen by the people at large. Assemblies in communist states had relatively large numbers of working-class members and all members retained their previous jobs, attending assembly meetings when required but not becoming professional politicians. Secondly, Marx's description of the Commune as 'a working, not a parliamentary, body, executive and legislative at the same time' indicates his approval for the combination of executive and legislative functions.

Lenin himself directly endorsed the practices of the Paris Commune, most notably in *State and Revolution*, where he saw them as replacing the 'venal and rotten parliamentarism of bourgeois society' with genuinely representative institutions as 'working institutions', including accountability and mechanisms of recall.[4] Communist-style representation was consistently contrasted in subsequent communist political theory with 'bourgeois parliamentarism', making this distinction one of the defining features of communist ideology. The denial of the separation of powers also characterized the communist systems that developed from

Leninist and Stalinist adaptations of Marx, though it was Lenin who originally established the principle of the 'leading and guiding role of the Communist Party'.

Soviet elections departed immediately from the proportional representation system used for the Constituent Assembly elections of 1917, the first direct elections to be conducted on the basis of a universal and equal franchise. Indeed, the Bolsheviks had fared relatively poorly, gaining only 23.62 per cent of the vote.[5] From 1922 to 1936 Soviet elections were indirect and conducted on the basis of a weighted franchise favouring urban workers and excluding those deemed to have been tainted by association with the old regime. This disenfranchisement of 'class enemies' reappeared in the form of limits to the franchise in the immediate postwar elections of independent Eastern Europe, when 'fascists' or 'collaborators' were excluded.

When the class enemies were declared defeated in the USSR in 1936, direct elections and a universal franchise were restored. Stalin prepared for competitive elections, but he suddenly took fright and reversed his position,[6] at the same time providing ideological justification: since parties were viewed as representing classes, and class harmony was the prevailing order, only one party was deemed necessary to electoral politics. This meshed well with the concept of the 'leading role' of the Communist Party. Thus from 1936 Soviet elections were held in single-member territorial districts, with (until 1989) a single candidate standing in each. The voter's task was to delete or endorse the candidate, whose democratic legitimacy was confirmed by the absolute majority requirement and whose accountability was ensured through his/her 'mandate' (specifying the issues and tasks he or she would undertake for voters, detailed in periodic reports by deputies to their constituents) and the electors' formal right of recall. It is interesting to note that the absolute majority requirement conformed to imperial Russian practice rather than to the procedures employed in the Paris Commune elections, which were governed by a plurality rule.

As the Soviet model spread into Eastern Europe, so too did its electoral practices. The communist assumption of power entailed the slavish adoption of the 'superior' Soviet political system, including the elimination of genuine party competition. Even where other political parties were allowed to exist,[7] as they were in most of Eastern Europe, they remained subject to the demands of class harmony and subordinate to the Communist Party in 'popular front' formations. Majoritarian systems based on single-member districts were introduced in all but Poland and the GDR, which had multi-member districts for much of the postwar period.[8] All countries maintained the requirement of absolute majority for election, though defeat of a candidate was generally rare and mostly localized.[9] The absolute majority was in most cases defined in terms of the eligible electorate, not the voting population, and it was generally combined with the stipulation that at least fifty per cent of the electorate had to vote for the election to be valid.

However, in some countries provisions for multiple candidacy, dormant in the USSR, manifested themselves quite early. In Poland one response to political upheaval in 1956 was the practice of having more candidates than seats, as well as the inclusion of independent lay Catholics (this was how the future Solidarity prime minister Tadeusz Mazowiecki gained parliamentary experience). Hungary also had some multi-candidate contests after 1966, although they constituted a small proportion of the total (in 1971 single candidates stood in 303 of 352 districts).

The use of a territorial basis for the distribution of seats must be seen more as default choice than as a positive adherence to a geographically based understanding of interests. Territorial representation was also a useful way of giving reluctant peripheral groups the impression that their interests would be listened to and 'their' people guaranteed a place in the decision-making process. There was formal cognizance of ethnicity in elections to the Soviet second chamber, the Soviet of Nationalities. There also remained some vestiges of functional representation in the role played by social organizations and the workplace in Soviet nominating and recall procedures. (This took on a specific form in 1989, when one-third of the seats in the new Congress of People's Deputies was reserved for social organizations.)

The basic precept underlying the concept of representation remained, however, the cross-section or mirror-image: as far as possible representatives should be 'like' their voters in terms of occupation, age and gender. The milkmaid in parliament became the symbol of communist superiority over bourgeois systems, since she not only served her electors but (as a part-time deputy) would not become part of an elite isolated from common concerns. To achieve this 'reflection' the Party issued guidelines regarding composition to 'assist' nominating committees. Thus there was a particular emphasis on the representative function of elections, accompanied by perennial concerns with improving the quality of 'socialist democracy'. Under Khrushchev (1957–64) there was greater emphasis on deputies' mandates and on the right of recall. It was also under Khrushchev that discussions again took place regarding the possibility of multi-candidate elections.[10]

From technical and legal perspectives, late-communist electoral insti-tutions differed little from those in established democracies. Voting hours were long, and the system provided exceptional ease of access to polling stations, which were organized on ships and in hospitals, with mobile ballot boxes to reach the infirm. Yet elections in the communist world were governed not only by formal laws but also by informal insti-tutions, notably effective communist vetting of nominations, and both negative and positive incentives to vote. The latter included ease of vot-ing in another district (Stalin was not the only leader to be returned with a majority of more than 100 per cent because of this), the provi-sion of scarce goods at polling stations, and tolerance of proxy voting. As a result, the system registered high levels of participation in the for-mal process of voting, but far lower levels of popular involvement in the actual selection of representatives. Western observers took a jaundiced view of Soviet-style elections up to the late 1980s. There was little if any genuine competition;[11] elections mainly served socialization and mobilization functions.[12]

During the late communist period, electoral reform in Central and Eastern Europe involved firstly the liberalization of the terms of contes-tation and secondly changes to seat allocation formulae. The relaxation of entry requirements gathered speed after 1985, with Gorbachev's reformist regime in the USSR. Reform had already deepened in Hungary in 1983 and in Poland in 1984–5 as a means of enhancing the legiti-macy of representative institutions. The limits on candidacies were loosened, and many of the filtering mechanisms which allowed the authorities to maintain control over the selection process were removed.

The Soviet Union was the linchpin of the communist system, and it was reform of the electoral system that heralded the Soviet collapse. Modest electoral reforms had continued to be proposed from within the ruling elite.[13] The first (limited) experiment with competition was con-ducted under Gorbachev at the time of the 1987 local elections, when approximately 5 per cent of deputies were elected in multi-member dis-tricts with limited choice.[14] Electoral institutions emerged as an issue in the public arena at the time of the design of voting systems for the Congress of People's Deputies, elected for the first and last time in 1989. There was not yet any real debate over the continued use of single-member districts; discussions focused more on nomination procedures and the new third element of the Congress, to be elected by All-Union social organizations, including 100 seats for the Communist Party.[15]

Such issues were again the main focus of debate in the rewriting of electoral laws for the various republic elections of 1990. The 'leading role of the Party' was shortly to be expunged from the Soviet Constitution, and most independent states of Central and Eastern Europe were preparing for fully free elections on the basis of new electoral laws. While most republics retained single-member districts in 1990, Estonia adopted (for that election only) the single-transferable vote and Georgia employed a mixed system. In six republics, Latvia, Lithuania, Estonia, Georgia, Armenia and Moldavia, non-communists gained a majority of seats, intensifying the acute fissiparous tendencies of the imploding Soviet state. The 'new elites' took charge of electoral reform here, while the 'old elite' retained its dominance in the remaining nine republics, including Russia and Ukraine.

All in all, the communist system provided a large measure of common experience across the region. However, considerable differences were evident among the communist states in the degree of readiness to experiment with reform, in the extent to which changes were elite-led, in the timing of change, and in the identity of leading pro-reform actors.

The distinguishing characteristics of post-communist electoral reform

Arend Lijphart has drawn a parallel between 'first-wave' electoral reforms and those that accompanied 'third-wave' post-communist transitions. Just as the relative decline of the support bases of the old Western European parties moved them to switch from all-or-nothing majoritarianism to proportional systems that would reliably deliver a modest return, so the post-communist transition gave representatives of the old regime reason to consent to reform once they realized that their position was under serious threat.[16] At the same time where new elites emerged, their interest was in institutional mechanisms that would challenge and remove the dominance of the old *apparatchiki* of the communist system.

Yet in many crucial respects the trajectory of electoral reform typical of Western Europe is *not* reflected in the Eastern European experience. Democratization historically involved two principal changes: extending citizen participation (franchise reform) and the liberalization of contestation (reform of candidate entry restrictions). In Western Europe the reform of contestation occurred upon completion of franchise reform and in direct response to it.[17] In much of the post-communist area, however, franchise reform was completed only under communism, and thus coincided with a radical restriction rather than an expansion of the terms of contestation. Once the 'class enemies' had been dealt with, the universal franchise was unproblematic, with voting rights denied only to the insane and those disenfranchised by a court of law. At the same time, there was virtually no genuine political competition.

This had important implications for the reform agenda that emerged at the time of the communist collapse. In most cases the formal terms of communist-era participation were accepted by the new democracies during the post-communist period. Few changes were made to franchise and voting regulations.[18] Nor were there significant demands for voluntary as opposed to automatic registration or changes in the age of voting. Indeed, we can note in passing that the post-communist states maintained very high rates of voter registration, unlike the Latin American new democracies, where some 10–33 per cent of the eligible population is not on the rolls.[19] This reflects the different non-democratic pasts and different levels of inherited state capacity in the two regions. The most contentious franchise issues were those of voting by immigrant minorities who did not qualify for citizenship in Estonia and Latvia, as well as voting by expatriates in Bulgaria, Poland and the Yugoslav successor states. Elsewhere the communist franchise was accepted. Though designed for ends other than those of democracy, its inclusiveness coincided with the needs of a democratic state. Thus unlike in Western Europe, the electoral reforms that accompanied democratic transition revolved mainly around issues of contestation, not participation.

A second key distinction between the two waves of reform is the relationship between electoral reform per se and the broader changes that were taking place in society. Though the enlargement of the franchise and subsequent changes in seat allocation rules at the turn of the last century had considerable consequences for political development in Western Europe, they were not associated with the kind of fundamental upheaval experienced in Eastern Europe from 1989 onwards.

In this regard Lijphart's explanation of reform in terms of changing perceptions of electoral strength ignores another striking feature of the communist transitions that differentiates them from the 'first wave' of Western European democratizations: the radical *institutional* dislocation that accompanied post-communist political transformation. Virtually all the Central and Eastern European states stepped out of or supplemented normal parliamentary procedures during the initial electoral decision-making process. At its least disruptive, this took the form of constitutional round-table talks at which informal but crucial deals were struck between the communists and the opposition (Poland,

Hungary, Czechoslovakia, Bulgaria). In other cases the violent suspension of existing decision-making structures enabled other actors to step in and legislate on electoral rules by decree (Russia, ⌊Romania⌉). In still other cases ordinary politics were at least partially suspended due to civil strife (Moldova, Georgia, Azerbaijan, Croatia). It is noteworthy that where such factors were absent, electoral reform was delayed until after the first multiparty elections (Ukraine, Macedonia, Albania), or democratization itself was delayed (Belarus, Armenia, FR Yugoslavia). Only in the Baltic republics of Estonia, Latvia and Lithuania and in Slovenia did electoral reform take place at the time of democratization under peaceful circumstances exclusively according to normal constitutional procedures.

It is clear, then, that electoral-system change in post-communist Europe was exceptional in several ways: its place in the reform process, the magnitude of the reforms in which it was embedded and the mode of its undertaking. Exceptional events are not always easily accounted for by existing theories, and several scholars have noted that conventional institutional paradigms fail to explain the shape of the emerging structures in Eastern Europe.[20] Previous research may be a better guide to subsequent changes in electoral law that occurred within the new institutional frameworks. However, those frameworks were themselves marked by instability, and uncertainty remained high in all post-communist states, as the changing identities of key actors, evolving perceptions of interests and fluid party configurations continued to reflect the dynamism of wholesale transformation.

How electoral systems are shaped

As suggested above, the post-communist transition process entailed two very different electoral reform contexts. When the legislatures were dominated by communist-era deputies and multi-party elections had yet to take place ($t = 0$), the choice situation was characterized by a different set of factors from that which informed it after the first multiparty elections ($t = 0 + 1$). Furthermore, this second stage should be in many respects similar to that following each subsequent election ($t = 0 + 2, 3, 4, ...$). It can be anticipated that different factors will have been important at different points in the reform process.

There are four identifiable approaches to explaining electoral system design. The first three focus on historical, external and wider contextual factors, the fourth on interest-based calculations by strategic actors. This section assesses the likely relevance of each approach in the post-communist context. There will be no attempt to demonstrate that one factor alone provides the explanatory key; it is highly probable in any context that a range of factors work together to determine political outcomes. The aim of this exercise is rather to hypothesize the relative contribution of each of the factors delineated.

Historical factors

Historical approaches abound within the discipline of political science, and history is often deployed as a factor in multi-causal analyses for good and understandable reasons. It is natural to suppose, as many observers of electoral reform have done, that the institutions previously employed in a state will have a bearing on the choices it makes when it (re)democratizes.[21] History is sometimes also mobilized as a residual explanatory variable. Matthew Shugart, for example, uses prior experience of parliamentary democracy to explain deviations from his model's expected outcomes.[22] Yet there is no clearly stated theoretical approach that specifies when history matters to electoral reform and when it does not. One factor is the nature of the historical experience: if positive, it may well be embraced; if negative, it is more likely to be rejected. Proportional representation was widely blamed for the ills of the Weimar Republic and the rise of Hitler, a negative association that helps to explain the adoption of Germany's mixed system, including a 5 per cent (then regional) threshold to counter party fragmentation.

Secondly, recent history will in all likelihood prove more influential than the more distant past. Blais and Massicotte's emphasis on the significance of the colonial legacy[23] does not have direct application in Central and Eastern Europe, where imperial legacies were both historically distant and far from democratic. Only the Austrian Habsburgs offered genuine experience of elections from the late nineteenth century; with universal male suffrage in 1907, the complex estates system disappeared and the two-round majority system was used in single-member districts. Reaction *against* Habsburg majoritarianism was one reason for the adoption of proportional representation in independent Czechoslovakia and Poland.[24] Likewise, pre-1918 Hungary's limited franchise, open voting and electoral 'management'[25] offered no viable model for a democratic electoral system, nor did it provide political experience for its constituent minority groups.

The territories that were part of the Russian empire had only one experience with genuinely competitive democratic elections: the November 1917 elections to the doomed all-Russian Constituent Assembly, conducted under a system of proportional representation. This experience was unlikely to be deeply embedded in collective memory or to provide an appealing model. Moreover, the more recent experience of the Soviet Union itself was not uniformly regarded as negative, with many adherents of Soviet-style practices remaining vocal across the post-Soviet landscape. Even in other Central and East European states, where political culture could be not just anti-Soviet but anti-Russian (as in Romania, Hungary and Poland), it was the lack of political competition rather than the single-member majority system per se which attracted the opprobrium of its critics. Yet, this does not make the Soviet and Soviet-inspired experience irrelevant. The view that one cannot attribute significance to a 'particular constellation of institutions that was little more than window dressing'[26] undoubtedly understates the socializing effects of lengthy experience, while also ignoring the frequent cases (such as Hungary in 1956 or Czechoslovakia in 1968) when the shell of sham institutions suddenly filled with substantive content. Moreover, patterns of representation can create vested interests as an element of local networks. For example, it is difficult to understand some of the bitter debates over nomination procedures without a grasp of the mechanisms of Soviet elections.

Also of potential relevance are the interwar experiences of the central European states. There were free elections everywhere in the immediate post-independence period except Hungary. Rothschild argues, however, that the franchise did not protect the mainly peasant populations from elite manipulation: in some cases '...universal suffrage functioned as the bureaucracy's tool for breaking the traditional power of "feudal" notables over their dependent peasant clientèles'.[27] Hungary did not even maintain the pretence of democratic elections, with the limited franchise and open ballot in rural areas maintained throughout the Horthy Regency.[28] Similarly, Mattei Dogan characterized the changes of power in interwar Romania as a form of 'mimic democracy' in which elections were nominally responsible for the replacement of governments but in reality changes were decided behind the scenes before the polls were called.[29] Throughout the 1930s King Carol, an acknowledged admirer of Mussolini, was the key figure in Romanian politics, even before the royal dictatorship (1938). Elsewhere too, the experience of free elections was limited, with almost all regimes succumbing by the 1930s to outright authoritarianism under which contestation was severely restricted. Bulgaria, for example, was noted for the violence of its politics. It experienced its first coup in 1923, when the powerful Agrarian Party was reduced to a shadow of its former self. The military took over in 1934, abolishing political parties and trade unions. When Tsar Boris took control a year later, the country effectively became a royal dictatorship until his death in 1943.[30] In Poland, with Piłsudski's 1926 coup and under the successor 'regime of the colonels' a strong executive-centred, semi-democratic system emerged. Opposition political parties continued to exist, but their treatment varied from administrative harassment to outright repression.[31] Only in Czechoslovakia were fully democratic, competitive multi-party elections held throughout the interwar period.

Proportional representation was the norm in independent interwar Eastern Europe, though the details of the proportional formulae used varied considerably. In Czechoslovakia closed-list regional PR with an upper tier generated highly proportional but fragmented parliaments in which between 16 and 19 parties were represented; however, party discipline and consultative practices generated reasonably effective coalition government. By contrast, the premium system operative in Romania from 1926 – a variation on the Italian fascist electoral law – stipulated that a party which won 40 per cent of the vote automatically won 50 per cent of the seats plus a number of remaining seats corresponding to its percentage of the total vote; the rest were divided proportionally among those other parties exceeding the 2 per cent threshold.[32] Thus the turbulence of this period and the weak hold that democracy had on most of the states in the region suggest that the interwar electoral institutions would not be particularly promising ground from which to mine institutional precedents.[33] But in the absence of more fruitful historical territory, the fragile interwar democracies might be expected to have provided some post-communist electoral system designers with a modicum of guidance.

This was indeed the case in Czechoslovakia, where free democratic elections took place in 1946. Czechoslovakia in effect resuscitated its 1920 law. In Hungary Soviet authorities supported the resurgence of major political parties in a 'popular front' strategy and pressed hard for a common list of parties in the provisional government. Bargaining with the Smallholders yielded agreement on a proportional system but with the proviso that the four-party coalition would continue regardless of the results of the 1946 election. In Poland, Romania and Bulgaria the communists were sufficiently strong to rig the first postwar elections and the electoral system hardly mattered.

The third factor which may be expected to increase the influence of past experience is that of timing. Decision-makers in a hurry may reach for the easiest acceptable alternative. An election deadline concentrates the mind wonderfully. Adapting historical exemplars may short-circuit decision-making when compromise seems otherwise unattainable.

Thus we have a tentative model suggesting that historical precedents will more likely be relevant if (1) the historical experience is viewed positively; (2) the experience was not too distant for contemporary relevance; and/or (3) the decision-makers are under pressure to reach a decision rapidly.

Foreign influences

Like the general historical approach, the role of foreign influences has been identified as a potential factor relevant to the shaping of electoral institutions. The transplantation of institutions was much in vogue after 1918 but soon went into decline, reflecting Mackenzie's quip that the 'only thing that can be predicted with certainty about the export of elections is that an electoral system will not work in the same way in its new setting as in its old'.[34] Still, there remains the possibility of direct or indirect influence. Certainly there were large numbers of electoral 'experts' from one country trying to engineer outcomes in another, and these usually gained at least a polite hearing.[35] But more often domestic institution crafters relied on foreign models without actual intervention.[36] Foreign experts were often called in *after* local policy-makers had already made up their minds and wanted outside counsel to validate their preferences. Here one should distinguish between advice given by foreigners and intentional replication or adaptation of a foreign electoral law, with or without advice from that country's experts. The degree of actual influence of foreign models can be expected to vary according to a number of factors. One is the availability of domestic experts in electoral system design. If they are few, there may be a greater temptation to take an 'off-the-rack' system from another country. Another factor is the level of cultural affinity with other countries, which may encourage institutional emulation. But overall it seems likely that most countries pick, choose and adapt in a process that owes more to *bricolage* than slavish copying or imposition, and that the adaptation of existing models involves a large measure of creativity. Foreign 'inspiration' might thus be a better term than 'influence', and we can anticipate that such inspiration will be refracted through a variety of factors specific to the domestic political context of the country in question.

Contextual factors

It is often held that electoral systems ought to be 'appropriate' to the social and political context in which they operate. But this does not mean that for each state there is an ideal electoral system. Subjective factors are vital in determining how 'appropriateness' is interpreted.

All social systems have numerous attributes that influence electoral outcomes; those that are most salient in a given state will depend on perceptions of representation and the professed aims to be achieved through the electoral system.

Multi-ethnicity is frequently considered to demand proportional representation in order that minorities can feel themselves properly represented through the election of people from their own group.[37] The introduction of proportional representation in Belgium in 1899, which began the turn-of-the-century wave of electoral reform in Europe, was motivated by the desire to accommodate minority interests.[38] The benefits of broad social inclusiveness in a democratizing state can be counted here as well. In establishing the constitutional basis for a new regime, it is often thought desirable to adopt a system that will provide the opportunity of representation to as many groups as possible, to avoid attempts at undermining the fragile new constitutional settlement.[39] Some more geographically concentrated minorities, however, prefer majoritarianism, as they can use the compactness of their voters to carry districts.

In other cases, views of electoral systems will be affected by the mundane economic considerations that impinge on electoral system design, such as administrative cost differentials across systems[40] and the cost of different systems to participants. The reluctance of the Albanian opposition to endorse single-member districts in 1991 was said to result from its lack of cars and the petrol necessary to mount grassroots campaigns in far-flung rural areas.[41] Economic considerations are more likely to affect decisions about aspects of the electoral law directly related to campaign financing, such as public subventions and spending regulations. In the post-communist situation where most political parties were new and the population experienced intense economic stress, it is not surprising that public funding became widespread.

The political context can also be expected to have been important in shaping perceptions of the role of electoral institutions. In the post-communist setting the aim of creating an institutional space for the promotion of alternative ideologies was initially prominent in political discourse. However, a variety of institutional outcomes are found in cases of high elite continuity or highly asymmetric power relations that advantaged old elites; similarly, countries with strong opposition forces did not necessarily adopt the same type of electoral system.

The capacity of electoral laws to shape party systems figured in many contemporary debates in which ideal party system types were linked – correctly or erroneously – to various aspects of electoral regulation.[42]

Herbert Kitschelt and his colleagues developed an argument which held that the type of communism experienced by a state (bureaucratic-authoritarian, patrimonial or 'national-accommodative') determined the strength of the (former) communists during the transition period, which in turn affected the type of electoral system adopted.[43]

The broad institutional framework also has an undeniable shaping role on institutions subordinate to the fundamental law. This is a factor that may be expected to distinguish the initial change of electoral law from subsequent changes. In many post-communist states constitutional amendments were needed to remove the Communist Party's legal monopoly, but full constitutional settlements came after the adoption of the first electoral law. Some countries then included general provisions constraining subsequent change. As in many Western European states (and effectively also the European Union), Poland, the Czech Republic, Estonia and Latvia introduced constitutional requirements that the assembly must be elected according to a given type of electoral system. In Hungary and Czechoslovakia (1990–2) change in the electoral law was subject to a super-majority in parliament. Yet at the outset there were no such restraints in the communist-era constitutions, leaving law-makers free to pass new electoral laws by majority vote. Constitutionalization may thus be seen as a second-order effect that must itself be explained by other factors.

One informal structure that requires specific attention in the early stages of post-communist transition is the device of the round-table among elites. Such round-tables were used to hammer out constitutional deals in Poland, Hungary, Czechoslovakia and Bulgaria. In Hungary and Bulgaria district design and seat allocation formulae were decided in these fora. Such deliberations took place outside formal institutional structures and were later ratified by parliament; the initial Polish case provided an example readily adopted by others.

A number of what Nagel terms 'disinterested actors' representing other institutions are also frequently involved in decisions over electoral laws.[44] In the post-communist context, however, such players cannot always be assumed to be disinterested. Institutional conflict is common in circumstances of ambiguous jurisdiction and the absence of precedent, and this conflict can shape preferences over the institutions that govern the composition and powers of the legislature. Presidents very often have perspectives on parliamentary and party-system development, as well as other political interests. Even weak presidents may play a role in initiating debate or in exercising suspensive veto powers. Other institutions such as upper parliamentary chambers and the judiciary, notably constitutional courts, may also play a role.

Finally, a force of potential relevance to electoral reform is that of public opinion, often expressed through the referendum, which played an important part in the New Zealand and Italian reforms. Though numerous referendums were held in Eastern Europe during the early stages of transition,[45] only in Slovenia was a referendum conducted on the shape of a proposed revision of the post-communist electoral law.

The relevance and nature of contextual factors will obviously vary from state to state according to the specific social, cultural, historical and economic situation that obtains. Under certain circumstances aspects of the electoral law that are given negligible attention in most places will take on overwhelming importance due to some specific feature of a state's socio-political configuration, as with non-citizen voting in Estonia and Latvia, registration options in Bosnia and expatriate votes in Croatia.

It is, however, possible to formulate several general expectations as to the likely impact of these factors. The political circumstances surrounding post-communism were invariably an important aspect of the contextual forcefield. It is also difficult to imagine a situation in which the existence of strongly demarcated ethnic groups played no role in shaping institutions (though more fluid ethnic barriers as found, for example, in Ukraine and Belarus may not be of great significance in determining rules of competition). Economic conditions seem less likely to have a strong direct impact on electoral laws, and the impact of other institutional provisions will be mediated by their actual or anticipated reciprocal structuring effects. The undeveloped nature of many institutions, including political parties, appeared to create considerable scope for contingency. Understanding contextual variations is vital to a number of perspectives, since differences in context may themselves help explain the shaping of interests and strategy.[46] The political setting influences the likelihood that individuals will pursue their aims through formal political parties, it shapes perceptions of the likely consequences of different electoral alternatives and of their overall desirability, and it can be decisive in determining who has the final say over outcomes.

Interest-based calculations

Interest-based approaches are prominent in much of the recent literature on the topic of electoral system design and reform. Broadly speaking, interest-based models can be classified firstly according to the types of actors assumed to be involved in strategic decisions over electoral laws, and secondly according to the goals those actors are held to seek. Theories developed in the context of states with established party systems tend to take parties as the main actors,[47] and a party-centred approach has been found to be useful in transition countries such as Spain and Korea as well.[48] In the post-communist context, many commentators followed in this explanatory path. They frequently argued, for example, that communists and ex-communists tended to prefer majoritarian institutions, including single-member district electoral systems; communists believed these would cater to their strengths in terms of candidate attributes and distribution of support. Emergent opposition groups by contrast tended to prefer proportional representation, which would emphasize ideology over personal characteristics and give representation to organizationally weak partisan groupings.[49] A formal elaboration of the party-actor approach in the Central and Eastern European setting is provided in the seat-maximizing model of Ken Benoit and his colleagues.[50] The basic assumptions of this model follow in the tradition of Stein Rokkan:[51] electoral systems change when a party or coalition of parties supports an alternative increasing its seat-share and has the decision-making weight to effect it. Electoral systems will not change when the party or coalition of parties with the power to adopt an alternative can gain no more seats than under existing arrangements.

However, analyses of transition contexts, and more especially of the dynamics of post-communism, have found that parties cannot always be assumed to be coherent actors, and that it thus makes sense to examine the interests of individual politicians in addition to those of collective partisan entities.[52] This will be the approach adhered to in this volume, where one of the main themes is that the very identity of actors is endogenous to the process of electoral system design: whereas at the outset individuals may have preferences over electoral system types that reflect their own personal likelihood of enhancing their political power, collective choices will generate collective actors – typically in the form of political parties – that will acquire interests over further electoral reform as a consequence of the initial choice.

Once the identity of the main players is conceptualized, it is necessary to postulate their aims. In theory the players in the institutional design process could seek to achieve any number of goals. They might be genuinely virtuous and strive to produce the fairest, most democratic electoral system (we might term this a 'justice-maximizing' or sociotropic model, where the public good takes precedence over self-interest).

But even the most virtuous system designers in all probability also look beyond the democratic aspects of the electoral system to the character of its outputs, and most would have ambitions to make substantive changes in politics and society as well as in institutions. We can therefore assume that most actors will have self-interested goals in addition to or in place of their desire to promote the collective good. Kathleen Bawn has, in the West German context, proposed what she terms a 'policy-maximizing' model, which holds that legislators will seek to maximize their control over government policy by maximizing their chances of gaining cabinet positions.[53] But those who have analysed post-communist transitions have generally found that levels of uncertainty are too high for such incentives to function, and that a seat-maximizing model is more convincing.[54] At the outset at least, the majority of politicians can be assumed to aim for a seat in the legislature whose electoral system is under consideration. Some may see a term in parliament as a stepping stone to sinecures in public administration, in which case their main objective may not be (re)election but to ensure that the subsequent parliament is structured such as to promote chances of success in some other domain. Alternatively, some may put the political composition of subsequent assemblies over their own future parliamentary success because the rise to power of political forces may threaten their non-parliamentary economic interests. But for the most part, it is probably safe to assume that most politicians involved in deliberations over electoral laws view their personal interests in terms of the likelihood that they will win parliamentary seats.

As mentioned above, the context of the first, 'zero-stage' electoral system design experience in the post-communist states was radically different in several important ways from post-zero-stage reforms. In seeking to account for the choice of electoral institutions in the region, it thus makes sense to distinguish between initial and subsequent change.

The founding stage

Strategic decisions at the founding state of the transition both bring about and reflect regime change. In the post-communist context decision-making at this stage is characterized by three features: the weak institutionalization of parties, high levels of uncertainty about electoral outcomes, and a common acceptance that the new system should be (seen to be) democratic. The implications of these characteristics for design outcomes will be considered in turn.

The transition process is one in which parties are formed as collective actors, and choices over institutions depend on the propensity of individuals to integrate themselves into parties, which depends in turn on the resources at their disposal. Matthew Shugart addresses founding institutional design as a struggle between individual preference-seeking and collective (party) preference-seeking. If politicians think they have better career prospects by keeping parties weak, thereby allowing the individual room to cater to local interests, then they will select an electoral system of single-member districts (offset by a strong president with the decree power to break legislative logjams). If, on the other hand, they prefer to stake their careers on association with a political party, they will opt instead for the party-centred system engendered by proportional representation (as well as a weak president). Shugart relates preferences to the way in which the transition to democracy began, specifically the how (pace and sequencing) of change and the who of decision-making (insiders or outsiders).[55]

Attention to the high level of uncertainty under which actors operated suggests additional constraints. The main interest of all players at the founding stage is to ensure that they remain in the electoral game. For individuals acting under conditions of high uncertainty, this may entail a strategy of multiplying channels of access to parliament by means of a mixed electoral system – an approach not incompatible with the preference for single-member districts predicted by Shugart. Considerations of high uncertainty also provide an additional clue as to why party-oriented actors have tended to prefer proportional representation. For collective actors, avoiding defeat means minimizing their greatest possible loss,[56] and the possibility of participating in government will most likely take second place to the desire to remain in parliament. We might interpret high uncertainty as being akin to a Rawlsian veil of uncertainty and hypothesize that under such conditions many partisan actors will choose a system that is fairest to parties in general – proportional representation.

Finally, there was a strong collective interest at the time of the founding elections in ensuring that they would reflect democratic norms so as to legitimize the representative system as a whole. This imperative can be expected to be manifest in a collective interest among elites involved in the electoral reform process to opt for institutional mechanisms that are perceived to reflect the values of democracy as commonly understood in their own political context. If a certain option lacks popular credibility, it may be in the interest of legislators to avoid it, even if it has the potential to enhance their ability to win seats.[57] In the context of post-communism we can expect the legitimacy imperative to generate liberal candidate entry requirements in the first post-communist elections, as communist-era restrictions on contestation are removed and normative commitment to equality is high.

All in all, the common features of the communist electoral systems cannot be expected to translate into similar post-communist founding electoral systems due to the diversity of the transitions experienced by individual states. The contingent circumstances of the transitions were important in structuring the fora in which initial electoral-system design decisions were made, as well as the identifications of the actors involved and their relative strengths. We ought thus to expect that this stage of the electoral-system design trajectory will be characterized by strategic diversity and that country-specific factors will loom large.

Post-zero-stage bargaining

Once a new democratic electoral system has operated in practice for the first time, the strategic context is altered. At this stage uncertainty decreases, actors become increasingly more knowledgeable and better aware of their interests, and successful contestants become institutionally embedded in the structures of the parliamentary chamber to which they have been elected. Likewise parliament becomes the main locus of decision-making. We ought to expect electoral systems to become 'sticky' at this point and path dependency may be an important explanatory factor.

An institution might be maintained for a variety of reasons, which can be classified according to structural factors on the one hand, and according to the interests (individual, party-centred and collective) they represent on the other. Structural impediments to change include formal constitutional obstacles, the constraints and transaction costs of the parliamentary process,[58] and the legitimacy the system may have acquired through use in the founding electoral events. When constitutional provisions specify the character of an electoral system, the nature of the amendment process (usually requiring a two-thirds majority) may serve as a barrier, as may super-majority requirements established specifically for electoral-law change. Change may also be difficult in the midst of post-communist economic reform, when a state may have other priorities and electoral change may be pushed onto the back burner. Finally, the repeated use of a law may convey either the legitimacy of familiarity or the sense that the law is genuinely good or appropriate.

Institutional inertia may also be due to the fact that elites retain the power to promote its reproduction, and because the status quo is supported by the cost–benefit assessments of individual actors. The 'power explanations' offered by some path dependency approaches stress that those who wield power gained through the existing electoral regime have little incentive to change it.[59] But although path dependency is often associated with the 'locking-in' of existing institutions, it does not assume that once generated, institutions are set in concrete. Explanations of change, in other words of deviation from the established path, depend on change in the elements promoting stasis. An exogenous shock may transform the functional requisites of the system. Actors may change their cost–benefit perceptions through learning and experience, including the emergence of unexpected consequences. The power or cohesion of the elite may weaken. Changes may occur in the values or subjective beliefs of actors. One cannot merely assume that institutional design will remain uncontested; indeed groups may perceive institutions as highly malleable, and stability is far from assured. Alexander hypothesizes that attempts to change institutions 'occur not only when groups try to reform or overturn designs which systematically privilege their opponents or when smaller or less electorally confident groups oppose win-concentrating designs, but also when strong and confident groups try to revise low-stakes designs in win-concentrating directions'.[60]

The strategies of political actors differ during the post-founding phase, depending not least on processes of party institutionalization. If individuals play a prominent role as independent deputies, then the question arises whether those who are politically well-endowed will seek to join parties or again try their electoral luck as independents. The answer to this will depend mainly on (1) the extent and cast of their reputations and (2) the material, organizational and human resources they can command. If they remain independent, they can be expected to favour institutional structures that benefit political entrepreneurs such as single-member districts, liberal nomination procedures and exclusively private campaign finance with no restrictive spending limits. If they decide to join parties, they will in all probability prefer open lists and small districts.

Where parties come to dominate the electoral reform process, their perspectives will to some degree depend on their internal cohesion and their ideological disposition. However, parties will also have increased information regarding their perceived electoral strength, the geographical distribution of their support and their linkage structures (all of which may well be inaccurate). This clearly facilitates the pursuit of seat-maximizing strategies. Large parties will favour high effective electoral thresholds (whether achieved though manipulation of district format, seat allocation formulae or formal thresholds). Likewise, parties whose support is based on personal or clientelist ties will tend to prefer electoral systems that favour the cultivation of personal votes, such as those with small district size and/or voter influence over the order of candidates over party lists.[61] We can expect that at this point their preferences will be both better defined and more accurately calibrated to maximize their interests as parties.

The third and final set of interest-based considerations concern those identified with the collective interest which may be more prominent during democratic transitions than during periods of 'ordinary politics'. The functionality of the system, or its propensity to contribute to the collective good, can be expected to be instrumental in ensuring its retention. The systemic requirements of a state such as its dependence on trade, the need to liberalize markets and its efficiency as a tool of governance have been hypothesized to affect choice of electoral system.[62] Empirical evidence has not always been found to support such claims,[63] and it has been argued that they are in any case not applicable to distributive institutions such as electoral systems.[64] However, such considerations must be borne in mind, especially in the context of transition, where virtually all political players have a common interest in a successful outcome.

Expectations and chapter plan

Like the first wave of electoral reform, the post-communist wave was triggered by a dramatic change, but that change involved the terms of contestation, not the terms of participation. And as we shall see, it was around various aspects of the terms of contestation that the reform debates in most cases revolved. These included criteria of eligibility, rules affecting the means through which contestants were able to mobilize support and rules governing the way in which the winners were ultimately decided ('electoral systems' in the narrow sense).

The overall explanatory framework advanced here is one that might be termed 'contextualized rationality'. Like many previous analysts of electoral system design, we anticipate that strategic calculations by elite actors will play a decisive role in determining the electoral systems that are adopted in the post-communist context. But we expect that contextual factors will prove more influential in the post-communist transition setting than they would be in an established democracy, or even a post-authoritarian state that had a usable pre-existing party system such as postwar Germany or post-Franco Spain. This is because the complex and varied circumstances of post-communism can be expected to be crucial in shaping the basic ingredients of the choice situation: the actors involved, the aims they pursue and the perceptions they have of design alternatives. In other words, we anticipate that shared contextual factors will tend to unify decision-makers within a given state, whereas rational calculations will divide them. The former will set the menu for choice, the latter will determine what is ultimately selected.

Further, we can expect that in states where ideologically oriented movements led to pronounced cleavages among the political elite during the transition with political parties coalescing early on, partisan affiliation will have been the strongest determinant of perceived interests, and members of parliament will have behaved in accordance with party or proto-party interests. But where ideological structuration was weak, legislators should have behaved mainly according to their (perceived) individual interests. This will be one of the main forces that shapes bargaining over electoral systems, such that party system and electoral system will structure each other. It is also likely that we will observe an increase over time in electoral entry requirements as successful players seek ways of locking out newcomers; this will both result from and reinforce party system institutionalization.

The chapters that follow will test the relevance of these different factors. In so doing they will shed light on the adequacy of the individual theories and on the ways in which they interact. The country studies will also point to problems with existing approaches and suggest alternative explanatory strategies. Finally, detailed attention to the texture of the debates surrounding electoral reform deepens our understanding of the way in which factors such as models, context and interest bargaining operate in practice, how they inflect debate, and the strengths of each type of argument. Appreciation of the mind-set of the actors involved in key decisions through analysis of the discourse of reform will enable us to gain access to the 'black box' of the policy process and will enhance our appreciation not only of *what* matters to electoral reformers, but also of *how* and *why* it matters.

The chapters are organized by country in a rough 'transition' chronology: Poland, Hungary, the Czech Republic and Slovakia, Romania, Bulgaria, Russia and Ukraine. Drawing on the explanatory framework outlined above, each chapter will seek to answer a series of embedded questions organized along the two main dimensions of process description and explanation. The first dimension encompasses the various features of the reform process. The main questions that will be addressed in this context are firstly, *the role of electoral-system design in the transition,* including the extent to which electoral reform was contentious during and after the communist collapse, the major players in the debate and how far the mass public was interested, informed and involved. Each chapter also addresses the *trajectory of electoral-system design*: when, where and what key decisions as to the shape of electoral-system design were made, and how firmly entrenched were the new rules. Accounting for outcomes entails analysis of the *menu for choice, the discourse of electoral reform and the role of strategic bargaining among actors*. We will be concerned here with which aspects of electoral law received the most attention, how actors deployed arguments in this debate, perceptions of different options, and the factors that determined ultimate outcomes. The final chapter compares findings across countries in order both to draw parallels and to explain differences.

2
Poland: Experimenting with the Electoral System

> If God were to write an electoral law, He would write a majoritarian one.
>
> (Andrzej Olechowski, Convention of the *Platforma Obywatelska* (PO), 24 January 2001)[1]

The electoral system used in Poland for the lower house of parliament (the Sejm) proved highly susceptible to change in the first decade of the new political system. Unusually, the law changed for three out of four elections (1991, 1993, 2001). Nor can the revisions introduced for the 2001 elections be viewed as final. Indeed, as Olechowski's view above shows, even basic premises of electoral system design remained contested. Here we provide an overview of the various electoral systems used for the Sejm and the circumstances of change. Then follows an analysis of the key political actors and the processes and issues that emerged.

First we should emphasize that the broad context was itself in flux. Political parties emerged and evolved, with significant changes in their nature and their relationships. The institutional context itself did not remain static. The round-table negotiations between the Communist Party (*Polska Zjednoczona Partia Robotnicza*, PZPR) and the Solidarity opposition in 1989 left an ambiguous institutional legacy. The new presidency was strong, if not clearly defined. The legislature was now bicameral, comprising the Sejm and the Senate. The Sejm was pre-eminent in regard to the accountability of government, but the Senate possessed extensive legislative powers. An interim Little Constitution (1992) clarified some jurisdictional conflicts while creating others. Both president and Senate saw an erosion of their positions by the time of the new 1997 Constitution. The presidential veto was weakened, with the vote needed to override it reduced from two-thirds to three-fifths, and the Sejm could now reject Senate amendments with a simple rather than two-thirds majority. Both the absence of a constitutional settlement up to 1997 and the 1997 Constitution itself served to shape the process of changing Polish electoral law.

Notwithstanding the interplay of institutions, in each case the final outcome was determined by the relative strengths of political forces in the Sejm itself and the ways in which they perceived their own advantage. In each instance of change 'learning' from previous experience was apparent. Although sociotropic arguments were not absent, a seat-maximizing approach provides the greatest insights into processes of electoral reform.

There was no appeal to historical precedent in Polish electoral debate. Poland's varied electoral systems were not associated with a flourishing of democracy. Its 1922 law used proportional representation and d'Hondt, as well as a national list allocating further deputies in proportion to the district seats won. In 1935 the authoritarian regime introduced (and then manipulated) a two-vote, two-member district plurality system. The year 1946 saw a return to the two-tier list system for a thoroughly rigged election. In 1952 the communist regime introduced a variant of Soviet-style majoritarianism, but from 1957 Poland permitted more candidates to stand than seats available.

With little in the way of clear reference points, the condition of uncertainty remained an environmental factor throughout, because of the changing institutional context, the vagaries of individual behaviour and unpredictable shifts in the fortunes of political parties. This uncertainty was itself variably perceived. Actors learned, but they did not always learn rapidly, and sometimes they learned the 'wrong' lessons. In no case did the chief architects of change prove to be its beneficiaries.

The impetus to electoral reform

What change?

The key developments that took place in Poland may be summarized quite briefly. All fall within Arend Lijphart's concept of a 'new' electoral system,[2] with clear changes in district magnitude, electoral formulae and thresholds (see Table 2.1). In 1991 open-list proportional representation replaced the complex majoritarian system of 1989. Candidature was easy, with a basic registration requirement of 5000 signatures. This was a limited requirement – in 1991 66 electoral committees did not attract even the 5000 votes of their signatories. Voters selected their

Table 2.1 Main changes in the law on elections to the Polish Sejm

Election year	Electoral system type	District structure	Seat allocation formula	Threshold
1989	Semi-competitive majoritarian	108	Two-round	n/a
1991	Two-tier PR (nl = 69)	35 (7–17)	Hare (c) modified Ste-Laguë (nl)	5% for nl
1993	Two-tier PR (nl = 69)	52 (3–17)	d'Hondt	5% party, 8% coalition, 7% nl
1997	Two-tier PR (nl = 69)	52 (3–17)	d'Hondt	5% party, 8% coalition, 7% nl
2001	Single-tier PR	41 (4–19)	modified Ste-Laguë	5% party, 8% coalition

c = constituency; nl = national list.

preferred individual candidate from their chosen party list to elect 391 deputies in 37 districts, ranging from five seven-member districts to the 17-member districts of Warsaw City and part of Katowice province. The calculation of seats took place in each district by the Hare-Niemeyer largest remainder system. Individual deputies were elected in order of votes cast. There was no threshold for the individual districts.

Seats for 69 deputies elected from national party lists were then determined by votes cast in the districts. Committees registering lists in at least five districts could submit a national list, composed of candidates on their district lists. Only those winning seats in at least five districts or at least 5 per cent of the total vote were eligible for national list seats.[3] The seats were allocated by the modified Sainte-Laguë formula (initial divisor of 1.4).

In 1993 the number of electoral districts increased to 52, while new thresholds of 5 per cent for a party/committee and 8 per cent for coalitions raised entry barriers considerably. The increased 7 per cent national list threshold and the shift of formula to d'Hondt for district and national list allocations also favoured larger parties. In 2001 changes were designed to strengthen the impact of medium-sized parties. The number of districts fell to 41, the national list was abolished, and the formula shifted again to modified Sainte-Laguë.

Some factors remained constant. The size of the Sejm was constitutionally defined at 460 deputies. After 1991, with the introduction of proportional representation, the open list system remained, while the exemption of registered national minorities from the national threshold requirement also continued – though both provisions were challenged.

Why change?

In each case changes resulted from broadly shared perceptions of perceived problems arising from the previous law. In 1991 and 1993 these were institutional problems. In 2001 the requirement for change was administrative, but the ensuing debates were intensely political. The greatest challenge and the most fundamental change was certainly that of 1991. The impetus to reform stemmed from the interim nature of the 1989 electoral law, a product of the Round Table. The free but only partly competitive election of June 1989 provided the effective mechanism for inaugurating the wholesale transformation of the Polish political system. Unlike Hungary and Czechoslovakia, where fully competitive 'founding' elections confirmed broad aspirations for democracy in spring 1990, in Poland the round-table election was not intended to inaugurate a new democratic political system. It was a mechanism of democratization, but not of democracy, with the Sejm's composition pre-determined by the electoral law itself. The unexpected outcome of the election created a whole new set of political relationships. The radical orientation of the new parliament put democracy on the agenda, and this required a law ensuring genuine political competition.

According to the law of April 1989 the Council of State determined the number of seats to be won by the PZPR and its coalition 'partners'[4] on the one hand and 'non-Party' (Opposition) candidates on the other. In each district at least one seat was reserved for a non-party victor. For each seat competition was intra-party for the 'establishment parties' (communist against communist, peasant against peasant…), but open for non-party seats. The basis for the Council's allocations was the proportions agreed at the Round Table: 35 per cent of seats for the 'non-party element' and 65 per cent for the establishment parties. The law also provided for an uncontested national list, drawn from the 'establishment' (Solidarity refused to participate). In the event 35 candidates stood on the national list.

This was a two-round majoritarian system save for the national list. The two leading candidates would go forward to any second-round run-off. Voting was by deletion of all but the desired candidate. For the (new) Senate, elected on the basis of unfettered competition, a block-vote two-round system was used: electors had two votes for two-member districts based on the 49 provinces (three votes/senators for Warsaw and Katowice), making a total of 100 senators.

The system not only 'fitted' the traditional communist majoritarian approach but appeared to provide the greatest certainty of outcome. Yet communist officials badly underestimated Solidarity's appeal. Although the decision to accept a freely elected Senate led some Party advisers to recommend a proportional electoral system for that body, the leaders firmly rejected this. They believed that stressing individual candidacies by well-known figures would be more effective against little known oppositionists than an overt campaign of 'Party against Solidarity'. They also set a tight election timetable on the assumption that Solidarity would find it difficult to respond rapidly. Nor did the PZPR expect the Church, which had affirmed its neutrality, to play such an active role in support of Solidarity.[5]

The mechanics of the system, the tactics of the contesting forces and the voters' response combined to generate the unanticipated elements of the result. Indeed, Solidarity's overwhelming victory came as a shock to both sides. The first departure from the script came with the national list debacle. So many voters deleted these candidates that only two obtained the required absolute majority. This result, in the context of the law's failure to anticipate such a contingency, left the establishment parties 33 deputies short (including their leaders), thus negating both the relative proportions negotiated at the Round Table and the constitutional requirement for a Sejm of 460 deputies. With Solidarity's passive consent, but conditional on the requirement that defeated candidates could not stand again, the Council of State amended the electoral law by a decree permitting additional district contests with new establishment candidates for the unfilled seats.

The second unexpected element – that all Solidarity candidates bar one emerged victorious – was a consequence of Solidarity's tactical sophistication, the PZPR's lack of control of its own party during the electoral process, and of course the behaviour of the voters. Critical here was Solidarity's placing of only one candidate in each contestable seat. Solidarity waged an efficient campaign, buttressed by a group of specialist commissions.[6] In contrast the PZPR's central authorities lacked effective control: numerous candidates contested the 'communist seats' in the Sejm and also, crucially, the Senate. Not only did these candidates split the communist vote, but some 40 per cent of voters deleted the names of all candidates for 'PZPR seats'.[7] The strategy of supporting 'distinguished', supposedly independent candidates in the 'non-party' contests also failed dismally.[8] The Party ran a lacklustre campaign. In the first round Solidarity's candidates won 160 of the 161 Sejm seats it was eligible to contest, and the PZPR won one of 'its' seats. Solidarity also won outright 92 of the 100 Senate seats and ultimately gained 99.

The second round restored the Party's nominal position to its planned complement of seats (38 per cent, with 27 per cent for the satellite parties); but without seats in the Senate and without its key leaders, the internal composition of its parliamentary contingent was very different from that originally foreseen. The PZPR could not rely even on its own deputies, and the satellite parties quickly defected from their alliance with the communists. After a summer of political crisis a Grand Coalition took office in September under Solidarity prime minister Tadeusz Mazowiecki.

Building democracy was high on the agenda, as the reformist parliament set about the business of system transformation. In June 1990 the Sejm debated proposed amendments to the 1989 electoral law, but deputies were unenthusiastic about a piecemeal approach,[9] preferring a fundamental overhaul. The Sejm had set up a committee, the Constitutional Commission, whose brief also embraced electoral reform.[10] By autumn two deputies had tabled the individual bills that formed the basis of subsequent deliberations. The (now direct) election of Solidarity leader Lech Wałęsa as president in December 1990 added another voice calling for speedy free elections, and hence a new electoral law.

The election of 27 October 1991 provided a new shock for the emerging political elite. The electoral system was widely blamed for the proliferation of parties, proto-parties and local groupings gaining representation under 29 labels. The problem was not simply these large numbers, but the absence of any strong party to anchor government formation: nine parties registered between 5.05 per cent and 12.31 per cent. Moreover, the two leading parties were Mazowiecki's Democratic Union (*Unia Demokratyczna*, UD) and the former communists' Alliance of the Democratic Left (*Sojusz Lewicy Demokratycznej*, SLD), and neither was an attractive coalition partner. The UD had seen a widespread reaction against its economic strategies of 'shock therapy' pursued under two Solidarity governments. The SLD remained 'communists', tainted by their historic role.

The difficult, protracted construction of Jan Olszewski's minority government reinforced these early concerns and encouraged reform initiatives. The Democratic Union articulated broadly shared aims of reducing fragmentation, especially to facilitate government formation and to strengthen political parties. However, a glut of legislation delayed parliamentary debate until June 1992, a period of intense political crisis; then Olszewski's defeat made the issue of government formation all the more serious. A year later the final debates took place in the shadow of another looming vote of confidence and in the immediate aftermath of the defeat of Hanna Suchocka's government. Although the president's subsequent dissolution of parliament was unexpected, the situation had imbued electoral reform with new urgency.

The second free parliamentary election took place in September 1993. The successor parties, the SLD and the Polish Peasant Party (*Polskie Stronnictwo Ludowe*, PSL), won a resounding victory, while most Solidarity parties suffered a traumatic defeat. Having designed an electoral system to favour larger groups and encourage alliances, the new parties remained fragmented, victims of their own hubris and misleading opinion polls. An exception was the merger of Labour Solidarity with the Social-Democratic Movement, both tiny in 1991 but now performing respectably as the Labour Union (*Unia Pracy*). The Democratic Union also succeeded, albeit with a reduced vote. Only two others crossed the threshold, the populist Confederation for Independent Poland (KPN) and Wałęsa's agglomeration of personal supporters, the BBWR (Non-Party Reform Bloc). Despite a reduction in the number of contenders, large numbers of local groupings stood again. The victors thus gained a huge seat premium from the enormous wasted vote of nearly one-third, with disproportionality further magnified by the failure of the KPN and the BBWR to achieve national list allocations (see Table 2.2).

The resulting SLD–PSL coalition had no incentive to alter the electoral law and ample parliamentary resources to block unwanted change.

Table 2.2 Party representation in the Sejm, 1993

Party	% vote	Seats	% seats
SLD	20.4	171	37.2
PSL	15.4	132	28.7
UD	10.6	74	16.0
UP	7.3	41	8.9
KPN	5.8	22	4.8
BBWR	5.4	16	3.5
German Minority*		4	0.9

* Thresholds did not apply.

Source: Państwowa Komisja Wyborcza.

President Wałęsa's proposal to reduce thresholds[11] was ignored, though many Labour Union proposals were taken seriously, including a change of formula. Some changes arose from technical considerations: regulations on the National Election Bureau in 1995; minor seat adjustments in March 1997 arising from a demographic review; amendments arising from the 1997 lustration law, requiring candidates to attest or deny past collaboration with the security services; and some changes in subsidy arrangements arising from the new law on political parties (June 1997). Essentially the law remained unchanged for the routine parliamentary elections of 1997.

The bitter blow for Solidarity parties in 1993 was followed by President Wałęsa's defeat at the hands of SLD leader Aleksander Kwaśniewski in December 1995. This double loss was sufficient to mobilize most extra-parliamentary Solidarity-derived parties into a new broad coalition, Solidarity Election Action (*Akcja Wyborcza Solidarność*, AWS). In 1997 AWS garnered many hitherto wasted votes, gaining over one-third of the total and benefiting from the seat premium for larger parties (see Table 2.3). Its coalition with the Freedom Union (*Unia Wolności*, which merged the Democratic Union and the Liberals in 1994) lasted until June 2000.

Government formation was no longer a problem; indeed Jerzy Buzek remained prime minister for the full parliamentary term. The need to adjust the electoral law now stemmed from the promulgation of the Constitution and administrative reorganization. The new Constitution permitted the candidacy of political parties and groups of voters, but not social organizations. The introduction of 16 provinces and a second county (*powiat*) tier required new boundaries for electoral districts. To these imperatives were added increasing concerns about corruption, leading to new initiatives regarding state financing of political parties.

Table 2.3 Successful contenders in elections to the Sejm, 25 September 1997

Party	% vote	Seats	% seats
Solidarity Election Action (AWS)	33.83	201	43.70
Alliance of the Democratic Left (SLD)	27.13	164	35.65
Freedom Union (UW)	13.37	60	13.04
Polish Peasant Party (PSL)	7.31	27	5.87
Movement for Rebuilding Poland (ROP)	5.56	6	1.30
German Minority*		2	

* Threshold did not apply.

Source: Państwowa Komisja Wyborcza.

AWS was anxious to strengthen its position, and it had campaigned in 1997 in favour of a 'majoritarian system', widely perceived as the means to entrenching political dualism. However, AWS had insufficient support to revoke the constitutional requirement for proportional representation. For a time speculation centred on possible AWS–SLD cooperation to introduce first-past-the-post. However, the SLD maintained its consistent endorsement of PR. Its spokesman argued that Poland had not yet matured sufficiently for a two-party system: the presence of two large and two medium-sized parties enabled stable government, while thresholds prevented excessive fragmentation.[12] Since AWS itself was never united on (nor ever clearly defined) its majoritarian preferences, battle ensued over the details of the PR system. In 2000 the main aim of AWS was to secure its own political advantage. In 2001 it joined a broad alliance seeking above all to limit the gains of the SLD.

The actors

Both the importance of institutional actors and the role and nature of the political parties altered throughout the 1990s. The Sejm itself remained the key forum for change, with the government notable for its absence. In 1990–1 the situation was at its most complex, with the 'contract Sejm' facing a hostile president, supported (for a time) by the Solidarity Senate. The interplay of these institutions was governed not only by rational calculation, but also by happenstance and personal loyalty. After 1991 the pre-eminence of the Sejm was unquestioned, with neither the president nor the Senate affecting electoral legislation.

Within the Sejm parliamentary commissions provided the main arena for substantive debate, with important elements of membership continuity across parliaments. In this respect the contributions of Professor Stanisław Gebethner of the University of Warsaw and Kazimierz Czaplicki, Secretary of the State Election Commisson, were of inestimable worth in helping to generate a body of expertise among commission members with technical advice, comparative analysis and simulations of proposed variants. Broadly speaking, deputies accepted decisions thrashed out in commission and defended in the Sejm.

Increasingly, political parties emerged as the instruments of structuring debate within the commissions and the Sejm. A considerable individualism marked the early debates of 1990–1 (the 'contract Sejm'). Ninety-one per cent of deputies lacked previous parliamentary experience[13] and within the broad reform consensus the organization of the Sejm into distinct parliamentary clubs was fluid. Following the PZPR's dissolution in January 1990 by no means all deputies joined its main successor, the SdRP (*Socjalno-demokracja Rzeczypospolitej Polskiej*), though most remained within the Parliamentary Club of the Democratic Left (PKLD). Solidarity too was in flux, as Mazowiecki's Democratic Union, Labour Solidarity (*Solidarność Pracy*) and a small agrarian element left the OKP (*Obywatelski Klub Parlamentarny*), Solidarity's Civic Parliamentary Club, leaving it effectively a federation of smaller groups. The former satellite, the United Peasant Party, maintained its unity and mutated gradually into the Polish Peasant Party (PSL). This process of division and realignment continued throughout the debates on the electoral law. By the eve of the first free election in October 1991 not only had the two large blocs shrunk from their original totals, but the remaining OKP deputies were rent by internal divisions. This made it difficult to unravel the precise nature of parliamentary gamesmanship as the Sejm commenced battle over the new electoral law, first internally and then with President Wałęsa.

In 1992–3 'parties' were adopting clearer positions and pursuing identifiable strategies. Many deputies of the small groupings did not vote, leaving the field to the larger entities. This continued after 1997, with the exception of AWS, whose main constituents began to act increasingly independently: AWS-RS (AWS-Social Movement, *Ruch Społeczny*) linked to the Solidarity trade union, the Conservative-People's Party (*Stronnictwo Konserwatywno-Ludowe*, SKL), the Christian National Union (*Zjednoczenie Chrześcijańsko-Narodowe*) and Christian Democracy (*Partia Chrześcijańskiej Demokracji*, PChD). By 2001, though 'political tourism' among deputies escalated as the UW and AWS began to disintegrate, voting was almost exclusively on (new) party lines.

This was, then, an elite game. The voice of public opinion was seldom heard. The significant exception concerned open lists, with their choice of individual candidate. President Wałęsa and his supporters advocated closed lists to strengthen political parties, but they were defeated in 1991, largely on the grounds that the immature parties were largely unknown. Subsequently a number of parties converted to closed lists, based on arguments that the early conditions no longer applied. Most then reversed their position, acknowledging polls showing massive public support for open lists as their reason. Individual deputies made similar references to such polls in the course of parliamentary debates.

The process of change

The Law of 1991

The first proposals for electoral reform came in summer 1990 from individual deputies of the Peasant Party and Solidarity respectively. Many recurring issues first appeared then, but there was a measure of consensus on the need to stimulate public involvement, with easy registration for both political parties and candidates, and to secure effective representation. Aleksander Łuczak's (PSL) bill[14] provided for PR along with the 'fairest' Hare formula, with open lists to maximize electoral choice. Henryk Michalak (OKP, then UD)[15] proposed a mixed parallel system, with 230 single-member districts and 230 deputies from multi-member districts allocated by the d'Hondt formula. He argued that deputies from single-member districts would 'raise and reflect local problems', while those elected from closed party lists would represent 'national interests'.

Key debates took place in the autumn,[16] with the main aim of guiding the Constitutional Commission on the fundaments of the new law. On 25 October 200 deputies voted for a proportional system and 110 supported a 'majoritarian' system.[17] Since a majoritarian system was not on the table, the minority vote was interpreted as supporting Michalak. As both bills were deemed to have 'useful provisions', both were referred to the Commission, which established a working party on electoral reform under Łuczak.

Deliberations were given shape by the expertise of Professor Gebethner.[18] The major problem, which ultimately determined the group's final recommendations, was that of district boundaries, linked to issues of representation. Some supported larger multi-member (13–18) districts to provide greater proportionality. Others opposed the detachment of electoral boundaries from existing provincial structures, as bigger districts would 'create too much distance between deputy and voters, while provinces are deeply rooted in popular consciousness'.[19] These views looked increasingly difficult to reconcile, and both mixed and proportional variants were explored. The working party spent some time on a 'German variant', offering some elasticity in the number of seats, and even a 'Hungarian variant', adding a third-tier national list to ensure that the existing political elite, heavily concentrated in Warsaw, would gain 'an honest route to parliament'.

As new implications emerged from successive attempts to find a solution to the definition of electoral districts, so members' views shifted. With successive meetings[20] attention finally concentrated on two systemic variants: (1) a mixed-member proportional system and (2) an open-list PR system with a national list and a low threshold. The working group preferred the second variant, but with an enthusiastic minority pressing for a mixed system;[21] it sought guidance from its parent, the Constitutional Commission, given 'the impossibility' of preparing two separate laws in the time available.

The Commission met on 14 February 1991.[22] To great consternation its chair, Bronisław Geremek, ruled that the vote – three for PR and 14 for a mixed system, but with 14 abstentions – constituted an endorsement of the mixed system. Since Geremek's party, the Democratic Union, favoured a mixed system, his ruling was seen as highly partisan.

Once this decision had been taken, deliberations proceeded more easily. The working party prepared a constitutional amendment to permit a flexible number of deputies and agreed an array of technical specifications before returning to the issue of boundaries.[23] Its final draft provided for 115 single-member districts and 345 deputies from 20 multi-member districts. The Constitutional Commission accepted most recommendations, but reinstated the open list, despite strong views that the opportunity for individual preference in single-member districts made it redundant. It also agreed to present the Sejm with several variants, notably in the choice of formula. Minority amendments were also tabled, concerning requirements regarding deposits, a 5 per cent threshold, the opportunity to campaign in churches, closed and preference list systems, and whether the franchise should include Poles resident abroad.[24]

Just as the final details were being added after months of deliberations, a new actor appeared on stage. President Wałęsa opposed the draft law and felt 'obliged to enter the process of preparing free elections ... to accelerate and facilitate the legislative process' to permit the holding of elections on 26 May. The president proposed a mixed parallel system not dissimilar to that of the original Michalak draft, but with closed party lists in one national constituency for the PR element.[25] On 10 March the Sejm referred the two drafts to the Constitutional Commission. Ten days later, however, a set of 'theses' arrived from the presidential chancellery. These proposed election of 391 deputies by closed-list PR with a top-up of 69 deputies from national lists. The working party patiently incorporated elements of this variant, making a three-tier system:[26] a national list with a 5 per cent threshold, 19–20 multi-member and 115 single-member districts.

The Sejm accepted this version,[27] specifying open lists, but increasing the number of multi-member districts to 35 in accordance with the president's preference. After a month (the delay itself a source of constitutional complications[28]), Wałęsa vetoed the law, accusing the Sejm of deliberate procrastination.[29] He criticized the law's complexity and offered two further versions, PR with a national list or a mixed-parallel system. This second variant was close to the Sejm's original (but mixed-linked) bill. Wałęsa reiterated his advocacy of closed lists to strengthen political parties.

The Sejm failed by seven votes to overturn the veto. The Constitutional Commission convened immediately, imbued with urgency as the October election deadline drew nearer. Informed by the Sejm debate (for example, large electoral districts had not found favour) and accepting the judgement that the law was too complex, it proceeded by a series of votes on key presidential points. Some were by a very narrow margin, including the fundamental decision to accept much of the president's PR variant. The commission retained Hare quotas for districts, with a 5 per cent national-list threshold to counter Hare's favouring of smaller parties and thus prevent 'excessive fragmentation'. For the lists it chose a half-way house, voluntary preference voting.[30]

The law passed on 15 June 1991, accepting the commission's version but reinstating open lists. Debate concentrated on the urgency of the matter and the need for compromise. Mieczysław Gil of the OKP and a presidential supporter said, 'The law is still a mess, incomprehensible and not adapted to our political reality, but it is an improvement.'[31] Speakers were critical but clearly willing to make concessions.

Although the Senate fully supported Wałęsa, the Sejm easily overturned its amendments.[32] The temperature had been visibly raised, with deputies seething at less-than-veiled presidential threats of dissolution. The issues had ceased to be centre-stage. At stake was parliamentary sovereignty, the 'political servility and obedience to be exacted from parliament' (Geremek), 'the genuine threat to our developing democracy' (R. Zielinski).

Wałęsa was furious. However, his unwarranted threats to dissolve parliament meant a looming constitutional crisis. Repeating the veto, he again argued for closed lists, claiming that '…the aim should be to limit intra-party competition in the electoral battle and thus to strengthen the fragmented and still weak political system.'[33]

Battlelines were clear. The Sejm 'should not fall to its knees, it must not submit to blackmail'.[34] The successor parties, the Democratic Union and a handful of other 'Solidarity' deputies argued for parliament, while most of the OKP proved loyal to the president. The Sejm easily overturned the second veto and a reluctant Wałęsa signed the new law.

No one fully approved of the law, though many defended it as the best compromise in the circumstances.[35] Both the president and the Sejm had variously endorsed both proportional and mixed systems before settling on variants of the latter, yet in the final version the majoritarian element disappeared altogether. However, most variants debated were more or less acceptable to deputies. The successor groups favoured PR, unsurprisingly in the context of their perceived weakness.

The president's second PR variant brought their preferred version back centre-stage, facilitated by a broad acceptance that the president was right about the complexity of the May compromise.

The Democratic Union preferred a mixed system to develop the deputy–voter linkages associated with single-member districts and to facilitate government formation. Opinion polls also appeared to give it (the illusion of) substantial electoral support, with expected victories for well-known figures in single-member districts. However, the UD would also gain from PR and it deplored the president's threats. Some incipient parties did manifest 'interests' on particular issues, for example the Christian groupings passionately supporting electoral campaigning on church grounds; the president supported this and it was ultimately conceded. To impute perceived party interest as the main motivator in a general sense was probably true, but to link party interests to advocacy of a particular electoral system is extremely difficult. Successor deputies supported PR, but they were not united on issues of the formula, the threshold or district magnitude. In the end much of the OKP ignored the issues and supported the president. It is thus highly misleading to see the law as 'designed to guarantee every grouping a fair chance of winning representation...'.[36] To refer to the law as 'designed' is itself something of a misnomer.

The president's role remains puzzling. Wałęsa's subsequent claim that he could not discuss matters with the undemocratic 'contract Sejm' was unconvincing. He had made no effort to woo parliament, nor to establish a clear political base among Solidarity deputies. His timing and inconsistency were inexplicable, and his confrontational style proved counterproductive. Some observers blamed presidential advisers from the Centre Accord (PC, *Porozumienie Centrum*) and the Christian National Union (ZChN), both of whom energetically supported a closed list system. One should also remember that opposing arguments were being put forward by the President's personal antagonists, notably from the Democratic Union. In the final analysis, however, the issues did not seem worth the candle.

The 1993 Law

Following the 1991 election, with its resulting high level of fragmentation, the Democratic Union returned to its initial preference for a mixed system, with three-quarters of deputies elected from closed lists. It aimed to generate the 'representation of political forces capable of engendering stable political camps forming government and opposition' and to 'embed political parties in the electoral process'.[37]

However, the UD found little support for its view that a mixed system would deliver the 'best of both worlds'.[38] Deputies of varied persuasion questioned whether the majoritarianism of the single-member districts would have the claimed consolidating effect. Many feared that it would encourage Independents, thus hindering the development of political parties (the 'Ukrainian problem'). The majority clearly favoured the threshold as the preferred mechanism for militating against fragmentation.

Following first reading the bill was referred to an Extraordinary Commission. Although this parliamentary committee was to deliberate for almost nine months, it spent much time on complex technical matters arising from the 1991 law, rather than on substantive, more obviously political issues. Indeed, its deliberations proved easier than those of 1991, not least because many of its members already had clearly developed views.

Having identified key issues, the commission proceeded immediately to a series of decisive votes[39] endorsing PR and maintaining the national list. Its vote favouring d'Hondt for the national list as opposed to Sainte-Laguë was much narrower (10–8). It agreed a threshold of 5 per cent, with 8 per cent thresholds for coalitions and the national list. It also returned to the strongly held view of a large minority in the previous parliament that electoral districts should coincide with provinces, except for Warsaw and Katowice. One argument was that deputies from combined provinces were not linked to a particular area, undermining bonds with their voters. A second was that smaller districts would favour larger parties, thus helping to reduce fragmentation. The commission also echoed the now-widespread sentiment in favour of closed lists. Another innovation (adopted) was the principle of a 20 per cent reimbursement of campaign costs on the basis of votes gained.[40]

More contentious was whether the national minorities should be exempt from the threshold requirement (confirmed, with a vocal minority maintaining that exemption undermined the equality of the electoral process),[41] and whether parties alone should have the right to submit candidates (a compromise specified parties, national minority organizations and, for one election only, trade unions).[42] From August, the commission also worked to accommodate the expected provisions of the new 'Little Constitution'.

The debate (the second reading of the now unrecognizable UD bill[43]) took place on 19 March (see Table 2.4).[44] Most favourable were the Confederation for Independent Poland (KPN) and the German Minority. The UD, the Conservatives (KP), Christian Democracy (CD) and the Liberal Democrats (KLD) preferred a mixed system but broadly

Table 2.4   Major party positions in March 1993

Party	Thresholds	List	Minorities exempt	Parties only to stand	Formula	National list
UD	As draft*	Open	Yes	Yes	d'Hondt	Yes
SLD	As draft*	Open	Yes	No	d'Hondt	Yes
KLD	Uncertain	Closed	Yes	Yes	Uncertain	Yes
PSL	District	Open	No	No		No
KPN	As draft*	Closed	Yes	Yes		Yes
ZChN	3%, 6%, 5%		No			Yes
Solidarity	4% or lower	Open	Yes	No	No view taken	Yes
KP	5%, 5%, 5%					Yes
PL	3%	Closed	Yes	Yes		
PC	As draft*	Closed	No	Yes		Yes
RdR		Open	No	No	Majoritarian system	No
MN	As draft*	Closed	Yes	Yes	d'Hondt	Yes
CD	None	Open	No	No	Other	Yes
SP	3%	Open	Yes		Other	
UPR		Open	No	Yes	Majoritarian system	

*   The draft envisaged 5% for parties, and 8% for coalitions and national lists.

Source: Based on the debate of 19 March: *Sprawozdanie stenograficzne z 40 posiedzenia Sejmu RP w dniach 18, 19, 20 i 31 marca 1993 r.*

endorsed the proposed changes, though the UD now supported open lists. Most small parties protested bitterly at the range of provisions favouring larger ones (thresholds, the d'Hondt formula, their reduced requirements for gathering signatures, the national list); Ryszard Bugaj of Labour Solidarity (SP) called the sum of measures an 'electoral swindle'. However, two – the Union of Political Realism (UPR) and Olszewski's new Movement for the Republic (RdR) – advocated a fully majoritarian system for reasons that remained unclear.

Two contentious issues were pre-empted by the decision to reject changes necessitating constitutional amendment. These were: (1) that only political parties and minorities might stand with, for one election, the trade unions; and (2) changes in incompatibility rules. Subsequent debate of the revised draft added little to well rehearsed arguments.[45] Given the large number of minority amendments, however, the Sejm

Table 2.5 Selected votes on third reading amendments, 1993

Issue	Deputies voting	For	Against	Abstained
Reject draft law	337	78	249	10
Remove national list	359	77	267	15
Remove thresholds	370	51	284	35
Party/coalition thresholds 3/5%	363	98	275	8
National list threshold 7%*	370	181	176	13
Remove minority exemption	363	137	212	14
Open list*	356	214	122	20
Signatures from 3000 to 5000*	354	193	103	58
Ban campaign from Church grounds	343	99	195	49

* Change from commission draft.

Source: Derived from *Sprawozdanie Stenograficzne z 42 posiedzenie Sejmu RP w dniach 15, 16, 17, 28 i 29 kwietnia 1993 r.*

requested a further report from the commission, provided for the third reading on 15 April.[46]

The Commission's recommendations were broadly accepted (see Table 2.5). The final vote on the completed law was decisive: 239 to 132, with four abstentions (18 per cent of deputies failed to vote). The clear view was that 1991 could not be repeated and that larger parties should be favoured. Yet strict party 'self-interest' was far from absolute in this context. None of the nine leading 'parties' was actually 'large', and party discipline was limited. Many individual speakers departed in debate from their party's stance.

The Sejm later accepted two Senate amendments:[47] 3000 signatures to support district lists (the original commission view) and the removal of the vote granted stateless persons.[48] The debate of 27 May[49] was brief, with a confidence vote looming. On 28 May the Sejm completed the final stages following its vote of no confidence in Suchocka's government. President Wałęsa signed the law on 1 June and called an election for 19 September.

The Law of 2001

We have seen that little change followed the 1993 election, despite extra-parliamentary concerns about the high level of wasted votes. There were several failed initiatives, notably to change thresholds and formulae.[50] However, after the 1997 election adapting the law to the new Constitution was imperative, and from 1999 the definition of new provinces implied new electoral boundaries. Politicians seized the opportunity to proffer their own initiatives, and what could have been a routine task became a political battle to secure advantage at the next election.

Five party drafts reached the Sejm between July and September: from the SLD, the PSL, the UW, SKL (AWS) and AWS-RS.[51] All parties accepted that districts must be based primarily on divisions of the new provinces, also respecting county boundaries. All accepted the maintenance of thresholds. All accepted that deputies and senators could not serve simultaneously as local, county or provincial councillors. All save RS favoured open lists (see Table 2.6).

The SLD version was most conservative, though it proposed that national list seats be allocated first, to the highest winners in the districts, and some reduction in district magnitude. (For the Senate, where it had done relatively badly, the SLD favoured a mixed system.) The UW and PSL proposals favoured smaller to medium-sized parties, with larger districts and a shift to a Sainte-Laguë formula. The UW also proposed quotas for women. The SKL proposed (even) larger districts. Like the PSL, it opposed the national list but left other major provisions intact. AWS-RS shifted its position, from very small districts and closed lists to agree with the SLD over open lists and district size, albeit with a reduced national list.

Given the complexity of adapting all electoral laws and the law on political parties to new constitutional and administrative requirements, the Sejm established the extraordinary commission known as NOW to consider the tabled proposals and a raft of others linked to these areas.[52] The Sejm's Administrative Commission continued work on state

Table 2.6   Proposals for electoral system change in Poland, 1999

Party	District magnitude	Thresholds	No. of districts	List	National list	Formula
(1993 law)	3–17	5–8–7	52	Open	Yes	d'Hondt
SLD	5–12	5–8–7	52	Open	Allocate 1st	d'Hondt
PSL	7–19	5–8	36	Open	No	Modified Ste-Laguë
UW	8–16		37	Open	Yes	Ste-Laguë
AWS (SKL)	10–19	5–8		Open	No	d'Hondt
AWS-RS	6–12			Open	Reduce to 50	d'Hondt

Source: Derived from party drafts.

financing of parties, later utilized by NOW. As before, NOW's members received publications detailing different types of electoral system and simulations of previous Polish elections, as well as again benefiting from expert advisers.

Only in spring 2000 did NOW began to address the ingredients stressed by the parties, identifying such key issues as the formula, the national list, the principles for establishing districts and incompatibility rules. Members accepted a minimum district magnitude of seven. With votes largely along party lines, the AWS–SLD majority initially supported d'Hondt and rejected the elimination of the national list. However, all but the SLD members agreed a reduction of the national list to 50 deputies.[53]

Further work resulted from NOW's decision to present a single, unified electoral law for both Sejm and Senate.[54] This led to linking the two chambers, with 41 Sejm and 40 Senate districts providing a uniform representational norm based on population (effectively, ten senators moved to the west side of the Vistula). In general, the precise boundaries of electoral districts were hugely contested, with battles for extra deputies in perceived party strongholds. The other issue causing bitter exchanges was the revived debate contesting the exemption of national minorities from national thresholds – on grounds that it violated basic principles of equality and non-discrimination.

On 12–13 July 2000 in an ill-tempered and highly partisan atmosphere NOW worked its way through 252 articles of its new draft[55] in preparation for the parliamentary debate. In June the UW had withdrawn from the governing coalition. SLD was riding high in the polls. Already some pleaded openly for an anti-SLD alliance to reduce the advantages for larger parties. When (AWS) Marshal Płażyński delayed the parliamentary debate, allegedly because the commission had not elaborated the financial implications of its draft, both the SLD and the UW saw this as a move to prevent an early parliamentary election. It could also be seen as a move to await the testing of the political waters in the forthcoming presidential election.

On 6 September the Sejm conducted an acrimonious debate[56] on NOW's new draft electoral law and amendments to the law on political parties.[57] There was a broad welcome for the greater openness and regulation of party finance, the innovative dimension of this latest stage of the electoral reform process. It included state financing of parties, an Election Fund through which all campaign expenditure would be channelled, prohibition of corporate and foreign donations, limits on total campaign expenditure and limits to individual donations. All current drafts (the Sejm's Administrative Commission had reached somewhat different conclusions on subsidies) were referred to NOW for reconciliation and refinement.

The general tenor of the debate was a predictable riding of individual hobbyhorses, some intelligent analysis and some rather contradictory perspectives. Those who opposed the national list as an anti-democratic elitist plot to strengthen political parties included some of its main beneficiaries. Splinter groups advocated majoritarian solutions while condemning provisions favourable to larger parties. In this vein one deputy congratulated 'AWS and the SLD on their cleverness in dividing Poland between themselves'.

However, AWS deputies were now far from confident of its strategy. The presidential campaign was going badly, leading to unsubtle delaying tactics in the NOW commission by AWS members.[58] Indeed, Aleksander Kwaśniewski's re-election that same month proved cataclysmic for AWS. Its candidate Marian Krzaklewski came an ignominious third and AWS began its protracted implosion. The election wrought havoc on the UW as well. Chunks of its liberal wing broke off to join AWS conservatives (SKL) in support of the new Civic Platform (*Platforma Obywatelska*), inspired by the creditable second-place performance of independent candidate Andrzej Olechowski. The SLD saw its former leader victorious on the first ballot and its own support topping 50 per cent in some surveys.[59]

The political situation evoked prospects of a massive SLD majority. The AWS Council suddenly embraced higher district magnitude, the Sainte-Laguë formula and no national list.[60] On 18 January 2001 NOW voted to support modified Sainte-Laguë for both districts and national lists. Its majority openly aimed for an anti-SLD alliance to limit the electoral gains of the SLD in the autumn. Yet despite earlier agreement that the electoral law should be subject to fast-track processes, the scheduled parliamentary debate was yet again postponed.

The law passed the Sejm on 7 March 2001,[61] with the revised NOW version largely intact.[62] Voting was on party lines, endorsing provisions deemed to favour medium-sized parties. Members associated with the new *Platforma* (PO) now strongly opposed state financing of parties, but their new-found endorsement of majoritarianism did not lead them to oppose the law. Only the SLD voted against it, along with four members of AWS and ten non-aligned deputies.

The signal departure from NOW's recommendations was the elimination of the national list, with consequent increases in district magnitude. Because of underlying anxieties about political fragmentation, the formula adopted was modified rather than 'classical' Sainte-Laguë. Thresholds, 5 and 8 per cent for parties and coalitions respectively, remained unchanged. Proposals for women's quotas failed, as did the withdrawal of national minority exemptions. The law introduced campaign expenditure limits and state funding of political parties, with a ban on party fund-raising or economic activity.

On 11 April the Sejm rejected the substantive changes proposed by the Senate, including opposition to state financing of parties, changes to some district boundaries and the substitution of classical Sainte-Laguë. Despite rumours to the contrary, President Kwaśniewski criticized but did not veto the law; given the support of all parties save SLD, the veto would easily have been overridden. Kwaśniewski signed the law and announced elections for 23 September. The next instalment of electoral reform was complete, but it was unlikely to prove the final chapter. Neither AWS nor UW passed the electoral thresholds in the election of 2001, which also saw the entry into parliament of four new political formations, including PO and two strident populist groupings. Of the latter the radical Self-Defence (*Samo-Obrona*) in particular appeared to have tenuous regard for the principles of parliamentary democracy. Again, the electoral system was deemed the main culprit, and all major parties announced a desire for electoral reform.

Conclusion

Poland's electoral law proved easy to change, but the process of change went through successive phases, with different actors dominating each stage. The law governing the semi-competitive election of 1989 was the product of elite bargaining between the ruling PZPR and the Solidarity opposition. This was a strange two-player game. The stronger side proved itself a prisoner of its own past. Assuming that the new rules would function just as the old rules had done, the communist elite badly miscalculated its position and made fundamental strategic errors. Choices and judgements that appeared fully rational from within the communist mind-set proved far from rational in terms of outcome. Solidarity, the weaker side in the bargaining process, was less laden with baggage, better prepared and more astute. From the communist point of view the 1989 electoral law was a massive failure of institutional design and political acumen.

Following Solidarity's dramatic achievement in 1989 the Round Table Parliament was striking in its broad consensus, partly despite and partly because of the unique, accidental character of its composition.

New political parties were in the first stages of formation as Solidarity crumbled, while the successor parties underwent internal crises of adaptation to new circumstances. The Social Democrats had identified a bedrock of support of some 10 per cent in the 1990 presidential election and had a sound organizational base. The Peasant Party also had realistic expectations of considerable support in rural areas. Otherwise there were few signs to guide the self-interest of aspiring politicians.

In this context the deliberations in 1990–1 over the new electoral law were at first highly individual, depending not least on the willingness of particular deputies to engage with the subject matter of electoral reform. At the same time a clear consensus prevailed within the Sejm on certain aspects of reform. The aim was to open up the political landscape, with few constraints on registering political parties, ease of candidature, media access and so on. Deputies were often content to take guidance from the working group, a subcommittee of the Constitutional Commission, where a body of expertise developed, taking as its reference points generalizations about the expected operation of different types of electoral system. This embraced both the mechanical, arithmetical perspective and the practical experience of other countries. Expert advisers were vital to this learning process. Yet the initial decision taken in 1991 to proceed with a mixed-member proportional system was almost accidental, depending effectively on a single controversial vote in the Constitutional Commission. When the president entered the fray with further PR and mixed variants, the electoral system became the arena for institutional conflict between president and the Sejm. Ironically the Sejm prevailed, but its attempts to compromise moved it away from its own mixed-system preference to the president's final preference for PR. In the end the Sejm had little difficulty in accepting a PR list system, albeit with a national-list threshold to prevent undue fragmentation (which materialized in any case).

As parties developed and the general institutional framework became clearer, parties contesting successive elections had a better sense of their own appeal and an emerging electoral geography. The SLD was especially well placed in this regard, garnering votes steadily over successive elections. Its refusal to abandon proportional representation was justified as in the public interest, but also served a legitimizing role to assuage anxieties about its thirst for a renewed monopoly of power. Within the PR framework the SLD pursued seat-maximizing solutions.

For other actors uncertainty remained high, as the Solidarity parties found to their cost in 1993 when the number of parliamentary actors was dramatically reduced by the cumulative effects of new measures designed as an antidote to the fragmentation of the 1991 Sejm. Both the Freedom Union (UW), once hopeful of reaping major electoral success but then resigned to at best medium-sized status, and the Peasant Party (PSL), limited by its rather narrow appeal, supported measures to assist such parties.

AWS was the strongest political force after the 1997 elections, but its shifts of view on electoral reform paralleled its decline in the polls and its defeat in the 2000 presidential elections. Its election manifesto endorsed a majoritarian system, then it supported PR with devices favouring larger parties, before shifting again to supporting the PSL's and UW's preferences for mechanisms deemed to support medium-sized parties. It was this coalition of parties seeking to forestall electoral disaster and a majority SLD government that triumphed in 2001 – though to no avail for UW and the remnant of AWS. That once again the electoral outcome did not meet the expectations of its architects was less a failure of institutional design than a result of the readiness of both party leaders and voters to abandon former allegiances.

We can see then both the advantages and limits of approaches focused on strategic actors and the concept of interests. While one must recognize that the concept of interests is itself multi-dimensional, Poland's parties came to act in accordance with seat-maximizing aims. At the same time they often underestimated the continuing uncertainties of 'transition'.

3
Hungary: the Politics of Negotiated Design

The view that the mixed Hungarian electoral system adopted in 1989 would be merely provisional was not borne out in practice.[1] The new system remained intact in all its essentials. It was a distinctive system in both its genesis and its nature. First of all, it was adopted almost entirely as a result of elite negotiations outside the existing formal institutional framework. Hungarian developments constituted the purest example of post-communist 'transition by pact', in a process of round-table discussions inaugurated by reformist elements within the Hungarian Socialist Workers' Party (*Mágyar Szocialista Munkáspárt*, MSzMP). At the outset their interlocutors, disparate elements of the Opposition Round Table, lacked even the legitimacy of popular recognition. Both internal desiderata and external developments shaped a situation in which the ruling party rapidly ceased to control the reform process. Unlike Poland, where the Communist Party lost control as a result of unanticipated outcomes of its own Round Table agreement, in Hungary the aims of the negotiations were system-transforming by the start of negotiations, and the balance of power shifted to the Opposition in the course of the National Round Table itself. Media coverage was limited,[2] while the core of the negotiations, gatherings of party and opposition experts, remained closed throughout the deliberative process.

The new electoral law was also distinctive in its complexity. It was indeed a 'fabulously incomprehensible electoral system'.[3] The arcane interweaving of the three elements of the mixed system meant that neither its architects nor its voters could anticipate the manner in which votes cast would be translated into seats won. There were no overarching principles of system design at work: neither proportionality, nor deputy–constituency links, nor ease of government formation. Though all these were adduced as 'reasons' for particular solutions at various times, the mechanisms adopted were a result of a succession of compromises and trade-offs in circumstances of ad hoc judgements of party advantage. No one anticipated the picture that would emerge as the pieces of the jigsaw were put together. To judge that 'Hungarians sought the best of both electoral worlds'[4] with a mixed electoral system is at best an oversimplification of this complex process. Nor is it correct to maintain that the Hungarian law was 'modelled basically on the German system',[5] from which it differs in fundamental respects.

After three elections considerable uncertainty remained about the impact of the electoral law, including how Hungary fitted into the broad category of 'mixed electoral systems'. What did appear clear, however, was that despite the anomalies, the process of institutional reproduction had begun and difficult hurdles faced advocates of fundamental change.

The origins of the origins

Electoral reform had been a persistent theme of Hungarian politics since the mid-1960s. Unlike most communist states, the Hungarian regime had moved much later to relinquish the list system, although PR became irrelevant in 1949 with a single 'government list' and no opposition candidates. In 1966 Hungary adopted the typical majoritarian system of the Soviet bloc, designed to 'strengthen links between deputies and their constituents'. Its provision for multiple candidacies was not widely utilized, and in 1970 the Central Committee called for an 'improvement in the electoral mechanism'.[6] That year the monopoly of the People's Patriotic Front in nomination proceedings was abolished, and voters were required to delete all but their preferred candidate. Still, though multiple candidacies declined or remained static,[7] they did not remain a complete dead letter. When generalized concerns about political participation and the strengthening of 'socialist pluralism' placed electoral reform on the agenda in the early 1980s to 'enhance the political maturation and voluntary participation of the citizenry',[8] increased electoral choice was the centrepiece of the new proposals. Choice would enliven elections and rejuvenate parliament. At the same time, the revised electoral law of 1983 included sufficient mechanisms to ensure that participation remained controlled, within carefully defined limits. Thus there were new provisions for mandatory multiple candidacies in each constituency, along with the right of individuals to submit nominations. Yet a new, uncontested national list virtually assured the election of selected luminaries, while all candidates had to accept the programme of the People's Patriotic Front in writing.

In general the scope for party control remained considerable, particularly in respect of nominating procedures,[9] and it proved easy to ensure the defeat of prominent dissidents in the nomination process. Local party committees were quite successful in persuading incumbents not to stand as part of the proposed 'renewal', but they had difficulty in finding 'matching pairs' of competing candidates to generate the desired composition of the new parliament. Multiple candidacies did improve the quality of political debate, and local issues emerged as central to the campaign; indeed, the 1985 election marked the 'arrival of local notables on the national political scene'.[10] Run-off contests were needed in 42 of the 352 seats, and 35 genuine Independents won seats in the new parliament along with the new breed of party members. The new parliament became increasingly active, both in the work of its committee system and in its public profile.[11] The concept of constituency service developed; it became an important reason for the subsequent emphasis on single-member districts in the 1989 electoral law.

The strengthening of parliament mirrored the government's own attempts to gain greater independence from the party *apparat*, a process which intensified after the sweeping away of the Kádárist Old Guard in spring 1988. Karoly Grósz, who became Prime Minister in June 1987, launched a campaign of public consultation, bringing in a wide range of expert groups to strengthen his own support. At the same time Imre Pozsgay, General Secretary of the People's Patriotic Front, was developing that organization as a political base for the growing reform wing of the Party. Pozsgay aided the establishment of the Hungarian Democratic Forum (*Magyar Demokrata Fórum*, MDF), formed in September 1987 to extend political dialogue to the 'populist' wing of the Hungarian opposition.[12] It was also Pozsgay who helped the Independent Smallholders Party (*Független Kisgazda-, Földmunkás-és Polgári Párt*, FKgP), the People's Party (*Magyar Néppárt*, MNP), and the Social Democratic Party (*Magyarországi Szociáldemokrata Párt*, MSzDP) to reconstitute themselves the following year.

In 1987 government and party bodies were working again on electoral reform, albeit still within the context of one-party 'socialist pluralism'. On 30 January 1988 the MDF held a conference on representative democracy, resulting *inter alia* in demands for a new democratic electoral law.[13] The ruling party's proposals for its own rejuvenation and for the modernization of all political, social and economic institutions intensified with Kádár's removal. The government prepared a new draft electoral law, submitted for public consultation in October 1988. Given the ferment of political debate, it was a surprisingly conservative document. The draft replaced individual nomination rights, restricting nomination to collective organizations, as well as proposing an enlargement of the national list. During the consultation process, the draft found few defenders.

New proposals were generated within a rapidly changing political environment, culminating in the relinquishing of the party's 'leading role' at its February plenum in 1989, and its formal commitment to the development of multi-party democracy. In January the new law on associations had effectively legitimized the formation of new political parties. For a brief period the leadership flirted with a 'Polish strategy', an interim negotiated sharing of the mandates with opposition representatives, with fully free elections delayed until 1995.[14] Its attempts to 'divide and rule' the main opposition bodies failed in March with the formation of the Opposition Round Table, whose commitment to fully competitive elections was central and non-negotiable. Even then none of the top leaders 'doubted that the HSWP would remain the largest party, or at least would become the dominant force in a coalition government after the next elections'.[15] In spring 1989 government experts drafted ten variants of a new electoral law[16] which 'already bore the imprint of the emerging multiparty system'.[17]

The negotiating parties

The National Round Table that conducted Hungary's negotiated transition convened discussions between the ruling party, the Opposition Round Table and the so-called third side representing social organizations, mainly through the Patriotic Popular Front. The third side had little influence, leaving essentially a two-element bargaining format. Of the groups that made up the Opposition Round Table, seven were 'political parties', one a trade union (the Democratic League of Independent Trade Unions), while the Bajcsy-Zsilinszky Friends' Society (BZSBT) and the Independent Lawyers' Forum were non-party groups of intellectuals. These organizations were not wholly distinct, and several had close links with one another and with the reformist Pozsgay, under whose auspices many had first developed. The most important were the new parties that had emerged from Hungary's increasingly pluralist ferment from the mid-1980s.

Of these, the Hungarian Democratic Forum (MDF) was the most prominent (it officially became a 'political party' in October 1989), originally conceived as a broad discussion forum to seek a specific 'Hungarian way', inspired by populist writers of the 1930s[18] and a concern to renew the decaying moral fabric of Hungarian society.[19] The MDF began to organize from summer 1988, becoming 'the only truly national movement'.[20] However, it had no formal programme, and it did not immediately abandon its middle position as a bridge between reformist elements of the regime[21] and the radical democratic opposition. At the National Round Table it was not however the Forum's leaders but the loosely associated lawyer László Sólyom, the historian György Szabad, and the museum director József Antall who played decisive roles. In particular the Round Table provided a stage for revealing Antall's strategic efficacy and negotiating skills. He became its star performer, and later the Forum's leader and prime minister.

The second major strand of the opposition was the Free Democrats (*Szabad Demokraták Szövetsége*, SzDSz), the core of which was a group of long-standing openly dissident intellectuals. SzDSz emerged from the Network of Free Initiatives, a loose alliance of burgeoning new groups, to form a 'political party' in November 1988. Its uncompromising goal was a fully Western-style liberal democracy, with strong, clearly defined civil liberties and a social–liberal market economy, buttressed by an 'unyielding anti-communism'.[22]

The third and less important of the new parties was the Alliance of Young Democrats (*Fiatal Demokraták Szövetsége*, FIDESZ). FIDESZ grew out of university discussion clubs dissatisfied with the education system to extend its concerns to the wider political system. It rapidly developed a radical political agenda stressing constitutionalism and human rights. It remained a youth movement (the age limit was 35) designed to appeal to the young, inviting their contribution to a 'new Hungary'. The regime initially opposed FIDESZ's participation at the National Round Table, and FIDESZ itself opposed premature negotiations or any strategy of 'national reconciliation'. Its future leader Viktor Orbán[23] came to public attention in June 1989 at the reinterment of Imre Nagy, the Hungarian leader of 1956. Orbán used the occasion for impassioned anti-communism, demanding the immediate withdrawal of the Soviet troops permanently stationed in Hungary since 1956. Yet FIDESZ proved less radical than many had anticipated, and its commitment to non-violent transition remained unswerving.

All three new parties enjoyed close links with one another. Their membership also overlapped with that of the Bajcsy-Zsilinszky Friends, which enjoyed a particularly close relationship with the Forum. The Democratic League of Independent Trade Unions, originally conceived as an alternative union movement, but developing as 'more think tank than trade union',[24] had close relations with SzDSz. The latter set up a separate secretariat to cultivate relations with the trade unions and encouraged its emerging local branches to assist the League's activity.[25] There were also some Fidesz members in the League.

The remaining 'parties' of the Opposition Round Table constituted 'historic parties', claiming direct legitimacy mainly from their pre-communist forebears, but also their temporary resurgence in Nagy's short-lived multi-party government in 1956. The Independent Small-holders Party had the strongest such claim, having achieved a stagger-ing 57 per cent of the vote in the free parliamentary elections of 1945. The Social Democratic Party had had a stormy postwar history, at first cooperating with the communists, then divided over its forced fusion with them, then briefly re-emerging in 1956. The Hungarian People's Party defined itself as the legal successor of the National Peasant Party, founded by middle-class intellectuals in 1938 to further the interests and representation of the peasantry (in 1956 it became the Petőfi Party). The Christian Democratic Party (*Kereszténydemokrata Néppárt*, KDNP) stressed its continuity with its interwar counterpart and prewar Catholic reform movements.[26] In March 1989 it was the last to emerge, as an endeavour 'to revive and represent...an institutionally autonomous Catholic world',[27] and was then added to the membership of the Opposition Round Table.

None of the historic parties proved to be a radical force. Indeed, elements of each had cooperated with communist rule and gained some rewards for doing so. Since they were not among the losers of the old regime, the Social Democrats found the 'formation of their opposition attitude' not without problems;[28] indeed, they remained beset by intense internal conflicts. Bozóki describes the Smallholders in November 1988 as more concerned with reviving political careers than with democracy as such, and hence as 'not radical' and 'happy to bargain with the MSzMP'.[29]

The strong informal linkages across the opposition movement were formalized in March 1989 at the initiative of the Independent Lawyers' Forum. The Opposition Round Table met on 22 March, with free elec-tions a central element of the proposed agenda.[30] While the ruling Party intensified its efforts to conduct separate negotiations with individual groups during February and March, Opposition members refused to attend a group 'preparatory discussion' with the MSzMP on 8 April, notably because of the failure to invite FIDESZ.[31] The outcome was not a foregone conclusion. At first the majority favoured participation, fearing that refusal would lend credibility to charges of sabotaging the regime's reform efforts. However, solidarity and a recognition of the potential power of the 'salami tactics' used in post-1945 Hungary won the day, and 'consensus became solidified as the most important principle of the Opposition Round Table'.[32] Desire to defeat the regime was the underlying desideratum, to which individual partisan interests were subordinate. On 22 April talks about talks began with a newly united Opposition facing an increasingly divided and beleaguered communist party. The opposition insisted that negotiations be undertaken with the MSzMP, on the grounds that the Party's Central Committee, not the government, remained the real locus of political power. The National Round Table began officially on 13 June, with the three-tier format of plenary sessions, a middle-level committee and an expert working committee. Effectively each side of the bargaining process had veto rights, but each side also needed to reach agreement.

The Round Table negotiations

During the spring government experts drafted a succession of electoral laws, and in May the Politburo approved that which most closely matched the existing system.[33] However, as part of the concessions that brought the opposition to the Round Table, the government agreed that the chosen draft would not be submitted to parliament, though it was published 'for consultation' on 5 June.[34] It also provided the starting point for initial discussions when Subcommittee I/3 of the National Round Table began its deliberations on 3 July. The subcommittee was imbued with some urgency, as elections were provisionally scheduled for December[35] (a timetable later pushed back with the partial collapse of the National Round Table over the mechanism for electing the Hungarian president).

On the governing, socialist side the negotiators were drawn from a variety of party and government institutions. The Ministries of Justice and the Interior provided constitutional and legal experts drawn from different sectors of public administration. Central Committee Secretary György Fejti was the party overlord with general oversight who briefed the Party Central Committee on the course of developments until his 'holiday' in August. Minister of State Imre Pozsgay's strategic role increased notably with Fejti's absence,[36] and Pozsgay also adopted an increasingly flexible position. Opposition groups also mobilized their contingent of sympathetic experts. In the negotiations on the electoral law the academic lawyer Péter Tölgyessy (SzDSz) emerged as the key political and legal strategist of the liberal–radical opposition,[37] while Antall (MDF) used his central position between the reformers of the MSzMP and the radical democrats of the Opposition Round Table to become an 'indispensable liaison person'.[38]

The government draft provided for 300 deputies elected in single-member districts by a two-round majority–majority system, with the two best-placed candidates going forward to the second round. Six hundred signatures would be needed for nomination. In addition, surplus votes transferred from the first round would elect 50 deputies from national lists using the Hare quota.

It is certainly the case that the Socialists believed they would benefit from the majoritarian thrust of their proposals, because they were the best organized and could promote known personalities, and because of the fragmentation of the opposition. This is a persistent theme of informed commentary on the National Round Table debates.[39] However, it is also true that the introduction of single-member districts had been seen as yielding positive gains in fostering links between deputies and their constituents. We shall see that such arguments, centring on the quality of representation, also provided the main emphasis of the subsequent parliamentary debate.

Moreover, there was a high degree of cross-party across-the-table consensus on the value of retaining single-member districts. The Opposition Round Table was divided, but its more significant elements rejected a proportional system based on party lists, despite its broad guarantee of seats roughly commensurate with electoral support. More predictably, the small historic parties, the Social Democrats, the Christian Democrats and the Smallholders, favoured a proportional list system, along with FIDESZ for a short time.

The Free Democrats (SzDSz) were less opposed to the Socialist draft, although they wished to reduce the proportion of single-member seats to three-quarters, rather than the 86 per cent of the government draft.[40] They argued that the strong majoritarian element would prevent excessive fragmentation (an argument which converted FIDESZ to their view[41]), while providing opportunities for the opposition to unite in the second round.[42] They also expected to do well in single-member districts, benefiting from the presence of eminent personages in their ranks and numerous lesser-known members whose skills would shine in individual contests.

The MDF, initially expressing no strong preference but endorsing the majority consensus for retaining a single-member element, proved pivotal. Its role was important because it was the largest opposition force;

by the same token it would expect to benefit from either a PR or two-round majoritarian system with the possibility of second-round alliances. It was the Forum that proposed the compromise unified position of the Opposition, combining the two elements endorsed by its members.[43] Antall had expressed a liking for a German variant (whose finer points he may well have misunderstood[44]). The resulting proposal was to abandon the Opposition's aim of a smaller parliament and opt for a two-vote mixed system, for 175 deputies in single-member districts and 175 deputies elected from national party lists. This was the simplest means of reconciling the views of all the Opposition Round Table participants, and it was a key decision of the negotiating process. It was not, as sometimes alleged, a government and opposition split between single-member and PR list systems respectively that generated the outline of the mixed Hungarian system. It is simply incorrect to state that the 'opposition wanted PR...'[45]

The socialists immediately accepted the principle of two votes, but they stuck to their 300–50 split (and hence the overall majoritarian thrust). Their view altered only with the testing of political support in four by-elections of July and August, forced by parliamentary resignations and opposition use of the recall mechanism. On 22 July the candidate of the united opposition won outright in the single valid election, with 69.2 per cent of the vote. Because of the dual constraints of the existing law, requiring a 50 per cent turnout and an absolute majority of votes with no provision for a run-off round, three by-elections had to be repeated. However, the first loss set alarm bells ringing within the MSzMP, and by its two further defeats on 5 August the Party's strategy had evolved substantially in four respects. First, it shifted from majority–majority to majority–plurality in single-member contests. Secondly, it altered its conditions for advance to the second round from the top two to all those gaining at least 15 per cent of the vote, with a minimum of three. Thirdly, it accepted the 50–50 split of single-member and list seats. Finally, it reinstated the compensatory seats, to be based on allocating losers' votes from the decisive single-member contests; the upshot was proposals for 150–150–50 split in a system with nominal, list and supplementary elements.

This was the source of the distinctive three dimensions of the future Hungarian electoral law. Growing uncertainty about immediate election prospects made single-member majoritarian contests less attractive to the socialists, especially given the demonstrated capacity of the opposition to unite. Both the list element, ensuring proportionality, and the compensatory seats, using otherwise potentially large numbers of wasted votes in single-member districts, suddenly gained appeal. The socialists were also cognizant of Polish developments, where the uncertainties generated by the June 1989 election were still being played out in an atmosphere of political crisis. Schiemann quotes Central Committee Secretary Györgi Fejti as acknowledging subsequently that the MSzMP moved to 'the principle of the smallest risk'.[46]

The Opposition for its part had gained its desired equal division of list and single-member districts, and it readily accepted the idea of a compensation list. Its leaders also proposed a further mechanism to ensure, as far as possible, that party elites (notably themselves) would be seated in the new parliament. This was the demand for simultaneous candidacy in all elements of the system: a candidate could stand in a single-member district, on the party list in two counties and on the national list. Since candidate choice was already provided in single-member districts, the closed list could not only serve elite interests but could strengthen their parties. The introduction of county lists rather than a single national constituency (now effectively provided by the compensatory tier) was the Opposition's condition for accepting the compensation list. It was particularly favoured by the historic parties, which (rightly) anticipated an uneven distribution of their support.[47] The MSzMP accepted county lists. The two sides also agreed to move to 4 per cent from their initial threshold positions of 5 (MSzMP) and 3 per cent (Opposition Round Table) respectively.

Some of the detail remained devilish, however, with contentious debates on second-round entry conditions and on the distribution of wasted votes to the national tier. Neither issue was resolved at expert level; they were referred to middle-level meetings. On the first, the Opposition finally acknowledged that no compromise could be extracted. Although its advantage lay with a straight Socialist–Opposition contest in the second round, the Opposition conceded the 15 per cent minimum three entrants and plurality decision. This would not ensure socialist success, but it could force the opposition to make strategic decisions on alliances and withdrawals in the second round (as it did so successfully in 1998). In exchange, the Opposition won a partial victory on the distribution of votes for allocating supplementary seats.

The Socialists had proposed that losing individual candidates' votes in the decisive round, whether first or second, would be aggregated nationally. With the Opposition's preference for a two-candidate run-off, and with most contests expected to go to a second round, most opposition parties would fail to have their votes transferred with this mechanism. The Opposition argued that remainder votes from the list element should be used instead. In the first stage of the compromise both sides agreed that surplus votes should be transferred from both Single Member Districts (SMDs) and list voting. Then the Opposition's concession on entry requirements led the socialists to agree that the first (valid) round should be used for surplus votes.[48]

There remained, however, the requirements for establishing candidacies and issues of district magnitude. For the single-member districts the MSzMP wanted to raise the number of signatures to 1000 from its original draft plan of 600. The Opposition had proposed 500 signatures but, as with thresholds, agreed to split the difference at 750, still a low figure. It was also agreed that a party would need to field candidates in at least one-quarter of a county's SMDs, with a minimum of two, in order to run a list in that county. To establish a national list a party must field at least 7 of the 20 regions (19 counties plus Budapest).

The decision to use the county as the basis for the regional element implied low district magnitudes for less populated counties. An unusual distribution proposal apparently came from the SzDSz's Tölgyessy,[49] but the reasoning behind it remains unclear. It provided for a limited largest remainder, with seats allocated to parties gaining a full quota of votes and then to those achieving two-thirds of the quota. Parties receiving seats without a full quota would have the missing votes deducted from their national surplus votes. At the same time seats not allocated by this method would be added to the national compensatory total. In practice it further helped the larger parties in 1990: had the largest remainder method been utilized without restriction, the 32 unallocated regional seats would mostly have benefited smaller parties.[50] The lack of controversy suggests that this was regarded as a technical detail, not a substantive one, however. Finally, following the signing of the Round Table agreement (but not by SzDSz or FIDESZ, still contesting the method of presidential election) the Opposition accepted the socialists' proposal to use the d'Hondt formula for the national list in order to strengthen larger parties. Schiemann argues convincingly that the small parties of the Opposition Round Table were now 'larger' than emerging parties outside the negotiations and hence had no objection to a shift from Hare to d'Hondt,[51] but it is not clear how far they were actually consulted.

The role of parliament

In the months both preceding and during the Round Table both the Hungarian government and parliament had become increasingly assertive, refusing to serve merely as passive pawns of the ruling party. The growing 'separation of party and state' was far from unique to

Hungary, but in Hungary the negotiations generated resentment that key decisions were being taken behind closed doors. Parliament had already jibbed at the government's agreement not to submit to it the original June draft. It was therefore unsurprising to see a vocal assertion of the 'old' deputies' collective *amour-propre* in the October debate.

The draft law generated by the National Round Table went first to the parliamentary committee on Law, Justice and the Legal System, which also received representations from individual deputies, several parliamentary committees, civic organizations and individual citizens during the brief consultation period. The committee itself rejected the notion of significant amendments on the grounds that such change would unravel the whole of the fragile consensus.[52]

Minister of the Interior István Horváth introduced the legislation, seeking, not wholly successfully, to counter some key critical arguments. These centred largely on the concept of representation, with concomitant proposals to increase the number of single-member districts.[53] Horváth stressed that democratic multi-party competition would alter not only the process of government formation, but also the nature of representation, with the role of the individual deputy now mediated by political parties. The issue would no longer be that of a particular individualistic relation of the deputy to his/her electors, but parties as a whole would seek to ensure the responsiveness of their deputies. At the same time, the mixed system would ensure representation of local and regional interests, but the appropriate balance had been struck: increasing the number of single-member districts would create a danger of ungovernability, with a parliament not fully reflecting the balance of forces in the country at large.[54] He also rightly argued that the national list would increase the proportional reflection of the voters' wishes. Kereszeti echoed this view for the parliamentary law committee, also arguing that change would disrupt the roughly equal support needed for each type of seat (then estimated at 25–30,000 for a constituency seat, 35–40,000 for a regional list seat, 45–50,000 for a national list seat).

Given the law's complexity, the debate[55] was short, but often heated, with some one hundred amendments tabled and much criticism of the illegitimacy of the Round Table.[56] When deputies 'looked at the map and saw that they had no constituencies, this released serious emotions'.[57] The substance of the debate centred almost entirely on principles of representation, with vigorous defence of existing bases of constituency representation and several approving references to Britain. Many speakers saw the new single-member districts as 'too large' for the effective representation of constituents' interests. Moreover the law effectively underrepresented rural areas, with many small towns losing their own representation; this raised the spectre of increased tensions between town and countryside. Outright hostility to political parties, the immaturity of parties, the 'faceless' nature of party election, voter confusion about parties, the 'excessive promotion' of parties were all adduced to support an increase in (or wholesale adoption of) single-member districts. People were 'accustomed' to the existing system, and historical boundaries should not be tampered with.

Few deputies tackled the system's mixed principles, though Ferenc Király attracted applause for his criticism of the inappropriate bases of the three tiers: some representatives will serve their constituents, he said, but regional list deputies would neither know their electors nor need to do so and 'certainly won't deal with Auntie Mary's fence', while those 'from the national list – well whoopee-dee ... The greatest problem worrying this representative, if he doesn't take a sleeping pill at night, is who on earth elected him? ...'

The strength of feeling led to change in only two main areas, however. (The Regional Development Ministry withdrew its amendment for a 5 per cent threshold before the vote.[58]) The first raised the number of SMDs to 176, leaving (a maximum of) 152 list seats and a national list of (a minimum of) 58 seats, thus increasing the size of parliament from 350 to 386. Secondly, deputies demurred at the multiple access of candidates, reducing it from four to three: candidates could run on only one territorial list rather than two (but still in an SMD and on the national list). The absence of provisions for minority representation, especially the national minorities but also the churches, attracted much criticism in the parliamentary debate, including from the neglected 'third side' of the Round Table. In its vigorous lobbying for the draft, the government neutralized this element by promising a supplementary law. The final vote registered a large majority in favour: 286 deputies, with 20 opposed and 24 abstentions.[59]

The law

The electoral law of 1989 provided a unique mixed system, with many individual elements recognizable from electoral systems elsewhere combined in a distinctive Hungarian *gulyás*. Unlike the mixed–parallel system adopted by many post-communist countries, its elements are 'fused', but in unusual ways.[60] It is a mixed–linked, majoritarian–proportional, two-vote system, with two-round majority–plurality and regional PR list elements and a compensatory national list.

There are 176 single-member constituencies, whose variation in size increased after 1990 because of population shifts. (Deviations from the national average and the difference between the size of the smallest and biggest constituencies are larger in Hungary than elsewhere in Eastern Europe.[61]) Candidates must submit 750 signatures in their support. Parties may nominate 'joint candidates'. A valid election requires a turnout of 50 per cent in the first round, 25 per cent in the second. The elector uses one of his or her two votes for an individual named candidate. For outright victory a candidate requires an absolute majority of votes cast (50 per cent plus 1). Otherwise candidates with at least 15 per cent of the vote, but at least three candidates, may compete in a second round (but may withdraw), where a plurality elects the winner. If the first-round turnout requirement is not met, all candidates compete in the second round, when the candidate with the most votes wins.

Twenty multi-member constituencies are based on county boundaries, with a maximum of 152 seats. District magnitude ranges from three four-member constituencies to the largest, Budapest, with 28. A party may register its regional list if it has candidates in at least one-quarter of the single-member districts within the constituency, but at least two. Voters use their second vote to support a particular party list. The contest is rerun if the 50 per cent turnout requirement is not met. In 1990 a 4 per cent national threshold operated, but this rose to 5 per cent in 1993. After an initial allocation of seats to parties meeting the Hagenbach-Bischoff quota (Total votes/(Total seats + 1)), largest remainders are used to allocate seats, first to parties with a full quota, then to those receiving two-thirds of the quota. Unfilled seats are transferred from the constituency to swell the total of national list seats.

There are at least 58 national list seats which may be allocated to parties fielding at least seven regional lists and gaining 4 (1990) or 5 per cent (1993 onwards) of the national vote. To the 58 are added all seats unfilled at the regional level. In 1990, 32 seats were added, in 1994, 27 and in 1998, 24. The national pool comprises the first-round votes for candidates whose parties did not ultimately win the seat plus the unused votes at regional level, with 'missing' quota votes deducted. D'Hondt is the allocation formula.

The aftermath

Effectively there were few important changes after 1989, other than raising the threshold. In 1990 the procedure for collecting signatures lent itself to abuses: nominating cards were traded and exchanged, and signatures falsified and even sold on the black market. Parliament amended the electoral law and passed a criminal sanction bill to prevent further abuses, though this measure came 'too late' for 1990.[62] In 1997 a general law on electoral procedures aimed to clarify certain provisions and to ensure unified application of the law. The law brought almost no changes in the content of procedures, and often little clarification. For example, redistricting regulations still lacked clear criteria and deadlines but the less than democratic feature of giving the government alone the authority to redistrict also slipped in.[63]

The 1994 local government electoral law provided for single-member districts, but with a guarantee of 40 per cent of seats for losing parties. Discussion also took place on extending the proportional element of the national law on these lines, but a scandal that occurred during debates on the local election law (the opposition left the chamber) and the weakness of Socialist PR adherents worked against reform in the 1994–8 legislature. In 1997 the super-majority Socialist (by now *Magyar Szocialista Párt*, MSzP)–Free Democrat coalition pushed through an amendment providing that each party on a joint list would need to meet the 5 per cent rule, rather than collectively achieving 10 per cent (for a two-party joint list). This was an attempt, reminiscent of that of Vladimir Mečiar in Slovakia, to hinder the growing unity of the opposition parties. Fidesz-MPP (from 1995 formally Fidesz-Hungarian Civic Party) had been busy negotiating alliances with the now shrunken Democratic Forum and the schismatic Christian Democrats, eventually constructing 'a formidable conglomeration of political forces stretching from the liberal centre to the populist right'.[64] However, the provision proved a dead letter in 1998, for the newly allied forces did not adopt joint party lists.

Over time, persistent voices in Parliament and the press favoured a smaller parliament and this found echoes in most 1998 party manifestos. In late 2001 Fidesz-MPP and the MSzP agreed (and had the necessary two-thirds of parliament's votes) to compulsory recounts in the event of close votes. Smaller parties opposed a proposal to double campaign spending limits (exceeding their own funding capacity), and also raised the spectre of a grand coalition between the then two major political forces.[65] The Socialists withdrew, however, in deference to their main ally, the Free Democrats.

The issue of minority representation persisted, not least because it was an unmet constitutional requirement. The government fulfilled its promise to parliament to legislate for the nationalities, and the law was duly promulgated in March 1990. It provided for the appointment of eight national minority representatives to be co-opted by the new parliament. However, the new conservative coalition government under

Antall was unsympathetic, and the law was quickly repealed. The complex system of minority self-governments provided avenues of local representation,[66] but the issue resurfaced. In the 1998 elections the forum of National Minorities fielded seven regional lists but without success. When the issue was discussed again in parliament, it met no response from the Fidesz coalition, now increasingly of a conservative–nationalist bent and toying with increased majoritarianism.

Assessing the outcome

Given the extraordinary dynamism of events, in Hungary and in the region as a whole, it is facile to judge the individual parties as having succeeded or blundered in their advocacy of particular elements of the electoral system by their results in 1990. However, it can be argued that the Socialists (from October 1989 the Hungarian Socialist Party (MSzP), essentially the reformist element of the old party) made a key strategic mistake in delaying elections because of disputes over the presidency.[67] The period between October, when the law was passed, and March 1990, when the first round of the elections took place, was one of significant further developments on a number of fronts. The Socialist Party lost support in quite a dramatic fashion.[68] The fortunes of FIDESZ and SzDSz also shifted, with both gaining visibility from their successful referendum campaign on presidential elections.[69] However, in theory some dynamic assessment should have been incorporated into self-seeking, seat-maximizing behaviour. The Socialists did this by shifting their positions at the National Round Table with new information; but they failed to anticipate their growing unpopularity or to hedge further against that risk. Thus in 1990 they, and all other parties save the Forum, would have gained (or their result have been unchanged in the case of SzDSz) from a system based solely on proportional representation.[70] The Social Democrats and the People's Party failed to gain seats in both the simulated PR and actual results, but their bargaining power was nil and they were but minor players.

The victor of 1990, the Hungarian Democratic Forum, was the first beneficiary of the system, but not always in ways that the architects of reform could have anticipated. The MDF gained not only from the single-member districts, but also from the threshold, the relatively small compensation element, and the use of d'Hondt for the national list. The benefits that accrued to the Forum in 1990 buttressed the Socialist Party (MSzP) in 1994 and Fidesz-MPP in 1998. Systems that yield highly disproportional results are prone to surprises, and although it is a mixed system, the single-member element is strong enough to create significant disproportionality.[71] The Hungarian system displayed some unusual outcomes, notably when in 1998 the Hungarian Socialist Party won most votes in both rounds of the SMD contests and most in the list element, yet gained fewer seats than its main rival Fidesz-MPP, which gained from alliances with declining parties.

If the distinctive nature of the electoral law made it difficult for the parties to predict its cumulative effects in practice, it is also clear that in other respects the system did not work as (some had) thought. One argument put strongly in parliament was that the single-member element offered considerable incentives to Independent candidates. Yet the system proved highly party-centred, not least because of the complex linkage mechanisms. The signature requirement hardly constituted an obstacle – in 1998 22 per cent of candidates did not gain 750 votes. However, the law virtually compelled parties to maximize their candidacies of both individuals and lists. Serious office-seekers cannot submit regional lists without sufficient single-member candidacies, and they need to maximize their regional lists to ensure passing the national electoral threshold. They cannot submit national lists without sufficient regional ones. Moreover, losing-votes remain valuable, as they constitute a party's national pool. The determined mobilization of collective action by parties proved difficult to counter for all but the most stunning of individual candidates, whose numbers declined at successive elections. In 1990 more than 10 per cent of candidates in single-member districts ran as Independents, with six elected. In 1994 that figure dropped to 5.5 per cent, with none elected, falling to 3 per cent in 1998, with one elected.

The incentive system of the Hungarian law

One reason why electoral systems do not change is that time itself generates both adaptation and inertia. In Hungary the two-thirds majority proved an obstacle, but not an insuperable one. In the event some evidence accumulated over three elections of the adaptive behaviour of both voters and political parties.[72]

As party structures developed, parties also learned more about the various strategies open for candidate selection. The possibility of simultaneous candidacy gave parties a strategic choice and an insurance policy, so different types of candidate could be selected for the different elements. Stars (but not necessarily party leaders, several of whom lost in SMDs) stood in single-member districts. Regional lists included regional notables, and often a balance to represent the localities. There was stronger centralization of decision-making for the list allocations, with the national leaderships and partly the regional committees taking the lead. The national lists reflected the top leadership of the party, while parties could also place key members high on both regional and national lists, as well as nominating them for a single-member district. Multiple nominations increased in 1994.[73]

The party incentive to forming alliances is an obvious dimension of the two-round system. The Opposition had already won by-elections under the old system by fielding jointly supported candidates, but in 1990 this practice was less widespread than might have been anticipated from the heated debates over the entry requirements for the second round. In 1990 parties were testing their individual strengths in an atmosphere of high uncertainty and rapidly changing survey recordings of their popularity. Their mutual bargaining power was weak. Only the Young Democrats and the Free Democrats ran 16 joint candidates and agreed to withdraw after the first round in favour of the higher-ranking candidate, though the Forum, Smallholders and Christian Democrats agreed to appeal to their voters to support the best-placed candidate of the three. The results did not match their expectations.[74] In 1994 the Socialists did so well in the first round that they proved virtually unchallengeable: they lost only eleven of the second-round seats they contested. Nor did the advantage of cohesion prevent the Smallholders from splitting and contesting the election as four separate parties in 1994. In 1998, however, alliances came into their own. Seventy-eight candidates were joint candidates of Fidesz and the Forum, while 229 candidates withdrew from the second-round contest, including 71 Smallholders, 28 Christian Democrats and 22 from the Forum in a strategy that generated significant gains for Fidesz-MPP.[75]

However, the final decisions obviously rested with the voters. In 1990, although second-round turnout dropped radically, indicating that some voters probably withdrew after their parties had failed, remaining voters moved massively to support the Forum. In 1994 the Socialists maintained their position and emerged as decisive victors of the election. In 1998 voters switched to Fidesz-MPP as exhorted by its allies.[76] Voters did not always need to understand the more abstruse elements of the system to behave strategically.

Conclusion

The genesis of the Hungarian law illustrates the centrality of utility-maximizing models of political negotiation. The parties to the

Opposition Round Table could not pursue unfettered particularist self-interest or pure seat-maximization because of the overriding priority of the unity necessary to confront the still-powerful ruling party. Moreover, the baseline of a system based largely on single-member districts also had an impact, the more so as for major constituents of the negotiating process (and for parliament) it also spelt the best kind of representation and ensured government stability. Moreover, as the system accrued in a series of compromises, no party was genuinely in a position to assess how votes would translate into seats. Even technical specialists could not produce effective simulations of possible results.[77] If the mixed system was in part an effort to generate a measure of proportionality, even the proportional elements generated a bias to the largest party. This was especially true in the conditions of 1990, when numerous parties failed to cross the threshold, and d'Hondt and the formula limit operated to the detriment of the successful smaller ones.

Nor was there much doubt that the intricacies of the system as a whole remained obscure to the voters, not least the mechanics of transferring votes to the national list element and the utility of losing-votes. Voters could not foresee what would happen to their votes, not least because of the transfer of unfilled seats to the national list allocation. This increased the role of the national list (and hence the party hierarchies) with implications for representation, especially in the small multi-member constituencies. Although calls for electoral reform were present in all party manifestos for the 1998 elections, and representation will certainly surface in the generation of a system for European elections, accommodation to the system seemed stronger than the incentive to change. Due to the two-thirds majority requirement parties must be flexible in their positions, which explains to a certain extent the vagueness of their manifesto commitments. Advocates of PR certainly emerged within the ranks of the Socialist Party after 1990, on grounds that PR better serves democracy, but their position within the party was too weak to ensure the legislative promotion of a radical change, especially in the context of a widespread belief in the benefits of the majoritarian component for government stability. Yet, the interest of some Socialists in PR, as well as changes in the party political arena (the strength of Fidesz, the virtual disappearance of the Forum, the fissiparous tendencies of the Smallholders, the entry into parliament of the radical right Justice and Life (MIEP)) contributed to preventing an MSzP-Fidesz agreement on a more majoritarian system that would save them the trouble of negotiating with the smaller parties (SzDSz and the extremist MIEP respectively). Thus the system stuck, and the voters were stuck with it.

4

The Czech and Slovak Republics: the Surprising Resilience of Proportional Representation

The Czechoslovak federation broke up in 1992 because, on some accounts, its two constituent republics were too divergent in their political cultures and policy preferences. While there may be some truth to this, at various times after the split the two independent states experienced very similar developments. One of these was the attempt to escape from the proportional representation system set out hurriedly in early 1990, shortly before the founding free election, which was held partly or largely responsible for the countries' alleged dependence on government by shaky coalition. In both states, there were attempts to shift toward a less proportional regime that would facilitate one-party or at most two-party government. In both countries, however, such efforts were thwarted or subverted.

This chapter explains the initial selection of proportional representation, the reforms that were proposed and enacted, and the surprising resilience of the federation's institutional legacy. It argues that the initial choice of electoral system was the product of party preferences derived endogenously through bargaining and in anticipation of expected results, but that these preferences were not solely self-interested. Like many statutory institutions during transitions to democracy, the new electoral system was seen not as locked in, but open to revision as its effects were clarified and party preferences shifted, again endogenously. Shocks exogenous to the electoral system were used to justify reform, but in fact the motor was the long-standing aim of the emerging beneficiaries of the new competitive politics to push the electoral systems in a win-concentrating direction. Although parties threatened by these revisions were able to mobilize the resources to stop, overturn or neutralize them, these episodes confirmed that statutory institutions do not account independently for the consolidation of democracy. Instead, they remain contested as long as parties distrust each others' intentions and the stakes of office are high.[1]

Initial choice of electoral regime

Following Shugart's rational-choice model of institutional design in new democracies, we would expect a country such as Czechoslovakia to opt initially for a party-dominated rather than candidate-centred electoral system. The model starts from the fact that the Czechoslovak transition was 'provisionary', in that the removal of a frozen post-totalitarian regime was induced by mass protests and round-table talks at the end of 1989, followed by the investiture of an interim government led by outsiders, who in turn set the pace in agreeing the rules for the founding of free elections. In these conditions, the rational interest of politicians was in an electoral system that enhanced the development of strong parties. The logic behind this prediction lies in the relative anonymity of most of the new democratic activists, whose careers would be best served by trading on the name of an uncompromised new party rather than on their personal reputations.[2] Since proportional representation (PR) usually empowers parties, some form of PR would be the expected first electoral system.

This model is supported to a considerable degree by what happened in Czechoslovakia in 1990, although it is impossible to prove that the motivation behind legislators' choice of electoral system was indeed personal career advancement. Also, the new democratic elite's preference for PR was not as immediate and obvious as the model would lead us to expect; it first had to withstand serious challenges from within the largest movements, Civic Forum in Bohemia and Moravia and Public against Violence in Slovakia. Polls in January 1990 showed support for the two movements at almost 30 per cent of the electorate, three times more than for any other contestant; their strategists were understandably tempted to rout rival parties under majoritarian rules.[3] One of the most talented, Civic Forum's Josef Vavroušek, acknowledged the appeal and rationality of that option:

> If Civic Forum in the Czech lands and Public against Violence in Slovakia behaved like classic political parties striving for the greatest share of state power, they would try to push through an electoral system that would allow them to use the spontaneous support of broad

swathes of the population based on rejection of the totalitarian system run in this country by the Communist Party. Both movements would most likely propose holding elections at the soonest possible date (for example, in February [1990]), on the basis of the majoritarian system used in past decades. The elections would then probably turn into a plebiscite, in which the movements Civic Forum and Public against Violence would receive a majority in most districts at the expense of the Communist Party. [...] But for Civic Forum and Public against Violence, there is more at issue than just electoral victory.[4]

As Vavroušek explained, several arguments steered the movements' leaders toward PR. First, men and women who until recently had been dissidents felt bound by their long-standing normative commitment to pluralism. A false unity had been imposed on Czechoslovak society for four decades and it was felt that the new federal legislature ought to be a more faithful reflection of its variety.[5] Civic Forum had actually embedded this objective in its organizational plan in December 1989, defining itself as 'a movement of citizens for political pluralism and the holding of free elections'.[6] As one Civic Forum leader, Petr Pithart, explained when an American political scientist advised him to go for a majoritarian system and trounce the Communists, 'We do not want to replace one dominant political force with another, so we shall not tailor the electoral system to benefit us and only us.'[7]

Second, it was recognized that parties were essential organizing elements of a democracy, and the system had to encourage their institutionalization before some day shifting the focus onto individual candidates linked to particular constituencies. Third, and more practically, Civic Forum and Public against Violence were constrained by the fact that a diverse multi-party system already existed, the combined inheritance of the sham pluralism of the National Front (the communist-controlled bloc that coordinated four satellite parties, the trade unions and other social organizations) and the genuine pluralism of dissident society. The consent of these other parties had to be secured in two special round-table talks held on 5 and 11 January 1990, in a cross-party experts' meeting on 19 January, and then in 18 legislative committees before a floor vote in the bicameral Federal Assembly on 27 February.[8]

Fourth, as they acquired greater appreciation of the state of the economy and the perils of its restructuring, Civic Forum and Public against Violence realized that they would do well to avoid sole responsibility for the hardships lying ahead, so a broader coalition government would be preferable and PR would facilitate that.[9] Finally, some strategists warned that the movements' national ratings in opinion polls might not actually convert into many victories in single-member districts, where locally respected independents or other parties could attract and aggregate support.[10]

The broad outlines of a PR system were quickly thrashed out by a working group and hotly debated in Civic Forum's supreme assembly on 6 January 1990. Although several of the movement's most celebrated figures argued for a single-member system that would allow independents greater opportunity to compete, they were gently but firmly overruled for the reasons enumerated above. The following day, Vavroušek distilled the assembly's discussion into three possibilities, which he directly linked to larger schemes for the restructuring of the federation:

1. PR in 12 multi-member districts, with a 4 or 5 per cent threshold, and an opportunity for voters to indicate preferences for particular candidates.
2. The West German additional-member system, with a 4 or 5 per cent threshold.
3. The use of option 1 for election of only one of the Federal Assembly's houses, the Diet of the People, in which Czechs and Slovaks were represented on a 2 : 1 ratio according to population size, while the Diet of Nations, divided evenly between the two republics, would be elected through single-member districts.[11]

Without consulting its own assembly or the public, the inner core of Civic Forum selected the first option. The second was rejected as too demanding of voters, while the third was quickly torpedoed by Slovakia's Public against Violence on the grounds that it would require a major constitutional settlement, which only freely elected legislatures would have the legitimacy to undertake.[12]

Subsequent talks with other parties swiftly led to general agreement on Vavroušek's first option, but the fine detail of the law remained to be written. Acute time pressure then became a powerful factor, as founding elections were scheduled for early June 1990. To expedite the bill's drafting, one of the former satellite parties, the Czechoslovak Socialist Party, dusted off the law used in the last largely free election, in 1946.[13] That law had been in turn a hasty revival (again, under time pressure) of the electoral system introduced for the new state in 1920, which in itself was a conscious reaction against the ethnically biased majoritarian system of the Habsburg monarchy.[14] The 1946 law had been superseded after the Communist seizure of power by a 1954 act that replaced PR with single-member districts; voters had the choice only of approving or rejecting the sole candidate fielded by the National Front.[15] The return to PR in 1990 was thus a replay of the break, seventy years previously, with the perceived injustice of majoritarianism.

The result of bargaining in early 1990 over a version of the 1920/1946 electoral law was a PR system using party lists in 12 multi-member districts (eight in the Czech Republic, four in Slovakia).

- To start with, electoral commissions would ascertain which parties had received at least 5 per cent of the vote in either the Czech or Slovak republic.[16]
- The Hagenbach-Bischoff formula (Votes/Seats + 1) would be applied to the total votes of qualifying parties in each of the 12 districts, to generate the quota for allocating seats.[17]
- After this initial district scrutiny, it was expected 10–20 per cent of the seats would still be unfilled, as no party within a given district would have enough votes remaining to meet the quota. The unused votes would be aggregated at the level of each republic, a new *republic* quota would be generated and the outstanding seats filled accordingly.

The main departure from the 1946 law was that Hagenbach-Bischoff (H-B) was used for the first and second quotas; in 1946, the first was generated by the Hare formula. It was hoped that the use of H-B would result in fewer seats to be filled on the second scrutiny, since party headquarters would have greater discretion in drawing up republic-level lists of candidates and centralized party power was an unpopular concept in 1990.[18] (A separate law governing elections to the Slovak republic legislature followed the 1946 model, but this was changed for the 1992 election to bring it into line with federal and Czech practice.[19])

Many speakers in the parliamentary debate on the bill reported that they saw strict PR as a short-term, transitional measure that should quickly yield to at least a mixed system. The expectation was thus present in Czech and Slovak politics from the very beginning that at some point soon a majoritarian element would enter the equation; polls in the autumn of 1991 suggested that a majority of voters would have welcomed it.[20] In fact, there was evidence of a long-standing public aversion to pure PR. During the liberalization of 1968, one survey found dissatisfaction with the practice of the single candidate, but not with

Table 4.1   Summary of Czechoslovak electoral laws

Election year	Electoral system type	District structure	Seat allocation formula	Threshold
1990	PR	14 multi-member districts 2 republic districts for unfilled seats	Hagenbach-Bischoff Hagenbach-Bischoff	5%
1992	PR	14 multi-member districts 2 republic districts for unfilled seats	Hagenbach-Bischoff Hagenbach-Bischoff	5% for single parties; 7% for alliances of two or three parties; 10% for four or more

single-member districts (SMDs). The most popular reform in 1968, preferred by three-fifths of respondents, would have been to retain SMDs while introducing true competition between candidates of the five parties of the National Front. Around one half, however, would also have welcomed multi-member districts with a mix of list and nominal voting. What united the most favoured options was the opportunity to choose individual candidates and not just a party. The *least* popular system was straight list-voting, with mandates allocated to candidates according to their rank on the ballot; more respondents preferred the unreformed status quo over a switch to that.[21]

The key features of the Czechoslovak electoral law are summarized in Table 4.1. However, sensing a general appetite for electoral reform, in late 1991 President Václav Havel submitted a bold initiative as part of a larger package of bills to rescue the federation from the constitutional crisis that beset it soon after the end of Communist rule. Havel had been one of the last leaders in Civic Forum to accept PR in 1990; as he explained a year later.

> I consider it one of the mistakes I have made in office that before the last elections I was not far more persistent in my struggle for a different electoral law. [...] To put it simply, it was a battle between a proportional and majoritarian electoral system. I clearly prefer the majoritarian. But I would be grateful also for a mixed system.[22]

The alternative proposed by Havel in 1991 would have introduced the supplementary vote, akin to that used for election of the Queensland

Legislative Assembly between 1892 and 1942, and more recently the president of Sri Lanka and mayor of London.[23] It allows voters to indicate first and second preferences among candidates standing in single-member districts. Should no one win an outright majority after first preferences have been counted, the weakest candidates would be eliminated stepwise and their second preferences assigned until one contestant had accumulated more than 40 per cent of the vote and won the seat. Should no candidate reach even that sum, each party's votes would be pooled with those from any other district in the Czech or Slovak Republic that had similarly failed to return a representative, the d'Hondt divisor would be applied, and the vacant seats awarded to parties proportionally.

The presidential bill had several attractive features. First, it introduced a stronger constituency link and accountability through the SMD and granted voters more power, since the 1990 law had contained only the narrowly circumscribed opportunity of approval voting.[24] Second, it allowed voters to signal what sort of coalition they might welcome after the election, as second choices could be read as acceptable partners. Third, it increased the likelihood of winners enjoying the backing of a majority of their constituents without second-round run-offs. Finally, it allowed local independents to compete while reassuring the larger parties of their overall pre-eminence, thus preserving the country from what the bill's backers called 'the Polish effect' (fissile governments held hostage by tyrannous micro-parties).[25]

The bill, however, died along with the rest of the constitutional rescue package in early 1992, primarily because the president failed to convince the parties that their place in the sun was not threatened by his plan. The pressure of time was again invoked to justify institutional conservatism, since the designation of SMDs and other technical demands might not be manageable with an election already fast approaching (the 1990 legislature, like that of 1946, was elected for only a two-year term).

Admittedly, there was one sizeable group interested in electoral reform: Václav Klaus's Civic Democratic Party (*Občanská demokratická strana*, ODS), the largest successor to the now-defunct Civic Forum. ODS, however, liked the French system of second-round run-offs; once it sensed that it could not build a majority for its preference, it shifted its energy into campaigning at least for the adoption of the d'Hondt algorithm, known to favour bigger parties, in place of the Hagenbach-Bischoff quota.[26] This effort likewise failed to find sympathy among the 15 diminutive parties in the federal legislature.[27]

The only substantial changes agreed in 1992 were the introduction of differentiated thresholds for electoral alliances (a coalition of two or three parties would need 7 per cent of the vote between them to qualify for seats, while a coalition of four or more would need 10 per cent), and a slight expansion in the opportunity for preference voting.[28] The threshold change compounded the disproportionality already generated by the 5 per cent cut-off, as shown in Table 4.2, with deviation rates comparable to those in countries with single-member plurality systems.[29]

Turnovec argues that this increased disproportionality primarily punished parties that favoured the federation's continuation, and manufactured a premium for the two parties that would unravel the union in the coming months: Klaus's ODS and Vladimír Mečiar's Movement for a Democratic Slovakia (*Hnutie za demokratické Slovensko*, HZDS).[30] The electoral law may also have contributed to the federation's demise by applying thresholds and quotas only through the constituent republics and not at the federal level; parties could therefore attract votes by

Table 4.2 Wasted votes and deviation from proportionality (*D*) in the Czechoslovak 1990 and 1992 elections

Assembly and year	Wasted votes (as % of all votes cast in Czech Republic)	D (Czech Republic)	Wasted votes (as % of all votes cast in Slovakia)	D (Slovakia)
Diet of the People 1990	16.8	11.2	15.1	7.2
Diet of Nations 1990	18.4	13.1	12.7	6.6
Republic legislature 1990	18.8	11.6	7.6*	3.6*
Diet of the People 1992	25.9	13.0	26.3	12.5
Diet of Nations 1992	26.8	13.8	20.5	9.6
Republic legislature 1992	19.1	8.6	23.8	11.2

* The threshold for seats in the 1990 Slovak legislature was 3 per cent.

Source: Author's calculations from election results in *Statistická ročenka České a Slovenské federativní republiky* (Prague: SNTL, 1991), pp. 629–30 and *Statistická ročenka České republiky* (Prague: Český spisovatel, 1993), pp. 437–41. Disproportionality (*D*) is derived according to the least-squares index proposed in Michael Gallagher, 'Proportionality, Disproportionality and Electoral Systems', *Electoral Studies*, vol. 10, no. 1 (1991), p. 40: the square root of $\frac{1}{2} [\Sigma (v_i - s_i)^2]$ where v_i is each party's share of the vote, and s_i each party's share of the seats.

catering to particular interests at the expense of the general, so no nationwide party system developed.[31] Czechoslovakia failed to emulate the crucial leap made by West Germany in 1953, when it moved from the original threshold of 5 per cent in one *Land* to the more demanding and integrative 5 per cent nationwide (or three district seats).[32] Consequently, the independent Czech and Slovak Republics came into being in January 1993 still under the PR regime hurriedly introduced without enthusiasm three years before.

The unintended consequences of the pursuit of stable government

Slovakia

Slovakia was the first to alter its system. Prime Minister Mečiar raised the possibility after the 1994 elections, which took place early owing to the collapse of his second government, and his third government's programme in January 1995 contained a vague promise of amendments to the law. A serious campaign, however, was not launched until March 1996. At that time, Mečiar told his party's congress that the lessons of 1994 (the fall of his government and the difficulty of forming a new one after early elections) showed that the 5 per cent threshold was not enough to ensure a manageable number of parties:

> We would therefore accept if the development of political parties' integration went towards the creation of another strong political subject so that in competition of the two (of course upon existence of all the others) the political system could stabilize. We can see that it will be necessary to change the system, to abandon the present system of relative [*sic*] representation – also our friends in Italy left the system that we have taken over and have been practising until now. And to switch to the majority system or a combination of the majority and relative [proportional] systems.[33]

Mečiar went into more detail during his concluding remarks to a closed session of the congress: 150 single-member districts, whose winner-take-all nature, he explained, offered 'a certain political hope'.[34]

Only three months later, however, Mečiar was reminded both of the reason for seeking this change and of the obstacles to its realization when a bitter feud erupted between HZDS and its junior cabinet colleagues, the Slovak National Party (*Slovenská národná strana*, SNS) and Association of Workers of Slovakia (*Združenie robotníkov Slovenska*, ZRS), over privatization spoils. Although the coalition survived, Mečiar learned that he could not expect his partners altruistically to support actions that would damage their own interests. As the two junior parties would be hurt by a law introducing severe disproportionality and HZDS held only 61 of the 150 legislative seats, coalition arithmetic forced Mečiar to retreat from majoritarianism.[35]

The bill's drafting was assigned to the Interior Ministry but after almost two years had passed, a group of parliamentarians including Mečiar's legal counsellor, Ján Cuper, assumed the task. That long delay, which may have been deliberate to deprive the opposition of reaction time, meant that the bill was not submitted until March 1998, only six months before elections were due. Containing a number of unconstitutional clauses,[36] the bill introduced three significant changes. First, the four existing electoral districts were to be collapsed into one, containing all 150 members. (The Association of Workers preferred eight multi-member districts, but was overruled by its coalition partners.) This huge rise in district magnitude would normally be welcomed as a boost to proportionality, but opposition parties interpreted it as a device to rob them of the campaign advantages of regional lists (which could be headed by locally popular figures), forcing them into a nationwide showdown with the charismatic Mečiar.

Secondly, preference voting, though formally untouched, was neutralized by the single district, as the application of the existing formula to such a large area made it practically impossible for any but the already most prominent figures to move up the candidate list.[37] Preference voting's impact was also lessened by a change in the procedure for filling a vacated seat – a common event, since deputies must suspend their mandates if they become ministers. Previously, it went to the recipient of the largest number of preferential votes who had not earned enough to move up the list into electable range; now the party leadership would have a free hand in selecting the replacement, to ensure that someone who had since become outspoken or even quit the party did not obtain a mandate.

Thirdly, the Hagenbach-Bischoff quota and 5 per cent threshold were retained but applied to each party, including the constituent members of an electoral alliance. (Electoral commissions would be able to determine the exact percentages garnered because allied parties would operate separate candidate lists.[38]) The amendment in effect rendered alliances redundant, as weaker parties could no longer piggyback on the stronger. (*Apparentement*, however, was not altogether abandoned: thanks to a motion tabled by the opposition, it was agreed that the votes of parties competing together successfully would still be pooled for the allocation of seats.) The reform was clearly directed at opposition moves to cluster small parties around the Democratic Union (formed in 1994 by defectors from Mečiar's HZDS and the Slovak National Party) and the Christian Democratic Movement and thereby minimize vote-wastage.

The day-long debate on 20 May 1998 consisted primarily of the governing coalition rejecting more than 200 proposed amendments from the opposition before enacting the bill largely as it had been originally drafted. The changes were clearly intended to disadvantage the diffuse opposition parties. Instead, they resulted in the merger of five of them into a shell party, the Slovak Democratic Coalition (*Slovenská demokratická koalícia*, SDK), with a single candidate list.[39] The three parties representing the Hungarian minority likewise coalesced into a single electoral entity. This arrangement removed the issue of thresholds while minimizing vote-wasting. In the September 1998 election, on a turnout of 84 per cent, only 5.5 per cent of the vote went to parties that did not win seats, a marked improvement on 1994 (13 per cent). More than half of the vote went to just two parties, Mečiar's HZDS and the SDK. The least-squares disproportionality index, 2.9, halved the 1994 score of 5.9, and was lower even than the rate from 1990 (3.6) when only a 3 per cent threshold applied. This ultra-proportional outcome left Mečiar completely unable to assemble a new majority coalition, let alone govern by himself. Instead of a government of one or at most two parties, the reform resulted in a new ruling partnership of ten.[40]

Even before the election was held, the opposition had filed with the constitutional court a case against the revisions of the electoral law. The court's ruling in March 1999, six months after the elections, struck down five contested sections, including the stipulations about filling vacated seats and candidate lists that made coalitions redundant.[41] As before, the initiative to prepare new legislation fell to a group of parliamentarians from the governing parties, this time to erase the defining features of the Mečiar reform. Going beyond the requirements of the court's finding, the amendment passed in August 1999 reinstated the threshold scale of 5 per cent for single parties, 7 per cent for alliances of two or three parties, and 10 per cent for alliances of four or more.[42] The single electoral district, however, remained.

This partial restoration of the *status quo ante* infuriated the opposition, now led by Mečiar's HZDS. Claiming that the country's new rulers were recondemning it to political instability, Ján Cuper, one of the authors of the 1998 law, even denounced multi-partism as unpatriotic because of the alleged harm it inflicted on the young state. In reply, the 1999 law's authors freely confessed that it was merely a stop-gap prelude to a systematic rethinking of the electoral system. Displaying the same lack of passion for their product as the designers of the original 1990 PR regime, they promised that the government would submit a major bill in the year 2000 but offered no hints of its content.[43] The following year elapsed without the promised legislation; the government's calendar for 2001 set a September target date but the bill was not a priority and remained off the crowded agenda. In the absence of executive leadership, the legislature itself produced two proposals for specific amendments:

- A working group of parliamentarians convened in the first half of 2000 and recommended a set of core changes, including the restoration of the four multi-member districts (although following boundaries different from those used in 1990–4), and easier conditions for preference voting.[44] Opposed by HZDS and backed by only half of the ruling coalition's legislators, the bill was voted down on its first reading in September 2001.
- In January 2001, a private member's bill was submitted by Robert Fico, leader of a new movement, *Smer* (literally, 'direction' or 'way'). Fico's bill aimed to raise the thresholds to 7 per cent for a single party, 14 per cent for an alliance of two or three, and 21 per cent for a coalition of four or more. Clearly intended to simplify the party landscape and award premiums to the successful (his own party was polling well at the time), the bill suffered the fate of most solo initiatives and died on first reading.[45]

With the next general election fast approaching, Slovakia had not undergone the thorough revamping of the electoral system that its political class deemed necessary (see Table 4.3). The reform introduced by Mečiar was largely undone, but with it went the powerful centripetal incentive of the 5 per cent threshold. Consequently, the SDK reverted to its constituent parts, which in turn were sundered by factional and personal rancour. Meanwhile, all of the ruling parties were damaged in public opinion by the painful austerity programme introduced to repair the fiscal disaster bequeathed by Mečiar in 1998. Ironically, the beneficiary of the reversal of the 1998 reform may be precisely the main sponsor of that reform: Mečiar's HZDS. If the 2002 election sees a rise in vote-wastage and disproportionality, it stands to gain, as the spell in opposition saw its support well above that for any governing party.

Table 4.3 Summary of Slovak electoral laws

Election year	Electoral system type	District structure	Seat allocation formula	Threshold
1990	PR	4 multi-member districts 1 national district for unfilled seats	Hare Hagenbach-Bischoff	3%
1992	PR	4 multi-member districts 1 national district for unfilled seats	Hagenbach-Bischoff Hagenbach-Bischoff	5% for single parties; 7% for alliances of two or three parties; 10% for four or more
1994	PR	4 multi-member districts 1 national district for unfilled seats	Hagenbach-Bischoff Hagenbach-Bischoff	5% for single parties; 7% for alliances of two or three parties; 10% for four or more
1998	PR	1 national multi-member district	Hagenbach-Bischoff	5% for all parties, whether standing alone or in alliance
2002	PR	1 national multi-member district	Hagenbach-Bischoff	5% for single parties; 7% for alliances of two or three parties; 10% for four or more

The Czech Republic

Mečiar's challenge to the 1990 PR model appears modest when compared to that attempted in the Czech Republic. As in Slovakia, the catalyst was a government crisis, which erupted in November 1997 and ended Prime Minister Václav Klaus's five years at the helm. As in

Slovakia, the causes of the crisis were the premier's style of rule, discontent within and defections from the largest party (ODS), the departure of coalition partners, economic woes and privatization scandals. A scapegoat, however, was found in the electoral system, because the 1996 election had returned Klaus's coalition to power two seats short of a majority. Although ad hoc deals with independent deputies kept the coalition alive, it was a precarious existence and encouraged brinkmanship by the junior partners. Whereas in 1995 Klaus had seemed content with the status quo,[46] in 1998 he targeted PR for replacement.

This choice of culprit was largely unfair. The 1998 election results showed that the existing system could sideline difficult extremist parties (the far-right Republicans, whose vote fell below 5 per cent) and produce a possible coalition of ODS, the Christian Democrats and the Freedom Union (recently formed by ODS defectors). Such a coalition would have had both a minimum-winning majority (102 of 200 seats) and policy contiguity. That option, however, was wrecked by intractable arguments over the premiership and ratio of portfolio allocations. Unlike the 1996 election, that of 1998 also produced an alternative minimum-winning coalition, of the Social Democrats (the largest party in the legislature), the Christian Democrats and the Freedom Union, which would have held 113 of 200 seats. Even though the Social Democrats offered huge concessions, going so far as to offer the premiership to the Christian Democrats, Freedom Union refused to join on personal and policy grounds.[47]

The impasse, caused not by the electoral system but by various parties' bluffing and stalling,[48] was broken in July 1998 when the Social Democrats and ODS came to a historic compromise: the former would be allowed to govern alone in a minority by the latter, under a set of conditions enshrined in a 'Pact on the creation of a stable political environment'. Article VII of this pact committed the two parties to writing within 12 months a bill that 'in accordance with the constitutional principles of the Czech Republic will increase the significance of the results of political parties' competition'.[49] This clause was widely interpreted as portending an electoral reform to benefit the larger contestants.

The constitutional proviso of Article VII was critical. The Czech constitution follows the example set in 1920 of marking the parameters of the electoral system. Furthermore, also as in 1920, it stipulates a bicameral legislature, with a Diet of Deputies (*poslanecká sněmovna*, to which the government answers) and a Senate. According to Article 18, the Diet of Deputies is elected by proportional representation, and the Senate by a majoritarian method. The intention was to give the country the best of both worlds without directly employing a mixed system.[50] The specifics of elections to the Senate were not agreed until 1995, due to a protracted intra-cabinet clash between ODS (again favouring the two-ballot majority system) and the Christian Democrats (arguing for the Australian alternative-vote system). The ODS eventually bullied the rest of the coalition into accepting its preference, using the illiterate claim that the alternative vote would not be sufficiently majoritarian to satisfy the constitution.[51]

Discussion of electoral reform in 1998, therefore, had to respect the requirement of PR for the Diet of Deputies or – and it was arithmetically possible at the time – include provision for constitutional amendment. Neither the ODS nor Social Democrats was internally united on the best approach: Klaus's lieutenants were divided between proponents of a one-ballot plurality method and forms of PR with naturally high thresholds,[52] while the Social Democrats debated whether any reform was wise when economic recession was eroding their own standing in opinion polls.[53] As the governing party dithered, ODS united on a plan inspired by a political-science undergraduate dissertation. They suggested fewer deputies (162 instead of 200) to be elected in 35 multi-member districts with the Imperiali divisor and a 5 per cent threshold without a second scrutiny.[54] While still technically a PR system, its disproportionality effect would be enormous, as an average district magnitude of 4.6 would create an extremely high effective threshold.

The Social Democrat prime minister, Miloš Zeman, signalled a sympathy for the ODS plan, but soon encountered resistance from his strongest in-house critic, Petra Buzková. Deputy chair of the party and of the Diet of Deputies, the very popular Buzková counter-proposed 14 multi-member districts based on the newly designated regions and the d'Hondt divisor.[55] Out of this confrontation within the Social Democrat leadership came a compromise position: 200 deputies elected in up to 36 districts but with d'Hondt rather than Imperiali.[56] An exasperated ODS put the country through a three-month crisis in the autumn of 1999, holding up passage of the budget and threatening to terminate the pact that kept the government in power, while sending out feelers to the parties with which it had failed to coalesce the year before. The Christian Democrats and Freedom Union, however, were now interested only in the highly successful 'Quad-coalition' (4K) they had formed with two mini-parties for the 1998 Senate elections.[57]

In this charged environment, ODS and the Social Democrats sealed a new pact, dubbed in characteristically regal style by Klaus a 'patent of tolerance', in January 2000. It committed the signatories to 'finding an electoral system that would significantly facilitate the formation of a functional majority government comprised of at most two political subjects'.[58] The outlines were close to those accepted by the Social Democrats in the summer of 1999, with 200 deputies to be returned from 35 multi-member districts. To accommodate the ODS demand for greater disproportionality, the Social Democrats invented a modification of the d'Hondt sequence, whereby the first divisor would be the square root of 2 (rounded up to 1.42) rather than 1.[59] The potential impact of this innovation is shown by Table 4.4, which compares the actual allocation of seats from 1998 using the Hagenbach-Bischoff quota with those that would have occurred under modified d'Hondt as well as the two formulas originally preferred by ODS (Imperiali) and the Social Democrats (unmodified d'Hondt).

In the course of the tempestuous second reading of the government's bill in May 2000, a final major change was introduced by the ODS club: in a more subtle version of Mečiar's reform, the differentiated threshold would be replaced by the requirement that electoral alliances of two parties should win 10 per cent of the vote, alliances of three 15 per cent, and alliances of four or more 20 per cent.[60] The rule skilfully avoided the accusation that it made coalitions redundant, since a two-party coalition could satisfy it by combining the support of 7 and 3 per cent of the electorate. In combination with an average district magnitude of 5.7, however, it would reinforce the new system's potential effective threshold of 14–17 per cent.[61] Had the 1998 elections been held under these rules, the least-squares disproportionality score would have been an enormous 20.2 instead of the actual rate, 5.8 (up slightly from 5.6 in 1996). Such a figure, which admittedly cannot take into account the strategic responses that small parties and voters would adopt to the new

Table 4.4   Allocations of seats according to formula, using the 1998 vote

Formula	Social Democrats	ODS	Communist Party	Christian Democrats	Freedom Union
Hagenbach-Bischoff	74	63	24	20	19
d'Hondt	88	71	22	11	8
modified d'Hondt	101	88	4	6	1
Imperiali	108	83	4	5	0

Source: Tomáš Lebeda, 'Přiblížení vybraných aspektů reformy volebního systemu', *Politologický časopis*, vol. 7, no. 3 (2000), p. 246.

rules, is comparable to the average for France under its two-round majority system, and nowhere near those for 'reinforced' PR countries such as Spain (average D of 8.15) and Greece ($D = 8.08$).[62]

The bill passed the Diet on 26 May 2000 and then the Senate a month later only with the support of ODS and the Social Democrats; Prime Minister Zeman threatened rebellious Social Democrat senators with expulsion from the party, while ODS had to drag three from their hospital beds to ensure ratification.[63] President Havel, once an ardent critic of PR but now opposed to a change so explicitly intended to skew the distribution of power, exercised his suspensive veto; the Diet overturned it on 10 July 2000 and the law was published in the official gazette.[64] Along with senators from the Quad-coalition (4K), Havel asked the constitutional court to strike down the changes, even though the 4K, like the Slovak Democratic Coalition in 1998, stood to benefit enormously from them if its recent surge in opinion polls were translated into seats (see Table 4.5). This paradox can be explained by the reluctance of the 4K's components to submerge their distinct identities, resources and leadership profiles permanently in an artifice they accepted only as a temporary survival mechanism.

The court had been involved in electoral system disputes thrice before: first regarding the 5 per cent threshold, then the introduction in 1995 of deposits refundable only to parties that won seats, and lastly the requirement that a party win at least 3 per cent of the vote to qualify for remuneration of campaign costs. In the first case, the court found that modest disproportionality was an acceptable externality of any PR system. In the second, it upheld the principle of deposits to deter frivolous campaigns. In the third, however, it objected to the reimbursement threshold as an excessive obstacle to political competition and

Table 4.5 How poll ratings would have translated into seats under the new Czech electoral system had an election been held in June 2000

	Social Democrats	ODS	Communist Party	Quad-coalition
Actual 1998 result (pre-reform)	74	63	24	39
Hypothetical 2000 result (post-reform)	27	56	46	71

Source: Miroslav Korecký, 'Průzkum: Na volební systém doplatí ČSSD i ODS', *Lidové noviny*, 19 June 2000, p. 1.

recommended its reduction to 1 per cent. The court's track record thus offered precedents for both sides: Havel and the senators could depict the new system as a limitation of political free play analogous to the rule on remuneration, while the Diet's team (led by its speaker, Klaus) could invoke the recognition of PR's unavoidable deviations and the value of 'integrative stimuli'.[65]

The court's ruling of 24 January 2001 found almost entirely in Havel's favour.

- While accepting that low district magnitude and the modified d'Hondt divisor individually were unobjectionable instruments, *in combination* they would give rise to 'some sort of hybrid [electoral system]' that conformed to neither of the general types – PR and majoritarianism – recognized by the constitution.[66] The supporting parties, moreover, had failed to supply a convincing explanation of their modification of the conventional d'Hondt sequence.

- Departing from precedent, the court overturned the requirement of a deposit of 40,000 crowns (equivalent to $1066/€1139 at the time of the court's ruling) in each electoral district. Most of the justices now viewed it as biased against poorer parties, redundant in the presence of a challenging threshold scale and rare in European states with PR.[67] The court repeated its earlier objection to the threshold for remuneration of campaign costs, now set at 2 per cent instead of the 1 per cent recommended previously by the court, especially as the amount of money awarded was to be drastically reduced and state financing directed more heavily just to parliamentary parties through an annual grant based on legislative seats. (The court struck down that change in a separate case in February 2001.)

- The one victory for Klaus came when a majority of the justices, in accordance with their earlier ruling on thresholds and the variety of policies and jurisprudence in other European states, upheld the new threshold scale for coalitions. They viewed it as politically motivated, but not unconstitutional.[68]

The verdict deeply divided the political elite and the political-science community: those who privileged stable (i.e. one-party) government condemned the court for discounting precedents of disproportional PR such as Greece and Spain, while those who deplored the bastardizing of PR rejoiced.[69]

The Social Democrat government quickly fell back on the scheme originally championed by its deputy chair Buzková (who had meanwhile resigned her party post in protest at the renewed pact with ODS): a straight d'Hondt divisor and 14 multi-member districts corresponding to the new regional tier of administration. The government's bill, which received its first Diet reading in June 2001, reduced the remuneration threshold to 1.5 per cent but audaciously replaced the deposit struck down by the court with a mandatory, non-refundable 'contribution to the cost of holding elections' of 15,000 crowns (around $400/€442) per district. As the government's bill retained the challenging thresholds of the 2000 law, senators from the Quad-coalition introduced their own to restore the old scale of 5, 7, 9 and 11 per cent. Thanks to their triumph in the 2000 Senate elections, the Quad-coalition needed the support of only two independents to assemble a majority in the upper chamber for their rival bill in August 2001.

In the ensuing intercameral game of 'chicken', as on so many previous occasions, the pressure of time proved decisive. A general election was due by June 2002, and the Social Democrats and ODS chose to call the Senate's bluff by pushing the government's bill through the Diet largely unchanged. They calculated that the Quad-coalition senators would yield, lest the latter's obstruction of the bill jeopardize the very holding of the election, an embarrassment that no country approaching the final stage of EU accession could afford to suffer.[70] In January 2002 the Senate grudgingly passed the Diet's bill, and President Havel signed it into law (see Table 4.6).

Table 4.6 Summary of Czech electoral laws

Election year	Electoral system type	District structure	Seat allocation formula	Threshold
1990	PR	8 multi-member districts 1 national district for unfilled seats	Hagenbach-Bischoff Hagenbach-Bischoff	5%
1992	PR	8 multi-member districts 1 national district for unfilled seats	Hagenbach-Bischoff Hagenbach-Bischoff	5% for a party; 7% for alliances of two parties; 9% for three; 11% for four or more
1996	PR	8 multi-member districts 1 national district for unfilled seats	Hagenbach-Bischoff Hagenbach-Bischoff	5% for a party; 7% for alliances of two parties; 9% for three; 11% for four or more

Table 4.6   (continued)

Election year	Electoral system type	District structure	Seat allocation formula	Threshold
1998	PR	8 multi-member districts 1 national district for unfilled seats	Hagenbach-Bischoff Hagenbach-Bischoff	5% for a party; 7% for alliances of two parties; 9% for three; 11% for four or more
2002	PR	14 multi-member districts	d'Hondt	5% for a party; 10% for alliances of two; 15% for alliances of three; 20% for alliances of four or more

Explaining electoral reform in the successor states

The pretext for electoral reform, as mentioned above, was the crises of government duration and formation in both countries between 1994 and 1998. Before we accept this motive at face value, we should consider alternative explanations in light of the experiences of other countries in recent years. Elsewhere, electoral reform has been attributed to a range of causes:

- Voters and elites enjoy greater freedom with the end of the Cold War to criticize the shortcomings of liberal democracy, so imperfect institutions untouchable in a more adversarial age can now be questioned.
- Countries have become more open to learning from each other's experiences, with possible gravitation toward mixed systems.
- Electorates no longer put up with the stranglehold on office of corrupt or unrepresentative parties and, in PR systems, wish to make individual elected officials more accountable.[71]

All of these explanations view electoral reform as at least partly the product of public pressure, not just of elite interests and bargaining; in Italy and New Zealand, for example, referendums played an important part in kicking off the process. This line of explanation does not apply so well to Czechoslovakia and its successor states. A shift to a more majoritarian system would indeed have been popular in 1991, but by the second half of the decade, especially in Slovakia, polls showed respondents preferring to stay within the bounds of PR. A 1997 survey, a year before electoral reform took place, found that 49 per cent of Slovaks wanted to stick with PR while 24 per cent favoured a shift to majoritarianism; the remaining quarter was undecided.[72] Once the outlines of the new electoral law became known in spring 1998, again only 24 per cent of respondents endorsed it while 500,000 people signed a petition against it.[73] Similarly, in the Czech Republic, polls in March and July 1998 (before and after that year's elections) found only 17 per cent favouring a majoritarian system, with commitment to proportional representation rising between the two surveys from 26.6 to 36 per cent. One-quarter expressed interest in a mixed system.[74] Single-member districts may remain an abstractly attractive concept for alienated citizens, but any shift to them could exaggerate and freeze the existing balance of power between parties; few voters feel moved to award bonuses on such a scale to the current incumbents.

Office-seeking provides the best explanation of moves to reform the electoral system in the Czech Republic and Slovakia. In each case, a major party had a selfish interest in maximizing its share of legislative seats in order to escape the constraints and exposure of multi-party governance. A key moment in both cases was the downfall of the pre-eminent political figure in each country – Vladimír Mečiar in 1994 and Václav Klaus in 1997 – owing to defections from his own party and coalition. (In both cases, their removal from the premier's office eventually led to early elections, which is unusual in post-communist countries.) These crises, however, did not change preferences so much as provide an opportunity to parties that ever since their foundation in 1991 had favoured majoritarian or mixed systems, and had always resented the PR regime that forced them to share power, resources and kickbacks with smaller, ever-obstreperous parties. Having survived the ordeal of their downfall, both leaders rallied, determined to minimize the number of parliamentary parties so that such power-sharing could be discarded.

It should also be noted that the underlying assumption of an inverse relationship between the number of parliamentary parties and cabinet survival, an axiom voiced not only by interested politicians but also (in the Czech case) by sympathetic political scientists,[75] is largely unsubstantiated. In fact, a bivariate correlation of 29 cases from all ten post-communist states applying for EU membership shows no relationship between the effective number of parties sitting in each newly elected legislature and the duration of the first post-election cabinet.[76] As in other new democracies, and some older ones, the causes of post-communist coalitions' early ends lie not in an excess of parties, but in the constraints on partner selection imposed by the presence of 'uncoalitionable' extremists, sudden events such as corruption scandals and economic crises, ego storms and the greater propensity of new parties to splinter rather than accommodate dissent.[77] Unwilling to accept those awkward facts, the strongest parties in both countries scapegoated overpopulated parliaments and sought a solution in electoral reform.

Conclusions

After a decade of competitive politics, elections in the Czech and Slovak republics remained governed by rules very similar to those agreed, quickly and with little commitment, at the start of the transition. Attempts at reform were stopped, overturned or diluted, but not before they produced a range of unintended consequences. Not least of these was harm, in the short run, to ODS and HZDS, the very parties that sought what their antecedents Civic Forum and Public against Violence forswore in 1990: the design of institutions to award seats and power well out of proportion to the victors' popularity. In both cases the mechanical effects of such manipulation were anticipated and neutralized by other parties' adroit mergers and voters' calculations (as shown in the 1998 Slovak elections, the 1998 and 2000 Czech Senate elections and the 2000 Czech regional elections[78]). In both cases the judicial branch intervened, decisively in the Czech Republic.

The experience of the two republics suggests two conclusions regarding electoral reform and the resilience of institutions. First, the Czech and Slovak party systems were already stabilizing at the time electoral reform was attempted, with the effective number of parliamentary parties falling to 3.7 and 4.4, respectively, comparable to the means for older democracies such as France and Belgium. Voter volatility and party replacement rates had also been declining, in line with the trend throughout Central Europe.[79] These cases thus confirmed that deliberate shifts toward greater disproportionality tend to be initiated in PR systems not in order to counteract fragmentation, but *after* a party system has begun to shrink and the fittest seek to push electoral systems in win-concentrating directions.[80]

Second, the creation of new electoral systems and their modification were the product of intense endogenous bargaining and horse-trading, and the parties involved proved capable of both self-interested and sociotropic motives. The Czech and Slovak cases thus tally with other findings in this volume, as well as studies of post-fascist Germany and post-Franco Spain that stress the political nature of major institutional choices, with some features selected to serve the public good and others to benefit only certain competitors.[81] The resilience of electoral institutions introduced hurriedly in 1990 was not an equilibrium outcome but an initially contingent process that generated uneven and unpredictable benefits which no one had the power to redirect even after new preferences were derived.[82] The perceived stakes of electoral institutions remained high as long as parties large and small, left and right, feared that victorious opponents would aggrandize their power and pervert public policy.

5
Romania: Stability without Consensus

In post-communist Romanian politics, electoral legislation was not a major point of contention and stability characterized the electoral system after 1990. The main principles of the provisional electoral law adopted prior to the first post-authoritarian election were maintained in legislation adopted by the first democratically elected parliament in 1991–2, and few changes were introduced thereafter (see Table 5.1). Romania has a bicameral parliament elected by closed-list proportional representation in 42 constituencies with a two-tier seat allocation.[1] The most important amendments introduced a 3 per cent legal threshold in 1992 and then raised it to 5 per cent for parties and 8–10 per cent for alliances before the 2000 elections. However, fuelled by dissatisfaction with politics, discussions over a radical change to a majoritarian system

Table 5.1 Main changes in the rules on elections to the Romanian Chamber of Deputies

Election year	Electoral system type	District structure	Seat allocation formula	Threshold
1990	Closed-list PR	41 (4–41)	Hare c + d'Hondt nl aggregated surplus/ remainder votes	No legal threshold
1992, 1996	Closed-list PR	42 (4–29)	as 1990	3%
2000	Closed-list PR	42 (4–29)	as 1990	5% for parties and 8–10% for alliances

c = constituency; nl = national level.

surfaced in the press in 1999. A government bill was planned for inclusion on the legislative agenda for 2001, but in early 2002 the focus of the debate shifted to issues of constitutional reform. The relevant debates thus occurred in 1990, 1991–2 and 1999–2001. They were lengthy, animated and highly partisan, yet, as we shall see, relatively uninformed and clearly dominated by short-term perspectives. A number of issues that were contentious in 1990 remained so throughout the decade, the most notorious being ballot format and the mode of presidential elections. The unequal balance between a strong communist-successor party and a weak, often incoherent, anti-communist opposition rendered the calculus of the former the dominant influence on institutional design in post-communist Romania.

Provisional institutions and the first post-communist electoral law

Street demonstrations and several days of armed battle led to the sudden breakdown of the communist regime and its government institutions in December 1989. All legislative and executive power passed to a provisional body – the Council of the National Salvation Front (CFSN), formed by dissident communists, oppositionists and demonstrators, and presided over by (former) communist Ion Iliescu.[2] Initial proposals for the 'Law on the Election of the Parliament, the President of Romania and Local Councils' were submitted to public debate by the Council on 1 February 1990. The preamble referred to the 22 December 1989 Programme of the National Salvation Front (*Frontul Salvării Naționale*, FSN), as well as to Romanian democratic traditions and the experience of established Western democracies as key sources for the ideas embodied in the draft.[3]

The text advocated the institutionalization of popular sovereignty, universal and equal franchise, human rights, political pluralism and free elections. A bicameral parliament, including 15 representatives of the army as non-elected senators, was proposed and justified as a continuation of interwar Romanian traditions. In joint sessions, the two chambers were to form the Constituent Assembly, possibly to continue as an ordinary bicameral legislature after the adoption of the Constitution. Direct presidential elections[4] and a majoritarian two-round system of elections in single-member districts[5] were envisaged. The text advocated 'proportional representation of all nationalities in parliament and local councils'. This implied a communist-style 'proportional representation', except that it focused on the representation of ethnic groups, not the demographic categories emphasized in communist-era assemblies. To ensure proportional representation all elected deputies were to declare their ethnicity; then compensatory seats would be allocated to minorities that did not reach the proportion of deputies indicated by their population share.[6] The proposals also provided for the right of citizens aged 18 years and over to contest elections; equal nomination rights for political parties, minority and social organizations;[7] free and non-discriminatory electoral campaigning; and a maximum of two consecutive terms for all elected offices. An independent Central Electoral Bureau, formed by judges, was to oversee the electoral process.

Public debate took place mainly in the press, and focused largely on some dubiously democratic aspects of the proposals, including non-elected senators and mandatory declarations of ethnicity. The choice of a majoritarian rather than a broadly proportional system and the lack of provisions conferring a significant role on political parties were other frequent targets of criticism.

After a meeting of the CFSN committee responsible for the draft with representatives of the then registered political parties on 3 February 1990, fresh proposals were submitted for discussion by the new legislative assembly, the Provisional Council of National Union.[8] In this provisional legislature, the 35 parties registered before 1 February and nine minority organizations had three representatives each, while the former CFSN received 105 seats, with Ion Iliescu serving as president. Although the CFSN thus ceased to exist, and these 105 assembly members did not consider themselves as representatives of a single political force, common parlance referred to them as 'the CFSN', a convention that will also be followed here.

The initial proposal for a majoritarian system was dropped as incompatible with the principle of proportional representation and as unconducive to strengthening political parties. The most disputed points centred on whether to define the political system as 'multi-party' or 'pluralist', ballot format, the second-tier seat allocation, party finance and various technicalities regarding polling procedures and penalties.

Arguing that the term 'pluralist system' did not guarantee the existence of several parties, the historic peasant (*Partidul Naţional Ţărănesc-Creştin Democrat*, PNŢCD) and liberal (*Partidul Naţional Liberal*, PNL) parties attacked the draft's preamble as fundamentally flawed. They feared that it could leave the door open to a 'pluralist' one-party system. But the majority of the assembly saw 'pluralist' as a broader term, incorporating 'multipartism'. Finally it was agreed to call the system 'democratic pluralist'.[9]

The new bill proposed list-PR based on regional constituencies. The CFSN still supported the idea of *territorial representation*, while most political parties focused on the proportional representation of each party's share of the vote. The minutes of the debates suggest that the CFSN accepted PR only after Iliescu declared publicly that list voting was better for Romanian democracy, despite its numerous complications. The key motive appeared to be a concern with legitimacy. Clearly, a majoritarian system would have strongly benefited the FSN at the time and better fitted its concept of representation. But it would have allowed for very limited, if any, parliamentary representation of the opposition, diminishing the democratic credentials of the new institutions. Moreover, elections organized according to a law not supported by the main opposition parties would not necessarily have been regarded as democratic by international observers.

Yet the CFSN remained eager to capitalize on the Front's organizational strength at local level and thus emphasized constituency representation.[10] This was the chief reason behind the vehement rejection of a proposal that national party lists could play a role in second-round seat allocation. Their inclination for a personalized form of voting was also fed by their particular conception of representation, to which many ex-communist deputies referred throughout the coming decade.[11] Finally, lack of familiarity with other electoral mechanisms must also be added to the list of plausible explanations for the initial CFSN opposition to compromise.

With the acceptance of regional party lists, it was agreed that a Hare quota would be used at district level, but different rules were to apply to the two chambers if seats were unfilled by full quotas. In Senate elections, the largest remainder method would be employed at constituency level. For the Chamber of Deputies, all remainder votes and unfilled seats were to be aggregated at national level, and allocated by d'Hondt.[12]

The debate on party finance focused on foreign donations and state subsidies for party campaigning. The core of the CFSN and a large number of small parties were strongly against foreign donations, seen variously as a form of 'interference in the domestic politics of Romania' and as unfair to less internationally connected parties.[13] The historic parties were the main targets, probably due to the CFSN's frustration with the support of émigrés and western NGOs for the historic parties, and perhaps to uncertainty regarding the electoral significance of the Democratic Union of Hungarians in Romania (*Uniunea Democrata Maghiară din Romania*, UDMR).[14] The final text of the law forbade the use in election campaigns of funds received from abroad or not publicly declared.

The bill also stipulated that ethnic minority organizations standing for election should receive seats in the lower chamber, even without sufficient votes to win them. Opponents considered this special representation to compromise proportionality and overemphasize ethnic cleavages. At the other extreme and notwithstanding the remarkable ease of registration, one CFSN representative proposed that each registered minority organization receive a seat even without standing for election. The rule eventually adopted – with the support of Iliescu and the minority representatives – stipulated that a duly registered ethnic minority organization must receive a seat in the lower house if it received:

- at least one-tenth of the minimum number of votes that a political party needed to win at least one seat; and
- more votes than any other organization referring in its name to the same ethnic group.[15]

Due to mutual distrust and suspicion, much time was spent discussing polling and counting procedures. Some new parties, especially the historic ones, were particularly concerned that, because of their own organizational weakness, the FSN might end up de facto overrepresented on local election committees regardless of legal provisions for parity between the contenders. Hence more and more provisions were proposed to regulate matters such as the opening hours of polling stations (6:00 to 23:00 was adopted), allowing ill people to vote at home, rules on possible suspension of polling,[16] and the composition and procedures of the local election committees overseeing and counting the votes.

The widespread view among commentators was that the Front could impose any legislation it desired since it had half the seats as CFSN, three additional seats as FSN – now registered as a political party – plus the support of several small satellite parties. Yet debates in the Provisional Council did not always reflect a bipolar confrontation between the FSN and the historic parties. Individual representatives often expressed views different from their parties. The parties were inchoate, and many assembly members genuinely believed that their function was to contribute their individual judgements, not to follow a party line. This belief was particularly pervasive in what outsiders called 'the CFSN'. Many of these deputies felt that they had been selected to be part of the CFSN (and then the Provisional Council) because of their personal past as dissidents or participants in the 1989 revolution, and some never became either members or candidates of the FSN. Moreover, although many small parties were more hostile to the historic parties than to Iliescu and the FSN, their loyalty to the latter was not guaranteed.

Note too that for many new parties debates in the assembly were more important as a means to become visible to the electorate – the sessions were transmitted live on television – than as an opportunity to influence electoral legislation. Matters were further complicated by the assembly members' limited knowledge of the matters discussed, as well as inexperience in negotiations and public life. Personal charisma, rhetoric and persuasive skills were essential in changing the balance of opinion.[17] Besides these factors, his position as chairman also helped Ion Iliescu.[18]

In a series of anti-communist demonstrations in the capital, demands were also raised, *inter alia*, that those who had occupied high positions in the Communist Party in the previous five years be barred from public office. Though the demonstrations had no impact on the election law itself, they shaped the opposition's political agenda for years to come.

The first elected legislature

In the May 1990 elections the FSN obtained a large majority of votes (66.3 per cent and 67 per cent) and seats (66.4 per cent and 76.5 per cent) in both houses of parliament, and Iliescu captured the presidency by a stunning margin. Otherwise, the Constituent Assembly was fairly fragmented, 17 parties plus nine ethnic minority representatives gaining seats in the lower chamber.[19] The adoption of a new constitution was its main task. The most controversial topics regarding representative institutions were whether parliament should be bicameral or unicameral, the prerogatives of the two chambers and the head of state, whether the monarchy should be restored and, if not, how to elect the president.

Most parties save the FSN[20] stood for a bicameral parliament, mostly for historic reasons, namely to show continuity with the interwar Romanian system. The extensive discussion on how to differentiate between the chambers raised already familiar issues such as ballot format, election of the Senate by municipal councils and non-elected senators. Most parliamentary groups reckoned that the Senate should be based on representation of place and the Chamber of Deputies mostly on representation of ethnicity and party. Directly elected senators in single-member districts was the preferred choice[21] but the mode of election of the two chambers was eventually left to be settled by the election law rather than the Constitution.[22] Other electorally relevant issues touched upon in the Constituent Assembly were the minimum voting age, the political rights of army and police personnel – granted the right to vote but not to be members of political parties or candidates in elections – and parliamentary representation for ethnic minorities.

The 1992 electoral legislation and the 1992 elections

After the adoption of the Constitution, the government submitted election bills to the two chambers on 17 January 1992. In the plenary sessions of the Senate alone, the debates totalled 45 hours and included 1215 interventions.[23] The government bill proposed to retain closed-list proportional representation for both chambers, based on 42 constituencies (41 counties and the capital Bucharest), a quota of representation (70,000 citizens for a deputy, 140,000 for a senator) to determine the number of seats per constituency, and the allocation of all seats at constituency level by the d'Hondt formula. The government, which could not expect majority support in the legislature after the FSN had split, set proportional representation as its primary goal, with the filtering out of numerous small parties, and argued that a single-member district system would undermine political parties.

The Senate first debated the bill on 9 March, but the Chamber of Deputies followed only on 23 April. The duplication and overlap of the functions of the two chambers presented numerous problems for this and virtually all other legislation. The same issues raised controversy but not necessarily to the same extent, and the versions initially adopted in the two chambers were so different that the final version only passed (17 June) after extensive mediation in committee and three joint plenary sessions.

The hottest topics included some familiar from 1990, that is the distinction between the two chambers, ballot format, *apparentement*, seat allocation procedures, party finance and some novelties such as the threshold. But the question of domestic election observers and the dates of legislative and presidential elections received most media coverage, probably because their less technical and more partisan nature raised their news value above other questions equally intensely debated by the legislators.[24]

The party splits of the period largely determined the attitude of individual parliamentarians and parties towards these two issues. At the national convention of the National Salvation Front in March 1992 former prime minister Petre Roman, leader of the more reformist and western-oriented faction, was elected party leader. In response Iliescu's supporters formed a separate party, initially called the Democratic Front of National Salvation (*Frontul Democrat al Salvării Naţionale*, FDSN).[25] Party fragmentation further increased as some smaller groups elected to parliament on either the FSN or the Democratic Convention of Romania (*Convenţia Democrată Română*, CDR[26]) ticket formed their own parliamentary clubs. The most significant was the historic National Liberal Party (PNL), the second biggest party in the CDR, the opposition umbrella organization that won the highest number of votes in the spring 1992 local elections. The FDSN and PNL needed time to organize and to make themselves known to the voters, hence they supported postponing parliamentary elections. In contrast, the Roman-led FSN and other parties in the CDR wanted to capitalize swiftly on the momentum gained in the local elections. These parties supported non-concurrent elections for president and legislature in order to prevent Iliescu from campaigning for the FDSN. Iliescu as ticket leader was expected to boost the FDSN vote in concurrent elections, while in non-concurrent elections the president of the country would not be permitted to campaign for a political party.

The most prominent arguments in the debate referred to the higher costs of non-concurrent elections and to the fact that neither the Romanian constitution nor the practice of foreign democracies clearly justified combining the two. Several alliances between the parties seemed possible on the two issues. In the end, FSN-Roman gave up on non-concurrent elections in exchange for elections in July 1992. However, since the FDSN did not deliver its part of the bargain, FSN-Roman refused to discuss the presidential election law. Yet, a reversal of a previous vote after the speaker of the lower house controversially ordered a repeat, and the support of some smaller parties, the Liberals and some deputies of CDR-affiliated parties led to an FDSN victory on both issues: concurrent elections were to be held at the end of September 1992.

The issue of domestic election observers was more controversial in the Senate than in the Chamber of Deputies. The historic parties, the government, the Hungarian UDMR and FSN-Roman emphasized that the (then) Conference on Security and Cooperation in Europe (CSCE) and Romania's western partners supported observers, and dropping them could raise doubts about the fairness of the elections. Some prominent FDSN parliamentarians fiercely opposed the idea, arguing that these observers could not be impartial since they had the right to express political preferences in the elections. Indeed, most domestic NGOs expected to volunteer for monitoring elections were believed to support the right-wing, which, in its turn, feared that a lack of activists could leave it underrepresented on local election committees. FDSN and nationalist (*Partidul Unității Naționale Române*, PUNR) senators abandoned their opposition to the presence of domestic observers only at the final joint plenary session of the two houses (19 June), when numerous provisions were added to ensure that observers could not 'interfere' with polling and counting procedures.

Though superficially covered in the press, debates on more substantive issues – voting and seat allocation procedures, party finance – were also lengthy and heated. The notion of a legal threshold came from the judiciary committee, not a party. Unsurprisingly, the smaller political parties (PSDR, ULB) argued against it, while the stronger ones (the National Salvation Front, Liberals, Christian Democrats, the nationalist PUNR and Hungarians) disagreed only on whether it should be 2, 3, 4 or 5 per cent. The experience of foreign countries was evoked in support of multifarious positions, not always with great accuracy. The Peasant Party (PNȚCD) supported the reintroduction of the 2 per cent threshold used in interwar Romania. A regional threshold was rejected on grounds that the aim of the law was to promote the consolidation of large national parties, not regional ones. The PUNR proposed a separate threshold for coalitions to prevent very small parties entering parliament with the help of an umbrella organization. The parties of the Democratic Convention, as well as the Hungarians (UDMR) and the Ecological Movement, vehemently rejected this proposal as unconstitutional. In the end, the law set a national 3 per cent threshold for parties and electoral alliances alike.

Debates regarding seat allocation procedures focused mostly on the proposed d'Hondt formula. Some smaller parties were categorically against it. The UDMR, FSN-Roman and PNL proposed retaining the system used in the 1990 lower-house election, which also relied on d'Hondt for second-round allocation at national level. This position eventually prevailed in the debate, but the discussions were prolonged, not least because of widespread misunderstanding about both d'Hondt and its alternatives. There was confusion as to whether d'Hondt was a 'proportional' system, whether it was compatible with the redistribution of remainder votes and whether a threshold was 'still needed' if d'Hondt were used. Whatever the party line, most parties remained internally divided on the issue. In the final version seats were to be allocated among the parties that passed the threshold by using a Hare quota at constituency level; remainders would be aggregated at national level and then distributed using d'Hondt. If the number of seats allocated to parties at the second tier is unproblematic and increases proportionality, the manner in which they are assigned to specific constituencies is neither clear nor transparent. The adoption of the almost incomprehensible algorithm specified in Article 66 of the law was not explained. Moreover it led to some anomalous situations, such as that in which a UDMR deputy secured a seat in a county where the party had received a mere 2000 votes.[27]

In the Chamber of Deputies, *apparentement* as a means to counterbalance d'Hondt's presumed tendency to favour bigger parties was proposed by the PUNR, the Liberals and the Agrarian Party (*Partidul Democrat Agrar din Romania*, PDAR).[28] The government displayed indifference and FSN-Roman supported it, speculating that small extremist parties would find it difficult to attract a partner. Yet the majority still rejected *apparentement*. Despite some arguments in favour of allowing votes for individual candidates, the straight vote for a closed party list passed easily following the government's argument that personalization of vote choice would be too complex for voters and electoral officials alike and would militate against the desired strengthening of political parties.

Both chambers discussed and rejected the proposal of the PNȚCD, PNL and UDMR to ban the candidature of those who had occupied senior positions in the party *nomenklatura* in the last five years of the communist regime. Other highly contentious points concerned technical matters such as the size of the space allotted to party symbols and the stamp marking the voter's choice, and whether and how to staple ballot papers into a separate booklet. These debates apparently emerged from the right-wing opposition's concern that local election committees would be dominated by the better organized FDSN and FSN, leading to bias in counting disputed votes. Although the government insisted that shortages of staples and staplers made stapling impracticable and could delay the election, parliament decided that ballots must be stapled.[29]

Campaign finance remained controversial especially in the Senate, which consumed an entire day debating the need for a separate law on campaign finance. Regarding foreign donations the same divide and outcome emerged as in 1990, but with the addition of more detailed provisions for state campaign finance. A number of FSN deputies (sitting on the FDSN and Greater Romania Party benches in the next legislature) strongly opposed public funding, arguing that the money could be better spent and that people uninterested in political parties should not be obliged to pay for them through taxation. Some nationalist deputies also tried to exclude the Hungarian UDMR from receiving public funding by insisting that it was a cultural association, not a political party.[30]

The debate on the protection of party symbols was related to splits in the Front and the Democratic Convention. The PNL and the FSN proposed that a label, symbol or logo used in a previous election by a party or alliance could not be used by another party or another alliance composed of different parties than the one that had initially used it. Thus, for instance, parties remaining in the Democratic Convention would not benefit from citizens' familiarity with the symbols and labels established when the PNL was part of the alliance. Similarly, FSN-Roman wanted to be the sole user of the FSN's name and its electoral symbol, the rose, to prevent the FDSN from using them. Despite predictable opposition in some circles the proposal was adopted. However, the rule did not bar a name or symbol *similar* to that of an existing party or alliance, thus in practice ballot papers remained filled with bewilderingly similar names and symbols of a variety of entities.[31] Indeed, easy access to the electoral ballot and the resulting media coverage led many irrelevant parties to register with names and symbols much like those of established parties, keeping the ballot paper brochure-length and highly confusing.

Throughout the debates, all parties represented somewhat incoherent positions as their representatives adopted different stances in the two chambers and over time, and individual deputies deviated from their party's position in a given chamber at a given moment. Divisions within parties and alliances also reflected shifting perceptions of the odds in the presidential race, which further complicated negotiations about the electoral laws. Various temporary alliances emerged on certain points, but the parties often reneged on their commitments. Momentary feuds, especially the emerging split in the FSN, often blurred long-term party interests, especially when, as frequently happened, they were coupled with misunderstandings about technicalities and their implications. Apart from the uncertainties created by the split, the main reason for retaining the existing PR-system was probably that many FSN-deputies were proud of the legislation they had adopted in 1990. As in 1990, the chairmen – the presidents of the two chambers – remained disproportionately influential, and the final text often ambiguous.

Reform proposals after 1996

Between 1992 and 1996 electoral reform temporarily left the agenda, while the party configuration underwent significant changes. The FDSN, subsequently renamed the Party of Social Democracy (PDSR), formed the government first in coalition with and then supported by the nationalist parties (PUNR and PRM). Despite its continuous decrease in popularity after 1992, the FDSN, subsequently PDSR (*Partidul Democratiei Sociale din Romania* – Party of Social Democracy of Romania), then PSD (*Partidul Social Democrat* – Social Democratic Party) remained the largest and most institutionalized political party in Romania, even when in opposition. The FSN (renamed *Partidul Democrat* – Democratic Party (PD) after 1992), CDR and the Hungarian UDMR were the 'democratic' opposition, the extra-parliamentary PNL joining the Convention before the 1996 elections.

The 1996 elections brought the first alternation in government in post-communist Romania as well as a new president. But disappointment soon followed as hopes failed to materialize and the right-wing coalition was marred by incessant conflicts as well as corruption and incompetence scandals. The government continued the previous practice of ruling by decree, since the legislative process in Parliament continued to be cumbersome, not least because of the symmetric jurisdiction of the two chambers. Almost all parties suffered splits and defections. In this context of disenchantment with the functioning of the political system, some journalists, NGOs and political parties – especially the PNL and a popular splinter group from the PDSR – advanced the idea of a radical reform of the electoral system, now blamed for the illnesses of Romanian politics.

Several parliamentarians proposed amendments to the electoral law and over time there were also several party proposals. Among them, the raising of the threshold and the creation of a permanent professional electoral commission were deemed necessary by most parties. Similarly to 1992, the first was meant to reduce the fragmentation of the party system and to ensure that only significant parties would be represented in parliament, thus increasing the chances of government stability. Although a permanent commission was suggested in successive CSCE/OSCE reports[32] and was in principle supported by all parties,[33] it never reached the parliamentary agenda.

A higher threshold was included in PDSR and PD bills submitted to parliament. In May 1999 the Chamber of Deputies began to debate a new electoral law, based on the PDSR bill; they adopted it on 9 June. It included a 5 per cent threshold, higher for alliances. Discussion focused mostly on technical points related to electoral administration in order to guarantee free and fair elections. Since the bill submitted to the Senate by the Democratic Party, and supported by its coalition partners and PDSR, was not placed on the agenda of the Senate plenary sessions, the 1996–2000 legislature never adopted a new electoral law.

Prior to the 2000 elections, however, the government introduced certain new provisions by emergency decree. The most significant raised the threshold to 5 per cent for parties and 8–10 per cent for alliances/coalitions (5 per cent for the first party, plus 3 per cent for the second, plus 1 per cent for each additional party up to 10 per cent). Other changes altered nomination procedures for minority organizations,[34] regulated the campaign in the broadcast media, defined an alliance and adjusted provisions regarding the date of the elections, voters' cards, polling procedures and the deposit of electoral materials.[35]

The threshold was only one among many proposals for electoral reform. The roots of the failures of representation and of the inefficacy of parliament – real or perceived – were believed to be deeper. Parliament was seen as remote from the electorate, slow, inefficient and unaccountable. Images of the parliament in television and newspaper reports included MPs reading or even sleeping during plenary sessions and certainly spending more time in the café than in frequently empty session rooms.[36] Moreover, although obliged to hold weekly office hours in their constituencies, deputies were still seen as largely ignorant of or at least uninterested in the concerns of their constituency. Consequently, the 'quality' of members of parliament was perceived as a crucial reason for the malfunctioning of the political system.

From 1999 on, an elusive person-oriented ('uninominal') voting system was presented as the solution by the press and some political parties, especially the National Liberals and the PDSR splinter Alliance for Romania. The central argument was that the closed list strengthened party leaders at the expense of voters. This reduced accountability, since MPs did not fear that poor performance would mean failure to be re-elected; rather their sole concern was with their position within the party. Following this line of argument, things would work in just the opposite manner if parliamentarians were elected individually, directly by the citizens in their constituencies and not via parties. This populist argumentation could capitalize on the mistrust of party-politics among journalists and citizens alike. Although the ideas had floated around for some time, support for them appeared unusually high and growing after 1999.

The most widely circulated quality newspaper *Adevărul*, the former daily of the Communist Central Committee and the champion of anti-corruption campaigns under the 1996–2000 non-communist governments, was in the front line of this 'crusade'. The reports and analyses in the paper did not enter into the technical details of this 'uninominal' system and thus did not specify a preference either for single-member districts with one or two rounds or an open list system; but the populist, anti-party tone was easily detectable. Moreover, a citizens' initiative law, submitted by a group including the president of 'Pro-Democratia', one of two main NGOs that deployed observers in the 1992 and 1996 elections, proposed a mixed-parallel electoral system for both chambers.

Among the significant actors, the liberals expressed the most radical position, proposing fundamental constitutional changes, including the election of the president by parliament and a majoritarian electoral system.[37] The historic parties had supported indirect presidential election since 1990, and this may be interpreted as a programmatic commitment, especially since its utility for PNL's electoral fortunes was doubtful. Majoritarianism was even less likely to benefit a party that, like the PNL, had 9 per cent of the seats in parliament and consistently hovered around 10 per cent in the polls after the 2000 elections. The most plausible explanation for this apparent anomaly lies in the long-term strategy of the party, seeking to become the centre-right alternative to PDSR.

It is highly significant that the peak of press interest in issues of electoral reform was reached during the 'long' election campaign of 2000. The PNL proposal was also launched at the beginning of the election campaign, and it received extensive coverage in *Adevărul*. PNL apparently believed that an increase in its credibility and electoral appeal would accompany such populist discourse. However, it is quite clear that the chief beneficiary of anti-system discourse and sentiment in the 2000 election was the extreme nationalist Greater Romania Party, which came second to the PDSR, while the Democratic Convention was excluded altogether by the new thresholds.

After their victory in 2000 the Social Democrats formed a minority government, with a programme embracing reform of the constitutional and judicial system. Constitutional reform was meant to render the bicameral system 'meaningful and efficient', thus restoring the authority of parliament. Even before the 2000 elections, the Social Democrats,[38] the PD[39] and the UDMR[40] saw a differentiation in the prerogatives of the two chambers as one way to make the legislature more effective. According to the governmental programme,[41] which was congruent with previous social-democrat positions,[42] the Senate should represent counties and oversee the ratification of international treaties and laws passed by deputies, without reproducing debate on individual points/ articles. The Chamber of Deputies should have the final word on legislation, and the government's capacity to legislate by decree should be determined (and limited) by law. The ruling Social Democratic Party (now PSD) justified the maintenance of bicameralism by public support and Romanian democratic tradition but it envisaged unicameralism in the long run, again congruent with its position in 1991–2. It also favoured increasing the quota of representation, thus reducing parliament to 220 deputies and 110 senators.

The biggest novelty in the government's programme was the proposal for a two-round majoritarian system – or at least a mixed system – to replace PR. Many 'hard line' ex-communist deputies had favoured such a system throughout the 1990s. They believed that it would benefit them, both because of their grassroots organizations and their recognition as public figures. The influence of communist principles of representation and a disbelief in multi-party competition accompanied by a preference for individual personalities as vehicles of political linkage between citizens and government could be detected behind this proposal. Yet, since legitimacy and image in the West were a constant concern for PDSR, in 1990 and 1992 as well as in 1999–2000, these voices had been marginalized in the party's official position. However ineffective the pro-majoritarian (pro-'uninominal') position inside FDSN/PDSR was until 2001, it was due generally to causes external to their party. Therefore, under more advantageous external circumstances when other parties, the press and public opinion also supported single-member districts, it was unsurprising that the party fully embraced the idea. Given its position of clear dominance of the party arena, a majoritarian system would favour PSD, both by creating a majority enabling it to govern alone and by diminishing the electoral chances of all opposition parties. This created a perfect situation for the PSD, pursuing its electoral interests while claiming at the same time to act on behalf of public opinion and civil society.

The Hungarian UDMR remained the only party consistently opposed to changing the electoral system in the direction of majoritarianism. In 1999–2000 the PNŢCD considered that majoritarianism would not be appropriate for Romanian democracy at that stage, while the PD supported a mixed system for the Senate. The UDMR consistently supported PR because it calculated that it would be disadvantaged by any type of majoritarian system: in few areas could it receive an outright majority of the vote, and it would not receive the support of other parties in run-off elections.[43] The UDMR also saw other ways to improve the quality of MPs, including internal party primaries such as those they themselves organized.[44] Moreover, the unity of UDMR as a party would be jeopardized in a majoritarian system, since its factions or other Hungarian contenders – independent candidates and small parties – would gain an incentive to stand in Hungarian-dominated areas.

In 2002, a superficial consensus on single-member districts seemed to emerge and the headlines were occupied by constitutional reform, especially on the mode of election and the function of the president. It is highly plausible that politicians feared a press campaign construing their opposition to the 'uninominal' vote as evidence of a desire to remain unaccountable. This would further delegitimize them, especially in the context of *Adevărul*'s coverage, which suggested that politicians expressed lack of interest because it would endanger their current positions. In contrast, the electoral support of UDMR was based on the pursuit of minority rights, so UDMR was immune to the danger of delegitimization on other issues. Therefore, it was easier for them to embrace positions unpopular with the Romanian language media, which are in any case not read by the majority of ethnic Hungarians. Further, it also appeared that the UDMR was the most aware of the likely impact of such a system, both on their electoral fortunes and on the structure of the Romanian parliament and party system. The other parties either do not have the same insight or their long-term goals took priority. The liberals applauded the governmental proposal and competed with the PSD for paternity of a new electoral system, thus assisting PSD not only in the legislative implementation of the new system but in their goal to maintain their image and democratic credentials.[45]

Conclusion

Until 1999–2000 the electoral system was not seriously contested and it had proved remarkably stable. In 1990, 1991 and 1992 all parties supported their positions with (sometimes inaccurate) references to Romanian interwar tradition, West European 'models' and major principles and values such as 'democracy', the 'people' and 'representation'. Yet both interwar traditions and foreign models served as legitimizing and time-saving devices during negotiations rather than exercising a direct influence. There were no specific appeals to the widely discredited communist experience, but both the proposals and their justifications often suggested its effective influence, especially on perceptions of representation.

The debates revealed a 'whole system' approach in terms of electoral and more generally institutional design, even if on occasion the parties misrepresented their electoral chances under one or another arrangement due to ignorance and unrealistic perceptions of their popularity. The parties tried to achieve advantageous arrangements by compensating provisions that would not favour them in the race for one institution with provisions that would favour them in another, as well as with provisions that would enable them to achieve goals other than electoral gain, such as international legitimization. Yet, contextual factors of the transition made the FSN (later FDSN, subsequently PDSR and PSD) the dominant influence on institutional design in post-communist Romania, a dominance enhanced by the weakness, disunity and incompetence of the anti-communist opposition.

Over time, the prime political interests of the ex-communist successor party remained twofold: electoral success and legitimacy. A directly elected president and concurrent elections were meant to ensure the former, proportional representation the latter. The balance gradually shifted between the two goals. In 1990, concerns over legitimacy were serious and fundamental, and uncertainty over election success low. The initial CFSN proposal expressed a particular conception of parliament and of representation closer to the communist concept of representation than to the liberal democratic one. Moreover, a majoritarian system would have ensured a near monopoly of seats for the FSN largely due to their superior organization. Yet, in the multi-party Provisional Council that replaced the CFSN, Ion Iliescu and the FSN supported a closed-list proportional system. This change must be interpreted as a consequence of the need to ensure parliamentary representation for opposition parties, but not as the yielding of concessions to the opposition parties, who were too weak and disunited to exact any concessions. Legitimacy became an issue in late January 1990 when violent attacks against opposition demonstrations by ordinary government supporters raised suspicions internationally regarding the democratic credentials of the new leadership.

In 1991–2, before and after the split of the National Salvation Front (FSN), uncertainty over the electoral chances of the successors of the FSN was high and issues of legitimacy remained important. Hence, both factions of the FSN supported PR and were not interested in promoting the single-member district system that some hardliners still suggested. The priority for the parliamentarians of FDSN was to ensure that presidential and parliamentary elections would take place concurrently in order to maximize their electoral fortunes by using Ion Iliescu as their ticket leader. The other faction – Petre Roman's FSN – naturally supported early but non-concurrent elections.

In the debate that began in the late 1990s, despite the position of some of its factions, the now 'social democrats' (PDSR) did not support a majoritarian electoral system until their success in 2000. After the 2000 elections, the minority government's programme comprised not only a proposal to reform the structure and prerogatives of the two chambers, but also an overhaul of the electoral system. If the first was congruent with previous official PDSR positions, the radical reform of the electoral system had not previously been part of official PDSR (then PSD) discourse. The system now envisaged was either a two-round majoritarian system or a mixed system, and the ideas included many of the initial points present in the 1990 CFSN draft. The electoral calculus behind this proposal is not difficult to detect. Given the disarray of the democratic opposition and the dominance of all levels of government by the PSD, the PSD did not fear that, as had all previous incumbents in post-communist Romania, they might lose the elections. Consequently, a majoritarian system would ensure their access to government at least in 2004 and thus entrench them in all the political structures of the state. Moreover, due to the presence of the extremist Greater Romania Party as the major opposition party and the wholesale disarray of the democratic opposition, their domestic legitimacy was also unusually high in this period, offering a golden opportunity to proceed with radical electoral reform. Last but not least, the majoritarian system was easily justified as a response to public opinion and civil society.

Electoral system design in Romania was largely dominated by conscious attempts to structure the party system, in 1990 to encourage party formation, from 1992 onwards to limit the number of parties and to maximize government stability. Despite the choice of PR, ideas of proportional representation did not occupy an important place in politicians' minds, unlike territorial representation and personalized links with the constituency. In the final analysis however, these ideas appear associated with strategies of party dominance and with the underlying dislike for political parties, rather than with accountability, and should thus be regarded as worrisome in terms of the quality of Romanian democracy.

Another broad objective of electoral system design is to ensure affordable and manageable elections.[46] This was indeed a major concern for Romanian politicians, as the number of provisions regarding polling procedures and penalties testify. Administrative issues meant to limit possibilities of fraud, some apparently related to detail, such as the 'mobile polling booth' and voters' cards, were debated at length in 1990, 1992 and again in 1999, and remained unresolved[47] in the view of most parties.

Finally, the public took little part in debates on the electoral system save in 1990 and in 1999–2001. Although in neither period did the issue occupy centre stage in public life – economic issues were always more pressing – street protesters in 1990 and the media in 1999–2001 were certainly active, influential and opinionated participants in the debates. Unlike in the 1990 public debate, journalists in 1999–2001 presented their own opinions as expertise rather than transmitting the judgements of experts and parties. Moreover, there was a significant difference in the form taken by the initiatives of 'civil society'. If in 1990, protesters in the University Square in Bucharest blocked the centre of Bucharest and demanded a ban on former members of the *nomenklatura*, by the end of the century NGOs had become legislative initiators.

6
Bulgaria: Engineering Legitimacy through Electoral System Design

The experience of electoral system design in Bulgaria during the transition from communism raises a number of interesting issues as regards the motives we attribute to those who propose and support new electoral systems. Three characteristics of this experience stand out. Firstly, Bulgaria was, by regional standards, a late starter in reforming its electoral institutions. Democratizing reforms got underway in Sofia only in November 1989, by which time virtually all the other states of Central Europe had already overthrown their communist regimes. By the time serious consideration of electoral legislation took place in the winter and spring of 1990, Hungary had already held competitive elections, which gave those considering options in Bulgaria a valuable pool of experience on which to draw.

Secondly, the process of electoral reform in Bulgaria was, more than anywhere else in the region, an iterative process. Discussion of the electoral system began at the Round Table talks held in the winter of 1990. These talks resulted, among other things, in an electoral law to govern the constituent assembly (known as a Grand National Assembly, *Veliko Narodno Subranie*) which met in 1990 and 1991 and drafted, in addition to a constitution, an electoral law. Subsequent revisions to that law were made by the parliament elected according to the system devised by the Grand National Assembly. Debates about the electoral law thus took place in three very different institutional contexts.

Thirdly, Bulgaria was the only country in the post-communist European region save Albania in which the ex-communists gained an absolute majority of legislative seats in the first competitive elections. Though the Bulgarian Socialists did not have the two-thirds majority necessary to dominate the process of constitution-drafting, they did have the requisite number of votes to push through ordinary legislation for which the Grand National Assembly was also responsible, including the electoral law.

Despite these three rather distinctive circumstances, the electoral laws adopted first under the influence of Round Table discussions and then by the Grand National Assembly were not at all atypical of the region. The electoral law agreed at the Round Table discussions was a mixed system, and the parliamentary electoral law adopted by the Grand National Assembly was list PR (see Table 6.1). The puzzle is why these particular systems were adopted under the rule of a party that, like its ideological counterparts elsewhere in Central and Eastern Europe, saw its advantage as lying in single-member districts. The answer, it will be argued, is that the Bulgarian Socialist Party (BSP) was not interested simply in maximizing the quantitative aspect of its control over the political decision-making process – as reflected in the number of legislative seats it held – but also in maintaining the legitimacy of its role in the face of economic difficulties and possible threats to its democratic credentials. Its strategy throughout the 1989–91 period was to try to encourage its rivals to participate as fully as possible in the institutions it had put in place and thereby to validate the regime itself. When possible, it even tried to include the democratic opposition in the exercise of power so as to spread the blame for unpopular policies. The main tool of the opposition was therefore the threat of non-participation, which enabled it to punch above its political weight in the institutional

Table 6.1   Main changes in the laws on elections to Bulgarian legislative assemblies

Election year	Electoral system type	District structure	Seat allocation formula	Threshold
1990	Mixed	200 single-member districts; 28 multi-member PR districts*	SMD: two-round abs. maj.; PR: d'Hondt**	4%
1991–2001	PR	31 districts (magnitude 4–13)*	d'Hondt	4%

* Seat distribution among parties is calculated at the national level, and seats are subsequently allocated to regional districts.
** No seat allocation formula is specified in the law; the CEC had discretion to decide. The d'Hondt formula was its chosen method in 1990; Maria Iordanova, 'Electoral Law and the Electoral System', in Georgi Karasimeonov (ed.), *The 1990 Election to the Bulgarian Grand National Assembly and the 1991 Election to the Bulgarian National Assembly: Analyses, Documents and Data* (Berlin: Sigma, 1997), p. 36.

bargaining process. These two factors – the willingness of the BSP to agree to institutional structures that increased the numeric power of the opposition and the opposition's ability to exact concessions from the BSP by threatening to withdraw from the process altogether – resulted in political outcomes that were far more favourable to the opposition than would be predicted purely on the basis of a theory of parliamentary seat maximization.

Also noteworthy from the point of view of interest-based theories is that the perceived manipulability of different electoral systems was a key factor which influenced the willingness of various political actors to support them. Concerns over possible electoral corruption appear to have been as important in the minds of the democratic opposition as the likely 'mechanical' and 'psychological' effects of the systems.

A final relevant aspect of the Bulgarian experience of electoral system design is the general lack of appetite for serious revisions of the electoral law after 1991. As noted below, frequent electoral reform was a prominent feature of Bulgarian constitutional history, yet the post-communist electoral law changed little following its adoption in 1991. With five renewals of the National Assembly between 1990 and 2001, Bulgaria had more parliamentary elections and more changes of power than any other state in the region, yet at the same time its electoral legislation remained among the most stable.[1]

Bulgaria's electoral history

The history of institutional design in modern Bulgaria dates back to the so-called 'Turnovo Constitution' of 1879, framed soon after Bulgaria had gained independence from the Ottoman empire. Under the Turnovo system, Bulgaria was a constitutional monarchy with a unicameral parliament, the Subranie.

Throughout most of the post-independence period elections were characterized by considerable state-sponsored manipulation and intimidation, with results often reflecting rather than generating changes in the balance of power at the top.[2] Mattei Dogan's term 'mimic democracy'[3] can without too much distortion be applied to Bulgarian electoral politics during this period (see Chapter 1). Most elections were nevertheless sufficiently competitive that consideration was often given to the design of electoral institutions, and electoral legislation during this period was marked by frequent changes.[4] Rumyana Kolarova and Dimitr Dimitrov note that between 1879 and 1939, elections were held under eight different electoral laws which were amended 27 times, and they comment that 'strategic electoral engineering has been a routine matter for each new governing parliamentary majority'.[5] The Subranie was initially elected according to a majoritarian system, then the European norm. In 1910 proportional representation was introduced for local elections, and this was extended to parliamentary elections in 1912. PR was gradually being adopted throughout Western Europe by then, so the reform was seen as a means of modernizing the Bulgarian political system.[6] Single-member district majoritarianism was reintroduced in 1923 as part of a move toward greater authoritarianism under Aleksandur Stamboliiski. A further reform introduced in 1926 gave a majority-generating premium along Italian fascist lines to the party which secured the greatest number of seats. PR was brought back again in 1931 in what was an unusually clean election.[7] The next parliamentary elections were not held until 1937, by which time personalistic monarchical rule was in place and political parties had been banned. PR was obviously not an option under such circumstances, and single-member districts were once again used. PR was brought back one final time for the last multi-party elections held under communism in 1953. From then until the breakdown of communism in 1990, majoritarian elections were the rule in Bulgaria as elsewhere in the communist world. Thus in electoral system terms, the period between independence and the advent of communism was characterized by a broad coincidence between proportional representation and democratizing moves on the one hand, and majoritarianism and authoritarian crackdowns on the other.

Bulgaria had since the nineteenth century enjoyed close relations with Russia, and these were maintained throughout the communist period. It is therefore not surprising that the collapse of communism in Bulgaria played itself out more in the manner of the elite-initiated Soviet collapse than of the popularly supported implosions of communism in much of the rest of Central Europe. The Bulgarian leadership had been under considerable pressure from Gorbachev to undertake reforms. There were tentative steps toward the introduction of multi-candidate electoral competition in 1987, when the law governing local and parliamentary elections was liberalized to allow for limited competition. This new law was first used in the local elections of 1988, yet the competitive nature of these contests seems to have been stifled to a certain extent by state manipulation of the results.[8]

The Bulgarian Communist Party (BCP) finally removed its ageing leader Todor Zhivkov on 10 November 1989 and agreed to undertake democratic reforms. Prompted by this initial move, an opposition umbrella group of dissident organizations was formed in December under the name of the Union of Democratic Forces (*Suyuz na Demokratichniti Sili*, SDS). By threatening widespread strikes, the opposition pushed successfully for Round Table discussions after the Czech, Polish and Hungarian models. The talks took place between January and May 1990; debate centred mainly around political reform, including the conditions under which competitive elections would be held.[9]

The Round Table talks and the electoral law for the Grand National (Constituent) Assembly, 1990

Bulgaria's transition to a multi-party system can be said to have been a 'guided transition', inasmuch as the Bulgarian Communist Party took the lead and, unlike in many other states in the region, managed to keep it through the first competitive elections. There are several reasons for this. Firstly, the opposition was, in November 1989, poorly organized – especially at grassroots level – and lacking in experience. Compared with their counterparts in the party itself, opposition leaders had had relatively little contact with western notions of electoral organization and strategy, and they were unprepared for the leadership's abrupt move toward change. In mid-November following Zhivkov's removal, the opposition was still describing multi-party elections as 'premature', while the new communist leadership was announcing to foreign audiences that elections were on the cards.[10] Yet even the lower ranks of the party had little inkling of what was to come until 11 December, when the new leader, Petur Mladenov, announced at a BCP meeting that within four months a new electoral law would be adopted and within 12 months the leading role of the party would be removed from the constitution and competitive elections held. The audience were said to have been astonished.[11]

Secondly, unlike in many other states in the region where communists sought during the transition to maintain as much power as possible, the BCP was making overtures to the opposition as early as December 1989, before the Round Table talks even got underway. Throughout the first eight months of 1990 – both before and after the June elections – the (ex-)communists appealed unsuccessfully to the SDS to join it in a coalition government. It appears that the ruling elite were seeking to extend limited power to the opposition in an effort to spread the blame for the impending economic crisis.[12] This is a time-tested communist strategy of rule via popular fronts, but it was also a far-sighted approach in that it gave them flexibility in their bargaining position and it served to preserve their popular legitimacy.

The desire to share power (and blame) was a crucial factor in the BCP's approach to the Round Table talks, which they initially viewed as 'consultations'.[13] The talks took the form of plenary sessions broadcast on radio and (in condensed form) on television, as well as closed 'contact groups'. The main actors were the communists-turned-socialists and the SDS. The ethnic Turkish Movement for Rights and Freedom (DPS) had failed to agree a mechanism whereby it could be included on the SDS side of the table.[14] The talks were held in three rounds, each of which produced a package of documents. The first package, signed on 12 March, was an agreement on the status of the Round Table itself, including an undertaking by the Communists that decisions agreed at the talks would be binding in that the parliament (still very much under their control) would automatically pass legislation resulting from the negotiations and would not attempt to amend it.[15] Also noteworthy is the BCP's extraordinary congress held in January–February 1990 (during the talks), when it agreed to remove the constitutional clause guaranteeing its leading role in politics, and to change its own name to the Bulgarian Socialist Party.[16]

The crucial elements of the electoral law were worked out in the second round of talks between 19 and 30 March. Once the basic architecture of the system had been agreed, there were discussions in the third round (April–May) on procedural guarantees to prevent fraud. Negotiations on the elections revolved around five key issues: (1) their timing – the BCP/BSP wanted polls no later than June 1990, while the SDS preferred September, to allow it time to organize and mobilize the vote. Given this preference, the SDS could credibly threaten to break off negotiations in order to play for time;[17] (2) the size and nature of the body to be elected: the BSP favoured holding ordinary parliamentary elections for a 200–250 seat chamber, while the SDS pressed for a larger Grand National Assembly along the lines of the Turnovo system; (3) whether or not Bulgaria was to have a directly elected president, which the BCP favoured due to the popularity of its current head of state, Petur Mladenov, and the SDS opposed for the same reason; (4) the status of political parties and the procedures through which they would be officially registered; (5) the electoral system: the BCP/BSP initially proposed a parallel mixed system in which 175 representatives would be elected by the current majoritarian system and 75 would be chosen through proportional representation.

In January and February the BCP/BSP side in the discussions submitted drafts of laws to the Round Table leadership on changes to the constitution to restructure the parliament, on political parties and on the electoral system. The draft electoral law was submitted for consideration on 26 February. Though there is little record of behind-the-scenes bargaining, the plenary sessions were recorded and subsequently published. The plenary debates on the electoral law took place on 19, 26, 27 and 30 March. The National Assembly had been due to discuss the electoral law on 28 March but agreed to put the topic on hold until an agreement had been reached at the Round Table, illustrating the priority accorded to the talks.

BSP representative V. Mruchkov opened the Round Table debate on 19 March by presenting the three laws and stressing their interdependence. He presented the 175/75 mixed law as a system in which majoritarian seats would lead to the victory of candidates who commanded 'the trust of the largest part of the population', along with proportional list seats, which would be a corrective.[18] At the same time, he indicated the BSP's readiness to adjust the proportions of seats filled through the two methods, which suggests that the BSP was prepared (and expected) to bargain on the matter. At this point debate over the body to be elected took over, and the electoral law was not discussed in great detail before the following plenary session on 30 March. But two representatives of the SDS side (Nikola Petkov from the Bulgarian Agrarian National Union (BZNS-NP) and an independent expert) noted during this initial discussion that the majoritarian system was undesirable under current circumstances; it was more open to manipulation than proportional list voting, in that majoritarianism is a winner-takes-all system which is prone to dirty tricks.[19]

The BSP's insistence on bundling these issues into a package set the ground for trade-offs, some of which had an important impact on the outcome of the discussions.[20] The main trade-off *across* issues appears to have been the SDS agreement to early elections in exchange for a BSP agreement to have the president, for the time being at least, elected by the legislature (in this case the Grand National Assembly). There also seems to have been a trade-off regarding the electoral law, with the SDS agreeing to a variant of the mixed system proposed by the BSP in exchange for the convening of a Grand National Assembly instead of an ordinary parliament.

The relative lack of knowledge in Bulgaria of modern democratic institutions and the paucity of contacts between Bulgarian intellectuals and those of democratic western countries has been noted.[21] In the domain of electoral system design this isolation from western institutional structures was probably an advantage in that Bulgarian electoral engineers had few preconceptions (or misconceptions) and they were free to invent their own solution to the situation they faced. The idea for the specific design of the parallel mixed system apparently came out of a number of visits to other post-communist countries in the region, including Hungary and Poland, each of which employed electoral institutions combining different principles – Hungary in elections to the unicameral parliament and Poland in different electoral systems for the upper and lower chambers.[22] It appears that the communist elite viewed Hungary and Poland as the most promising models for peaceful transition,[23] making them favourably disposed to those countries' electoral institutions.

The parallel mixed system had three further advantages linked to the circumstances of high uncertainty that surrounded the first post-communist elections. Firstly, the provision of two means of winning a seat in parliament and the fact that individuals were allowed to stand as candidates in both parts of the system represented a form of insurance or bet-hedging. Should they fail to win a single-member seat, prominent members of the major parties could rely on the fall-back route to parliamentary power via the party list. (As in Hungary, this safety net proved essential to the electoral fortunes of some high-profile politicians in 1990, especially those from the BSP; Minister of Defence Dobri Dzurov, BSP spokesman Filip Bokov and Minister of Culture Krastyo Goranov all lost in the SMD contests to SDS competitors but won through the BSP party list.[24]) Secondly, the use of single-member districts allowed the BSP to de-emphasize its party image and promote the professionalism, experience and other personal attributes of its political figures in a way that would not have been possible under a pure PR system. In some parts of the country – especially rural regions – the party label was not a problem, but in major cities communism was tarnished enough for the BSP to want to distance itself from its image, and the party went so far as to support independent candidates in some places.[25] As elsewhere in the post-communist region, one main advantage of the Bulgarian ex-communists was that they had candidates familiar to the public, whereas most opposition figures were virtually entirely unknown outside elite circles. There is evidence that the Socialists acknowledged this asset openly and made strategic use of it during the electoral campaign by declaring that individual attributes were more important than party labels.[26] Single-member districts also provided an opportunity for independents to win seats, and the communists evidently believed that non-party deputies would support them. Finally, the combination of systems in parallel made it easier to foresee the probable result of the elections than was the case in the complex Hungarian system, and it could be anticipated that the outcome would be more majoritarian.

During the debates the SDS bargained for a larger number of PR seats as a means of playing to its own strengths as a democratic opposition and minimizing the extent to which the BSP could draw on its organizational and personnel resources. The final agreement, worked out at the Round Table on 30 March, was for a 400-member Grand National Assembly. Two hundred deputies would be elected through an absolute majority in two rounds in single-member districts with a 50 per cent turnout requirement, and 200 from 28 regional districts (representing Bulgaria's traditional administrative districts) through list PR with seat allocation at the national level by d'Hondt and a 4 per cent national threshold.

The relative ease with which agreement was reached through essentially splitting the difference may be due to the fact that all involved viewed the system as a temporary structure rather than a permanent part of the Bulgarian electoral process.[27] A possible additional factor is that, unlike in ordinary legislatures, the 50 per cent threshold was not relevant to constitutional decisions in the Grand National Assembly, which required a two-thirds majority. Neither of the main parties expected to gain two-thirds of the seats under any electoral system (and the communists viewed such an eventuality with actual trepidation, as it would have undermined the legitimacy of the constitutional reforms made by such a body). This meant that that the details of the system eventually chosen were less crucial in determining constitutional outcomes than they would have been had an absolute majority been required. Also noteworthy is that the Agrarian BZNS, part of the Communist-led front organization until 1989, favoured PR.

The Grand National Assembly Election Act was duly passed by the National Assembly on 3 April, when parliament also set the date of the elections for 10 June. By the end of the Round Table talks there had also been a compromise on the presidency. Whereas the BSP had initially wanted directly elected presidential elections to be held simultaneously with parliamentary elections, an agreement was eventually reached to allow the then National Assembly to elect the president (Mladenov), whose term would continue to the end of the Grand National Assembly.

Of the 200 single-member seats in the June elections, only 81 had to go to a second round. The final result gave the BSP an absolute majority of seats – 211 out of 400, of which 114 were won in single-member districts and 97 from party lists. The SDS came a weak second with 144 seats overall, with 69 won in districts and 75 on lists. The BSP had as predicted been advantaged in the single-member districts, but official results showed that they had also gained more list votes (47.2 per cent) than the SDS (36.2 per cent). This last fact led many to question the legitimacy of the electoral process itself. The suspiciously high turnout of 90.8 per cent in the first round prompted the SDS to make numerous allegations of corruption. Its parliamentary party even split over whether to recognize the validity of the elections. The majority of SDS leaders eventually agreed to participate in the parliament (partly due to western pressure[28]), but the conduct of the electoral process loomed large in subsequent debates over the law for parliamentary elections.

Several independent reports at the time suggested that local BSP notables and bureaucrats had manipulated the electoral process, with the electoral commissions in many cases proving helpless to prevent it.[29] It is noteworthy also that the official results were never published in full. A parliamentary investigation three years after the event uncovered many instances of multiple voting. The parliamentary commission reported on 24 March 1993 that at least 10 per cent of the votes won by the BSP were of dubious validity and that about half a million extra votes were probably cast.[30] Though allegations of fraud were evidently justified, the BSP ran a far more professional campaign than the disjointed, poorly organized and inexperienced SDS, and virtually all opinion polls showed the ex-communists to be in the lead prior to the first round.[31]

The outcome of the elections did not confer as much legitimacy on the BSP as it might have desired, yet the bargaining strategy of the two main actors in the electoral system design process was strongly conditioned by the (ex-)communists' need for such legitimacy and by the SDS's recognition of that need. As Kolarova and Dimitrov argue, the main issue of discussion at the Round Table was 'what are the concessions that the BCP is ready to make?'; but rather than a sign of weakness, the willingness to make concessions was a legitimating device for the BCP/BSP in demonstrating the seriousness of the party's stated intention of giving up monopoly power voluntarily.[32]

At the outset the reform process in Bulgaria was similar to that in the Soviet Union, yet by the end of the Round Table talks it had taken on a very different character. The removal of the ban on alternative parties before the election and the institutionalization of opposition in the talks brought Bulgaria closer to the Central European mode of transition. At the same time Bulgaria was in a unique position in holding its Round Table talks so late. Not only did actors on all sides have the experience of other countries to go by, but they also faced rather different threats. Whereas the threat for early democratizers such as Poland (and, to a lesser extent, Hungary) was of possible Soviet intervention to quell moves toward democracy, the threat in the Bulgarian case was the 'Romanian variant' of the forceful removal of the communists themselves.[33] This meant that the Bulgarian democrats were in a far better bargaining position. But because of their lack of grassroots organization and extensive popular support, even the achievement of relatively favourable institutions was not enough to give them electoral victory.

The parliamentary electoral law of 1991

Following the June 1990 elections, the BSP tried once again to lure the SDS into coalition, but the latter resisted. It did, however, accept the presidency for its leader Zhelyu Zhelev in August, by which time Mladenov's position was no longer tenable following the disclosure in June of remarks he had made on video calling for the violent repression of dissidents the previous November.

The Grand National Assembly was the seventh of its kind in post-independence Bulgarian history, and like its predecessors, its main task was to adopt a new constitution. At the same time it also served as an ordinary parliament, passing legislation by absolute majority. Discussion of the electoral law had to wait till after the constitutional deliberations were over. Elections had originally been planned for May 1991, but the BSP successfully delayed the constitution-making process to maintain their assembly majority for as long as possible. The SDS, for its part, was eager to have fresh elections prior to the adoption of the new constitution, notionally to validate the fundamental law in the eyes of the people, but most likely also because it believed its share of the vote would be higher than it had been the previous year. This effort came to naught. Debates on the constitution took place between May and July, and the document was finally adopted on 12 July by a vote of 309 of the Grand National Assembly's 400 deputies. It called for what was essentially a parliamentary system with a weak, directly elected president with powers of suspensive veto only. The National Assembly, for its part, was to have 240 members, to be elected for a term of four years. The design of the electoral law was not constitutionalized.

The SDS had never been a cohesive organization, and it began to fray seriously during the constitution-drafting process. Portions of the more radical anti-communist wing preferred a fundamental law that made a cleaner break with the past. A group of 39 such deputies left parliament on 14 May and staged a hunger strike in protest at what they viewed as a 'communist' constitution. In a symbolic gesture, President Zhelev refused to sign the document when he assumed power in August. Once these difficulties had been overcome, the assembly soon turned its attention to provisions for the forthcoming elections.

The Grand National Assembly dissolved itself immediately after the constitution was passed (it continued to function as an ordinary parliament), and elections were called for the end of September. There was no question of retaining the law adopted in 1990 for the parliamentary elections. Debates over the electoral law governing the elections to the Grand National Assembly had always been just that: debates over a transitional body, not plans for the parliamentary electoral law itself (which was a separate document that supplemented but did not supersede the electoral law for the Grand National Assembly). This meant that there was very limited time in which to act.

Kolarova and Dimitrov identify four principal stages in the two-month process of electoral system design: (1) the period between 18 and 30 July when the basic decision on proportional representation was made; (2) the period between 31 July and 22 August when the provisions of the law were debated in plenary session of the Assembly and it was passed, followed by a suspensive presidential veto; (3) the opposition revolt on 22 August against the agreed seat distribution formula; and (4) the debate over ballot colours which lasted until an amendment on this matter was passed on 12 September. This periodization provides a convenient heuristic device for the present analysis.[34]

In contrast to the situation during the Round Table talks, it was now in the BSP's interest to delay a decision as long as possible during this new round of bargaining over the electoral law. Even before the onset of debate, a broad consensus had emerged on the introduction of pure proportional representation for the National Assembly elections.[35] Debate centred around the overall district design to be adopted. The BSP leadership undoubtedly saw cleaning up the elections as a way of removing power from the unreconstructed *apparatchiki* who still dominated at the local level. Single-member districts were believed to be part of the problem, so the party elite sought alternatives that would still enable it to preserve its electoral advantage. They initially considered a Greek-style premium system (allegedly suggested by connections in the Greek Socialist party), but this was rejected on the grounds that it was not sufficiently democratic.[36] Following the disputes over the 1990 results, the SDS had made it clear that it would never accept a law that included single-member seats. They threatened to boycott the elections altogether if this institution was retained in the law in any form. Their reasoning was that it was far easier to swing the results if the change of only several hundred votes was required than if thousands of votes had to be shifted.

The result of this debate was a relatively unusual system in which there were 31 regional districts but the distribution of seats to parties was done on the basis of national-level results, with seats then allocated to districts by means of a quota formula. Though there were some later moves to alter this system to make the results more equitable at the regional level, the major parties proved relatively content with the system, and it remained in force more or less unchanged after 1991. In many respects the 1991 law represented a generalization of the regulations governing the proportional portion of the ballot in the 1990 elections. The possibility of introducing preferential voting was discussed, but closed lists were preferred by the larger parties; the 4 per cent threshold was judged too low by some and too high by others, but it too was retained. The law passed on the first reading on 30 July.

The second stage revolved around the definition of the actors who would play the electoral game, and debate over the terms of contestation in August was just as intense as debate over the terms of competition had been during July. Two principal issues were at stake: the rights of citizens who lived abroad to vote and the right of candidate nomination.

The electoral rights of citizens living abroad was, as in many parts of the Balkans, a delicate issue due to the country's history of population movement. An estimated 350,000 ethnic Turks had left Bulgaria in the 1980s following a campaign aimed at repressing their ethnic identity. It was believed that such people would support the Movement for Rights and Freedom. Given that the DPS was loosely allied with the SDS, allowing voting by expatriates would likely have benefited the opposition, and the SDS argued for this provision on the grounds of basic constitutional rights.[37] The result was a compromise. Whereas an earlier draft of the law had required voters living abroad to return to Bulgaria to participate in the electoral process,[38] provision was made in the final law for registration at Bulgarian embassies, though such voters were still required to return on election day to cast their vote. This represented a restriction inasmuch as overseas voting at embassies had been possible at the time of the Grand National Assembly elections (though its logistics had been fraught with procedural difficulties[39]).

There was also debate over the nature of the contestants. According to the final law, non-party organizations were not allowed to nominate candidates, though independent candidates could stand, provided they gathered 2000 signatures. A requirement in the first draft that independents pay a monetary deposit of 2000 leva[40] was subsequently removed. On this question the large parties had an interest in blocking access to the electoral process to non-party groups, yet considerations of fairness made a deposit politically unacceptable at this point.

The law finally passed its second reading on 14 August by 169 to 36, but President Zhelev vetoed it on the grounds that it violated both freedom of speech and the rights of Bulgarians abroad. At this point the BSP majority in parliament amended the law, but not the sections to which the president had objected. Instead they imposed a two-tier seat allocation procedure, dubbed the 'Videnov variant' after BSP member Zhan Videnov. This envisaged distribution of seats at district level by Hare quota and distribution of centrally pooled remainders by the d'Hondt method (retaining the 4 per cent threshold). The SDS objected strongly, arguing that the difference in district size would result in varying effective thresholds, which would be discriminatory, and that all parties should be subject to the same national thresholds at the level of each tier.[41] By threatening to boycott the elections, they won the return of the single-tier d'Hondt method.

The final phase of the electoral reform process involved debates over a topic that had plagued Bulgarian electoral history since the start of the transition: the unusual practice of providing, at state expense, separate coloured ballot papers for each party. According to this Bulgarian electoral tradition, ballots were colour-coded to match the colours of the various ideological tendencies they represented – red for the BSP, blue for the SDS and so forth.[42] The new Bulgarian party system proved very fractious, and the question of parties' rights to ballot papers of given colours was closely tied to issues of party continuity and thus to voter identifications and the ability of political organizations to gain the trust of distinct sectors of the electorate. The decision to allow colours to individual parties was left to the Central Election Commission, which was appointed by the president (and composed largely of party representatives, most of whom were required to be legal experts). This gave President Zhelev indirect and weak, but still significant, control over the electoral process which somewhat counter-balanced the role of the Socialist-dominated National Assembly in drafting the law. Given that the president was at that point a member of the main opposition party, this can be seen as a device to placate the opposition by conceding some powers while still maintaining control over the basic design of the law. By yielding powers associated with electoral administration and thereby distancing itself from the electoral process, the BSP may well have being trying to protect itself against allegations of fraud and abuse.

The Socialists' majority in the Assembly enabled them to impose many aspects of the electoral law over the objections of the opposition. But there were two limitations on the BSP's power in this domain. Firstly, it was anxious to maintain (or restore) the credibility of the electoral process. It was therefore willing to give in to opposition demands on certain issues of electoral administration. Secondly, the SDS had the power to undermine the legitimacy of the BSP by threatening to boycott the elections. This was a tactic used during the Round Table talks, and it still represented a credible threat that allowed them to win concessions on questions of districting and the seat allocation formula. Yet there were some areas in which all the established parties had an interest in maintaining their advantage over newcomers, and during the last two days of the assembly's term, it passed various tax exemptions for party-linked foundations as well as campaign finance legislation favouring larger political organizations.

The outcome of the October 1991 elections was the long-awaited defeat of the BSP. The SDS nevertheless failed to win an absolute majority, taking 34.4 per cent of the vote to the BSP's 33.1. This translated into 110 seats for the SDS and 106 for the Socialists. The SDS then formed a coalition government with the Movement for Rights and Freedom, which had won 24 seats. These elections were generally seen as a great improvement over the 1990 polls in terms of their conduct,[43] vindicating the SDS's claim that proportional list voting was a more democratic system less prone to abuse.

Post-1991 changes to the electoral law

Between 1991 and 2001 the Bulgarian electoral law remained remarkably stable, especially in the light of the numerous changes undergone by its pre-communist counterparts. Most changes involved details of electoral administration. This may in part be because all except the 2001 elections were held prior to the end of the parliament's normal term, and there was thus little time to consider major overhauls. Nevertheless, each new election was preceded by efforts to alter the law.

In the summer and autumn of 1994 electoral reform was again addressed by parliament. There had been demands for pre-term elections, and the BSP was keen to revert to a mixed electoral system, which it believed would allow it to win an absolute majority as in 1990. The BSP could have had its way if it had been able to convince enough small parties to agree with it. This was nearly accomplished through a deal with several centrist parties that were willing to accede to a mixed electoral system in exchange for an agreement to postpone the elections until the natural end of the parliament's term. But the deal fell apart when the Socialists pushed also for another of their main aims: a constitutional amendment to further limit the powers of the president.[44] There were also allegations of collusion among the three largest political forces – the SDS, the BSP and the DPS – within the party-dominated Central Electoral Commission to regulate the electoral process in such a way as to restrict access to smaller parties after 1994.[45]

The BSP-led coalition won an absolute majority of 125 in 1994 even without a mixed system. Following the local elections of 1995, the Socialist government separated provisions on local elections from those on parliamentary elections (they had since 1991 been part of the same act). But since the administrative structure required for parliamentary elections relied to a certain extent on that established for local elections, some provisions governing local elections were maintained in the parliamentary law, though the bodies they referred to did not always exist in the same form. This led to a highly anomalous legal situation in which the CEC was required to interpret an incoherent law as best it could.[46]

Nevertheless, there was no significant change to the substance of the parliamentary electoral law prior to the 1997 elections. The Socialists tried but failed to lower the threshold to 3 per cent to allow more of their potential coalition partners to gain seats: the relevant legislation was passed by the National Assembly at the tail end of its session only to be vetoed by President Petur Stoyanov of the SDS. Though the Assembly needed only a 50 per cent majority to override a presidential veto (and thus had the capacity to push through the electoral legislation), it never had the opportunity to do so: it was dissolved on 19 February before the law could be considered a second time. In the event, the SDS-led coalition easily won the 1997 elections on a majority of 137 to 58.

Given the incoherence of existing legislation, the desirability of introducing a new electoral law was clear, and a new 'Elections of Members of Parliament Act' was adopted in April 2001 prior to the June parliamentary elections. The reform process was facilitated by the fact that for the first time since 1991 the parliament sat for a full four-year term. This at last gave law-makers adequate opportunity to consider a completely rewritten law. Seven drafts were considered by the Subranie, but that eventually adopted – a draft prepared by the CEC – brought little change. Renewed BSP proposals for a mixed system and a 3 per cent threshold were rejected, as were suggestions for preferential voting. The CEC's proposal to introduce signature requirements for new parties was eventually dropped in the face of opposition protest. There was already unease at the stringent party registration procedures in a new law on parties, and the introduction of additional hurdles was seen as a blatant means of preventing newly popular monarchist parties from competing. The new law retained the controversial coloured ballots, despite the fact that they had been abolished for local elections with the 1995 reforms, and despite the recommendations of international observers.[47] The nationwide seat distribution procedures and the threshold also remained unchanged. The main achievement of the new law was to clarify and rationalize election administration procedures (though this did not prevent allegations of manipulation on the part of the opposition).

The remarkable stability of Bulgarian electoral legislation during the first post-transition decade can largely be attributed to the dominance of two large, relatively equally matched organizations with a common interest in maintaining a system that allowed them to alternate in power. The situation changed dramatically, however, when the June 2001 results gave half the seats in the parliament to a new populist/monarchist political formation which had mobilized around Simeon Saxecoburggotsky, Bulgaria's former king. The subsequent victory of BSP candidate Parvenov in the presidential elections increased the political turmoil, as did the lack of experience of the ruling National Movement for Simeon II (NDSV). The parliamentary election results were widely interpreted as an indication of the depth of the Bulgarian citizenry's discontent with political parties in general, and renewed consideration was given to preferential list voting. Elements within the NDSV strongly supported this move at the point when they officially established themselves as a party in April 2002,[48] and there were indications that the other parties would not oppose such a change.[49]

Conclusion

After fifty years of institutional stasis under communism, the Bulgarian tradition of electoral engineering was revived. This resulted first in a mixed law for elections to the Grand National Assembly, then to a proportional representation system for subsequent parliamentary elections. In both cases the legitimacy of the democratic institutions was the main focus of discussion; debates over the principal elements of electoral system design were framed in terms of the degree to which different institutional options would leave the process vulnerable to manipulation. At the time of the Round Table, preferences over different electoral institutional arrangements were determined largely by the different organizational capacities of the competing forces. As elsewhere in the region, early debates also included deliberations as to who should be the main actors of the elections. It was in the ex-communists' interests to promote individual politicians, whereas the opposition believed it would benefit from the championing of political labels. But after the Grand National Assembly elections this debate was less prominent. The Socialists saw that their party image was not an impediment to winning votes, and the opposition had by this time gained political experience and its developing structures reduced the socialists' organizational advantage. By the summer of 1990 political parties had been established as the common currency of Bulgarian politics, and with politics dominated between 1990 and 2000 by two large political organizations, there was a broad consensus on many issues surrounding electoral institutions. Procedural aspects of the electoral process became the main focus of debate. Lingering fears (and allegations) of vote falsification and other forms of electoral malfeasance served to motivate proposals for changes to the system of ballots, the operations of the Central Electoral Commission, campaign finance regulations and voter registration procedures.

Bulgarian politicians consistently used electoral engineering as a means to help them achieve their ends. Yet this did not in all cases involve crude seat-maximization. In 1990 the BSP favoured a system that would increase the chances of the opposition in order to enhance the legitimacy of its reforms. And in 1997 the same party proposed that the threshold be lowered to increase the electoral chances of its coalition partners. This is a rare example in the post-communist region of a case in which seat-maximization was less important for a party than maximizing its chances to form a government.[50] However, district design and seat allocation procedures were evaluated as much for their propensity to facilitate electoral corruption as for their 'psychological' and 'mechanical' impacts. When procedures are not effectively embedded, their embeddedness itself becomes an issue that can overshadow issues of formal design.

It is significant that the debates over the electoral systems were largely a parliamentary affair. Though the Bulgarian Constitutional Court was active and influential in other areas, such as the delineation of the powers of the various branches of government,[51] it did not play a great role in adjudicating questions of electoral law.[52] It mainly focused on defining the terms of contestation. The Court's decision to allow the DPS to participate in elections despite the ban on ethnic parties, and its support of a refusal to register Simeon's party were perhaps of greatest direct relevance to electoral politics. Nor was the president a major actor in this domain, though he was at times decisive in preventing change (as in 1997), and his control over CEC appointments represents a partial 'separation of electoral powers'.

A final interesting aspect of Bulgarian electoral system design is that it was not only influenced by examples in other countries, but Bulgarian election experts see it as an example for others. Japanese experts were said to have made several trips to Sofia to study the effect of the parallel mixed system prior to the adoption of a version of this system in their own country.[53] The Japanese system then served as a model for other countries, and the 'parallel electoral system' became an established variation on the mixed system type following its adoption in Georgia (1990), Lithuania (1992), Croatia (1992), Russia (1993), Armenia (1995), Azerbaijan (1995), Ukraine (1997), Tajikistan (1999), Kazakhstan (1999) and Kyrgyzstan (1999), as well as a number of countries outside the post-communist region. That it gave way in Bulgaria itself is due to the discrediting of single-member districts, with the introduction of full proportional representation providing a means of legitimizing the democratization process.

7
Russia: the Limits of Electoral Engineering

Two interesting questions surround the process of electoral system change in Russia during the post-communist period: why, when Yeltsin was able to impose the system of his choice in 1993, did he choose a mixed system, and why, given the circumstances under which this system was imposed, was it not subsequently changed by parliament? This chapter will argue that a combination of high levels of uncertainty and multiple aims account for the adoption of a mixed electoral system, and that once in place, it generated interests that served to entrench it.

Three distinct phases of electoral reform can be identified: the late-Soviet period of electoral liberalization, first in the all-Union elections of 1989 and then in the Russian republican elections the following year; the period between the collapse of the Soviet Union in late 1991 and the 1993 parliamentary elections, in which Russia's mixed system was first designed and introduced by decree; and the post-1993 period when certain minor changes were made. The analysis that follows seeks to assess the factors that influenced the adoption of the mixed system in 1993 and the reasons for its subsequent retention.

In studying the dynamics of electoral system design in Russia, we are fortunate in being able to rely on a base of previous research. Unlike a number of other cases studied in this volume, the Russian electoral system has been the subject of a sizeable secondary literature. The strategy of this chapter is thus both to provide a critical assessment of this work and to supplement it with additional primary source materials where appropriate.

Late Soviet electoral liberalization: 1989–90

Prior to the first multi-candidate elections to the Congress of People's Deputies (CPD) in 1989, a number of measures were taken to ensure continuing Communist Party control of the process. These included the establishment of a bloc of seats chosen through state-linked social organizations, such as the Communist Party, trade unions, scientific associations and veterans' groups; the election of an inner working parliament (the Supreme Soviet) from within the CPD; and the requirement that where more than two candidates had been nominated, pre-election meetings be held to vet candidates and refuse their nominations if they failed to satisfy the participants (who could often be controlled by the Party *apparat*). When provisions for the republican elections of 1990 were considered, the republics were initially under substantial pressure to institutionalize these devices at their level as well.

The previous elections to the parliaments of the Soviet Union's 15 constituent republics took place in March 1985, shortly before Mikhail Gorbachev came to power, and thus well before *perestroika*. The 1990 elections represented the first point at which electoral reform was seriously debated at the republican level, and they came at a time when change was accelerating rapidly. The Communist Party itself was increasingly differentiated, with incipient 'platforms' belying the still official ban on factions. Not surprisingly, criticisms of the existing system formed the starting point for debate on republic laws. Both the communist leadership and the emerging opposition had learned a good deal about competition from the previous year's all-Union federal elections.[1] Most republics did away with the nested legislature introduced in 1989, even though the CPD had taken on greater powers vis-à-vis the Supreme Soviet than had been anticipated. Russia alone maintained this structure, and along with it the practice of electing some (900) of the deputies from territorially based districts and some (168) from districts based on its subfederal (ethnic) administrative divisions.

Much of the discussion about electoral procedures concerned the mode of nomination, as this was perceived to be the point at which the authorities had regulated and (partly) controlled competition in 1989. The practice of nomination by work collectives, social organizations or groups of voters remained unquestioned, although there was some liberalization of the terms and conditions.[2] The necessity of pre-election candidates' meetings was questioned, as survey findings indicated public support for their abolition.[3] Polls also found that only 27 per cent supported the idea of reserving a bloc of seats in the Russian assembly for social organizations, and a number of candidates in the CPD elections had promised in their campaigns to do away with them if elected.[4] In the end, the republican law omitted reserved seats and pre-election selection meetings.

Although republican elections were regulated by laws passed at republican level, the centre retained – in theory at least – considerable control over the process. One curious feature of the Soviet system was that although elections were of relatively minor political significance, the provisions governing them were accorded pride of place in the Soviet constitution, which devoted an entire section to their conduct. Because the constitutional provisions governed elections at all levels, the republics were able to introduce electoral innovations only in those areas on which the constitution was silent. But by this point republican elites were becoming far more assertive, and many republics adopted electoral laws that violated the federal constitution. This forced the all-Union Congress of People's Deputies to alter the fundamental law to give the republics more leeway in this domain.[5] The alternative was to declare all the new republican laws unconstitutional, which would have incurred too great a political risk.[6] Electoral reform was thus a complex drama involving two interlinked processes, one at federal level and one at republican level.

The first draft electoral law for the Russian Federation was published in mid-August 1989, and like its federal forerunner it envisioned multiple candidacies without a multi-party system. Press briefings at the time assured the public that there would be no limits on contestation, while the bill stipulated that selection meetings would be held only when more than ten candidates were standing in a constituency.[7] Nine hundred deputies would be chosen in single-member districts, and another 168 to represent the constituent parts of the Russian federation. To win a single-member district, a candidate had to obtain an absolute majority; failing that, the top two contenders would enter a run-off two weeks later. It was conceivable for the run-off to be won on a plurality: voters indicated their choice by crossing out the name of the candidate whom they did not support, and in theory they could delete both of them, so the winner would be the one deleted least often. As in the past, 50 per cent of registered voters had to participate for the results to be valid.[8]

The law was revised over the next few months and eventually passed on 27 October 1989, with the pre-election meetings removed altogether. There were complaints at the time among Russian legislators that the law had been insufficiently debated and pushed through the Supreme Soviet in the manner of old,[9] and certainly there was less debate at this level than in the Congress of People's Deputies. The direct election of the republic's president was voted through at the same time, over Gorbachev's opposition.

The republican parliament elected in March 1990 came to constitute the first parliament of independent Russia, so its composition acquired considerable importance. How far it reflected the will of the Russian people remained contentious (and of course both politics and public opinion shifted sharply over later months). At the time of the elections, the Communist Party was the sole legal political party. In February 1990 its Central Committee had consented to the amendment of Article 6 of the Soviet Constitution which ensured the Party's political monopoly, but this revision did not take effect until after the first round of the Russian elections. Thus the only opposition groups around which candidates could mobilize in March 1990 were local voters' clubs and the so-called 'informals', grouped into blocs such as Elections-90, Democratic Russia and the far-right Patriotic Bloc, along with various groupings within the Communist Party itself.

Certainly from a numeric point of view the elections were competitive: 6705 candidates competed for the 1068 seats, a mere 121 of which were filled in the first round of voting.[10] Malapportionment also apparently decreased between 1989 and 1990.[11] Yet reformers won only about a third of the seats, leading to speculation that the results had been manipulated by conservative *apparatchiki*. Though some commentators claim that state resources were deployed selectively to the benefit of candidates favoured by local elites,[12] others contend that the election was generally fair, and that the relatively poor showing of reformers reflected the current state of popular opinion, which remained conservative in many rural regions.[13]

In assessing electoral reform in the run-up to the Russian elections of 1990, one should bear in mind that Russia was then still also the centre of the Soviet Union, with all that entailed for the perceptions and preferences of the actors involved. Not all the proposed changes were in the direction of western-style democracy. In local elections held simultaneously with their republican counterparts, there were several 'experiments' with factory-based electoral districts designed to increase the representation of workers.[14] This institutionalization of the 'production principle' was clearly at odds with party-based competition, and it demonstrates the diversity of opinions as to what democracy meant for the electoral process. Indeed, Boris Yeltsin himself opposed the idea of a multi-party system in the USSR, even as his Central Committee colleagues were voting to legalize it.[15] Moreover, a detailed analysis of All-Union-level debates over electoral reform concluded that for members of the Congress of People's Deputies social representation of citizens on the basis of their gender, occupation, ethnic group and so on was a desirable outcome which ought to be one aim of electoral system design.[16] The parameters within which these debates were conducted suggest that few political actors seriously questioned the fundamental institutional structures of the USSR or Soviet concepts of representation.

If the 1990 election law had a longer-term effect, it was that it engrained the practice of each voter completing two ballot papers, one for the single-member district and another for a part of the federation. In sustaining the core principle of the 1989 Soviet elections that representatives could be returned to a chamber on more than one basis, it may have contributed to the adoption of a mixed system for independent Russia.

The 1993 electoral decree

Upon the demise of the Soviet Union at the end of 1991, Russia assumed sovereignty with its late-Soviet institutions intact but their occupants facing vastly different challenges. The elections of 12 December 1993 were the first multi-party elections to be held in Russia in some 75 years; however, the absence of attendant constitutionalism meant that the process of electoral system design was even less democratic than it had been four years previously in the Soviet Union.

With new parliamentary and presidential elections provisionally scheduled for June 1994, work began on a new legislative electoral law. Drafts emerged in spring 1992 from two committees in the Russian Supreme Soviet, one under the leadership of centrist Viktor Balala, and the other led by the reformist economist Viktor Sheinis. The two drafts were similar in most respects: both 'westernized' the provisions for the nomination of candidates, for campaigning and for campaign financing. They differed, however, in the electoral formula.[17] The Balala draft called for exclusive use of single-member districts according to a plurality rule, on the grounds that the non-communist parties were still too weak for proportional representation to be appropriate and that PR would exaggerate the power of Muscovite elites, old and new. The Sheinis variant was a mixed system, with a minority of seats elected from party lists under PR. The intention was to combine the direct accountability and localized focus of single-member districts with PR's incentives to institutionalize new parties[18] – an argument we also encountered in Poland and Hungary. Crucially, this model did not build in a link between the two elements, so it was not a true additional-member system. Although Sheinis was reportedly inspired by the German example, he appears not to have grasped its essential dynamic.[19]

The Sheinis draft was discussed by the Russian Congress of People's Deputies in June 1992, but growing opposition to pre-term elections meant that the bill had to be shelved. It was revived in January 1993 and began to be widely debated after a referendum in April demonstrated that the diverse Russian peoples had lost confidence in their parliament. When Yeltsin dissolved the Congress of People's Deputies on 21 September, he simultaneously decreed elections under a mixed electoral system, with a preponderance of single-member seats (270 to 130 in the proposed 400-seat chamber, to be known by its pre-revolutionary name, the State Duma). Although a number of top presidential aides had originally inclined to the Balala model, Sheinis sided with the Kremlin during the constitutional quarrel and this loyalty partly explains the triumph of his version. The President's Chief of Staff, Sergei Filatov, was put in charge of hammering out the details, and ten days of intense reflection compelled several presidential advisers to reconsider the content of the initial decree.[20] Even before the dissolution of the Congress, Sheinis had concluded that the new legislature should consist of an equal number of members elected from party lists and from single-member districts. Backed by the chairman of the Central Electoral Commission and the president's legal department, Sheinis convinced Yeltsin of the merits of this even split in time for its inclusion in a second presidential decree on 1 October, number 1557.[21] (Yeltsin was apparently in a more pro-party mood at the time, since he could be persuaded that the recent success of the speaker of the Congress of People's Deputies, Ruslan Khasbulatov, in mobilizing legislators against the presidency derived from the absence of countervailing parties.[22]) A 5 per cent threshold was joined to the PR formula. Subsequent decrees specified guidelines both for the Duma elections of 12 December and a simultaneous constitutional referendum, and passages perforce written in great haste later caused more than their share of confusion.[23]

Sheinis and his allies marketed the mixed system as a compromise that offered concessions to different groups. Like many of Yeltsin's advisers, Sheinis saw proportional list voting as a means of strengthening parties, and he assumed that reformist forces would do well on the party lists dominated by Moscow-based elites, but poorly in the single-member districts, where conservative local notables had clout and better networks.[24] As he put it, 'no proportional representation, no parties'.[25] He also viewed PR as a means of structuring parliament, and even society at large.[26] Others of Yeltsin's advisers viewed a pure single-member system as a way to establish a two-party system in which reformist forces would become one of the major players.[27] SMDs were seen by Sergei Filatov, head of Yeltsin's presidential administration, as a means of catering to regional interests.[28] There was also discussion as to whether the single-member district elections ought to be governed by the traditional two-round system employed for Soviet elections or by plurality. Some feared that the pro-reform vote might fragment under a plurality rule, allowing the communists to sweep the single-member seats; but others saw in plurality an additional stimulus for the formation of a two-party system.[29] Although many fine arguments were made, the deliberations were characterized by tremendous uncertainty and a dearth of hard facts. The unpredictability of the variants' effects was compounded by not knowing which parties would be competing: the Communist Party of the Russian Federation (KPRF) was suspended by decree on 4 October along with several other parties, though it was allowed to resume activities in time for the election.

Given that the law was imposed by decree in a time of conflict rather than through structured negotiation, it is difficult to see it as a bargaining outcome as the Hungarian and Bulgarian mixed systems have been interpreted. It also took rule-making out of the hands of the legislators, who are the demiurge of most interest-based models (see Chapter 1). Final authority rested with the president, and 'at that time, no individual or institution in Russia was in a position to stop him'.[30] At the same time, detailed analysis of the genesis of the law has shown that it was the product of lengthy deliberations involving a range of partisan and institutional actors, some of whom were planning to stand for the new parliament.[31] Several explanations of the outcome have been proposed, the most comprehensive of which is by Robert Moser and Frank Thames.[32] They identify five sets of competing aims that shaped the process of electoral system design within Yeltsin's entourage.

- The inclusion of a PR element served the goal of encouraging a new party system.
- The SMD element would ensure elected representatives' sense of responsibility and connection to voters, and facilitate presidential patronage of regional clients.
- The various incentives of the mixed system (including the treatment of Russia as a single electoral district for the allocation of PR seats and the rules for registration of party lists) were intended to force parties to operate nationwide, as a party system based on regional divisions could engender ethnic unrest among the Russian Federation's diverse ethnic minority groups, with worrying separatist potential.

- The system's authors wanted to promote pro-reform parties but could not predict confidently how they would perform under pure majoritarianism or PR, so the mixture acted as an insurance policy, hedging against liberal failure under one of the elements.

- The elimination of a run-off for the SMD element was inspired by the belief that a one-round plurality contest would encourage the emergence of a two-party system, as in the United States and Great Britain, since the second round in France appeared to allow numerous parties to survive. A similar effect in the PR realm was also predicted, as a result of the 5 per cent threshold's impact on the range of competition.

The mixed system was thus the product of competing aims vis-à-vis party system development. Closed-list PR was a party-strengthening and nationalizing force, whereas single-member districts gave voice to local interests and were also believed to favour a small number of large parties.

The desire for legitimacy appears to have been prominent in the minds of those in charge of the law, though it is a factor rarely mentioned explicitly. When the law was imposed by decree, there was a keen awareness among Yeltsin's people that this was not the ideal circumstance for the birth of a democratic party system. The mixed system had the advantage in this context of being 'moderate', seen to cater to the needs and interests of all political forces. It could also be put forward as 'progressive', and the innovation it represented was milked for all it was worth by its authors.[33]

The mixed electoral system adopted in 1993 can thus be seen as the product of three main factors: high levels of uncertainty, attempts at party system engineering and the desire for legitimacy. In the absence of clear evidence as to the likely outcome of one system or the other, the mixed system allowed the reformers to spread their risks. There was no obvious strategy to ensure their victory. But their virtual monopoly over the design process provided the drafters of the law with the opportunity to make the electoral system do as much work as possible. They were clearly looking beyond the expected outcome of the approaching election, to the new system's inter- and intra-party effects, and they had an interest in building a political order that would benefit Russia's fledgling market economy. Their calculations were thus structured by short-term as well as long-term horizons, and at a time when partisan interests were viewed in both a narrow sense as supporters of the president himself and in a broader sense of support for a democratic, pro-market regime. It is not surprising that this vision, which was both 'fuzzy' and 'double', engendered a mixed electoral system. As in Bulgaria, Russian electoral engineers saw in the parallel-mixed model a formula that would allow them at once to satisfy competing demands among the reformist elite and in the population at large, to generate relatively balanced outcomes and to prevent hostages to fortune.

The resulting system was an even split among PR and SMD seats, 225 deputies being elected to the Duma through each mechanism on separate ballots.[34] The single-member seats were filled in a single round by plurality, with a 25 per cent turnout requirement, while the PR seats were filled from closed national party lists with a 5 per cent threshold (up from 3 per cent in an earlier draft). The two tiers were not linked, and candidates could stand in SMD races while also appearing on a party list, such that losers in the former could still enter the Duma under the latter.

In the turbulent conditions under which the elections were held, there was a widespread perception that they would be flawed. A poll taken in mid-October showed that only 49 per cent of respondents thought it would be possible to have democratic elections.[35] The perception of illegitimacy lingered well after the polls, as full district-level results were never released to the public and rumours persisted that turnout had been massaged to bring it up to the 50 per cent required for the validity of the simultaneous constitutional referendum. There were also allegations of fraud in the parliamentary elections,[36] but the parliament nevertheless took office under the new constitution and served the full two-year term for which it had been elected.

Contrary to the designers' expectations, the PR–SMD mix did not lead to party system consolidation, largely due to the fact that the SMD races resulted in even greater party fragmentation than the PR contest.[37] One anomaly of the system was that party affiliation was not listed on the ballot in the single-member races; this was intended to deprive the Communists of their local advantage, but it had the unintended consequences of making it difficult for voters to coordinate their two votes and of lessening the importance of parties in these races.[38] Moreover, 121 of the 225 deputies elected in SMDs had no party affiliation. No single party won an outright majority of the Duma seats, but the opposition nationalist Liberal Democratic Party of Vladimir Zhirinovskii did far better than expected, gaining 64 of the 450 total seats and 59 of the 225 PR seats on the basis of 22.9 per cent of the list vote, while the pro-Yeltsin Russia's Choice won 62 seats overall and only 15.5 per cent of the list vote. The Communists, for their part, did relatively well in the party list component of the ballot, winning 32 list seats and only 10 in the SMDs. The institution of the Duma Council, which organized the chamber's business, imposed a powerful incentive for all deputies to affiliate with a faction based around a party, and made them (rather than committees) the dominant organizing force.[39] A total of eleven clubs emerged, however, though only eight parties had cleared the 5 per cent threshold under PR. The gravity of these factions was too weak to induce loyalty or discipline, making the passage of legislation extremely laborious.[40]

In theory Yeltsin and his advisers were ideally positioned to design an electoral law to suit their needs, and, as detailed above, the available evidence suggests that interest-based calculations were prominent among the factors that influenced the design of the system employed in 1993. But interest-based calculations are effective only inasmuch as they are accurate, and as other commentators have also noted, the law did not work to the partisan advantage of those who had crafted it.[41] Nor was this their only aim. There appears to have been a clear link between political reform and the development of strong political parties in the minds of those responsible for the law. Their project was as much one of actor-creation as it was an effort to favour one set of actors over another. The outcome of the 1993 elections demonstrated that Yeltsin's advisers proved as unsuccessful in devising a system that fostered party development as in securing a pro-reform majority in parliament or generating a sense of legitimacy. White and McAllister claim that in 1999 the electoral law was 'still under active discussion, at least in part because of the circumstances of its introduction'.[42] But Yeltsin had been careful to legislate for a transitional parliament with a term of only two years, and the first post-communist elections served as a valuable lesson for the Duma members when it came to drafting a law for the 1995 elections.

The 1995 electoral law

The point of departure for the debate on the new law was the Kremlin's conclusion that the wrong parties – Zhirinovskii's Liberal Democrats and the Communists – had benefited from the PR element of the mixed system. By contrast, the more amenable Russia's Choice had performed best in the SMD races, and it was expected that the new 'party of power' associated with Prime Minister Viktor Chernomyrdin, Our Home is Russia, would do so also owing to its extensive regional contacts and resources. Accordingly, a bill drafted in late 1994 by the president's staff retained the overall number of Duma deputies (450) but reweighted them, such that 300 would be chosen in SMDs and only 150 from party lists. This nakedly biased turn was masked by more sociotropic claims of concern for the quality of representation (regarding both the merits of the deputies and their bond with the electorate) and the diffusion of power beyond Moscow.[43]

The presidential bill found little sympathy among the parties of the Duma. While this is unsurprising in the cases of parties expected to suffer from the change, even putative beneficiaries such as Russia's Choice were largely opposed to it. In this respect, the parties were united along the ideological spectrum by their common interest as a form of political organization and as members of a constitutional body. Party leaders enjoyed the control over candidate selection and ranking that closed-list voting afforded, while an increase in independents from SMDs would undermine the parties' hold on Duma business and leave the chamber more at risk of manipulation by the presidency. Since no majority could be mustered for the president's concept, or for the preference of the Communist KPRF and Liberal Democrats for a 100 per cent PR alternative, the status quo was the only option that could succeed. Even the deputies themselves elected in the SMDs exercised loyalty to the chamber, supporting the 50/50 mix lest no law be passed and the fate of the electoral system be decided again by the president rather than the legislature.[44]

The Kremlin and the upper chamber of the Federal Assembly, the Federation Council (representing each constituent part of the federation by parity), resisted the Duma's own status quo bill but, with memory of the confrontation of 1993 still fresh in everyone's minds and time again running out as the next election approached, they conceded the battle in June 1995. In the ensuing conciliation talks, Yeltsin had to abandon a bundle of amendments: to raise the threshold to 7 per cent for alliances of two parties, to reintroduce the run-off for SMD contests to ensure victory by majority and not just plurality, to bring back the requirement that at least 50 per cent of voters participate for an election to be valid. Two changes were agreed:

- Parties would be permitted to subdivide their candidate lists by region, with only the top 12 names being 'national', so that voters would feel a stronger connection to deputies chosen under PR.
- The process of registering parties for list voting was made even more demanding (parties had to collect 200,000 signatures, and only 7 per cent could come from any one region) to deter frivolous bids and to ensure that no party entered the fray on behalf of only one unit of the federation.[45]

Despite the climbdown, Yeltsin's advisers stuck to their hope that the December 1995 election would fulfil their project of trimming the extremist ends of the spectrum and distil party politics to two centrist forces, Our Home is Russia and a movement based around Duma speaker Ivan Rybkin.[46] The Russian electorate refused to cooperate, and instead the Communist KPRF capitalized on, and aggregated, votes of discontent at the expense of smaller leftist and nationalist forces. Taken all together, pro-reform and pro-government parties also increased their share of the vote, but did not play the electoral system as rationally as the Communist KPRF, so became victims of the 5 per cent threshold (thereby repeating the mistake of the Polish right in 1993). The more demanding registration rules did not deter proliferation (43 parties stood compared to 13 in 1993), and with 49.5 per cent of the vote going to parties that failed to enter the Duma, the KPRF could convert its 22.3 per cent of the list vote into 44 per cent of the seats.[47] This outcome had been foreseen to some degree in the aftermath of the Georgian elections held on 5 November 1995, in which 62 per cent of the vote went to parties that failed to clear the threshold. The response of many Russian parties, however, was not to merge but to push at the last minute, in vain, for lowering or removing the 5 per cent barrier.[48]

Yeltsin's plan to reduce the PR element would not have greatly changed the outcome, as the KPRF outperformed all rivals in the SMD contests as well. Nevertheless, in late 1997, the president resumed his campaign against PR, this time to eliminate it completely. He used the pretext that the high vote wastage of the 1995 election represented a violation of voters' rights, since so many did not see their preferences reflected in the legislature.[49]

Again, he encountered a united front of Duma parties committed to the status quo, and the opposition of the high-profile chairman of the Central Electoral Commission (who did, however, support reintroduction of the SMD run-off and of the 50 per cent turnout requirement).[50] A year later, in November 1998, the Constitutional Court entered the discussion when it was asked to rule on the legality of the PR–SMD mixture. The case had been brought to the court by the legislature of the Saratov region, formally out of concern for equality of voter rights, and ended up striking directly at the PR element. The court upheld the law but, in a burst of judicial activism, ruled that the 5 per cent threshold was constitutional 'provided that the application [...] allows the seats to be shared between at least two political groups that together represent more than 50 per cent of the poll'. This opinion was supported by the claim that democracy in Russia required a multi-party

system and an opposition, and the mathematical despotism of the
threshold would have to bend to that higher constitutional goal.[51]

The electoral law in the context of 'managed democracy'

The system adopted in 1993 consistently displeased those observers
who wanted it to do more, in particular to produce a small number of
sustainable parliamentary parties. It survived, however, as everyone's
second preference, being not to anyone's particular advantage but the
least prejudicial in conditions of persistent uncertainty. A whole new
text of the electoral law was passed in June 1999, ahead of the next
general election; drafted largely by the activist Central Electoral
Commission in consultation with party leaders, it kept the defining features unchanged and passed with the support of almost 80 per cent of
Duma deputies.[52] The most important innovation was the introduction
of a deposit, as an alternative to the old requirement of 200,000 signatures, for the registration of a party or individual. These deposits would
be returned to any candidate receiving at least 5 per cent of the vote and
to any party receiving more than 3 per cent. Intended to compound the
system's selectivity in rewards, the move was justified by reference
to frequent allegations of signature fraud and maladroit attempts to
disqualify parties on the eve of previous elections.[53]

Although pre-emptive mergers occurred and fewer parties (26) contested the December 1999 election compared to 43 four years before,
the system clearly did not present the sort of deterrent that advocates
of a tidier party population wanted. One of the main culprits, as in the
past, was not the PR component of the system (as Ordeshook claims[54])
but Article 39, which allowed candidates both to appear on party lists
and stand in SMDs. Politicians interested only in winning a seat for
themselves could set up vehicles that would receive air time and funds
like all parties standing under PR, and benefit thereby from the extra
publicity and resources. Around 65 members of the Duma entered the
chamber in 1995 in this way, evidence that the system provided an
inadvertent incentive to party proliferation.[55]

The 1999 election consolidated the KPRF's hold on votes of the left
while creating a stronger centre ground, represented by hastily assem-
bled movements linked to the new prime minister, Vladimir Putin, and
one of his predecessors, Evgenii Primakov. Six parties cleared the 5 per
cent barrier, compared to four in 1995, while in the single-member districts the heightened involvement of local powerholders, especially
governors, had an unprecedented impact on candidate selection and

outcomes. As a result, the number of independents elected in SMDs rose from 77 in 1995 to 85 in 1999; only two political parties (KPRF and Putin's 'Unity') outnumbered them in seat share.[56] Events in the following months dashed Moser's initially upbeat conclusion that the combination of PR and SMD was proving to be the best way to promote party institutionalization in Russia because it forced parties to devote energy and resources to local party-building as well as national campaigning.[57] Primakov's Fatherland-All Russia movement, which seemed to exemplify the rational response to the dual incentive structure of the electoral system, collapsed as an organization and submerged itself into a pro-Putin ensemble at the end of 2001.[58]

The perceived failure of the electoral system to have its expected and desired simplifying effect forced the passage of supplementary legislation, which took on a special meaning after the sudden resignation of Yeltsin and his replacement by Putin at the end of 1999. The new president, like his predecessor a fan of an SMD-only system, soon came to be accused of pursuing a 'managed democracy', one that had little patience for free play, unpredictable outcomes and diversity of (critical) opinion.[59] One cause of this accusation was a bill (drafted, again, by the Central Electoral Commission, with the Kremlin's support) on political parties. In the form approved in July 2001, the law introduced several additional requirements for access to Duma elections, the most demanding of which was that each party should have at least 46 local branches with no fewer than 100 members in each; any extra local organizations would have at least 50 members. This threshold, plus clauses in the 1999 electoral law withholding deposits and compelling unsuccessful parties to return any funding they had received from the state toward their campaign costs, was expected to effect the radical cutdown that had not taken place at previous elections.

Conclusion

Electoral system design in Russia was marked by conflict and misperceptions, as well as inchoate and changing interests. The relative stability of the system is thus somewhat surprising, especially as it was first imposed by decree in the wake of the forcible and violent dissolution of the Russian parliament in September 1993. This is a good example of a case where the law, once imposed, generated an interest in its continuation even without being the majority's first preference.

All the evidence suggests that the 1993 law was the product of electoral engineering in the aim of maximizing the seat share of pro-Yeltsin reformists. In this sense it was based on instrumental motives. Urban sees in this act of electoral engineering a continuation of undemocratic Soviet-era practices.[60] But though the design and imposition of the electoral system was extraordinary in that it took place outside the legislative framework, there is nothing inherently undemocratic about an electoral system that is generated by one group of politicians to the disadvantage of others. Such is often the case when one party has a parliamentary majority. What is interesting about the Russian electoral law is that it is a compromise solution when there was no *political* reason to compromise. As in Hungary and Bulgaria, the electoral law of 1993 was a product of bargaining, but in the Russian case the compromise was not among distinct ideological forces but rather among different beliefs as to what the results of the elections might look like under alternative formulae, as well as among the multiple political goals of the drafters.

Also worthy of note is the fact that, as in Bulgaria, those who wrote the law were playing a long game. Though they certainly had one eye firmly fixed on the elections of December 1993, they also took into consideration the long-term shape of the Russian party system. As Moser and Thames remark, 'Despite the preponderance of power President Yeltsin held throughout this process, the system was not crafted exclusively for the interests of a particular party or ideological camp.'[61] Those in charge of drafting the law had multiple interests – personal, ideological, institutional – and these multiple interests generated a system that served to entrench them by providing multiple channels of access to legislative power.

8
Ukraine: the Struggle for Democratic Change

Of all the states studied in this volume, Ukraine was the slowest to reform its electoral institutions following the collapse of communism. There was nevertheless considerable legislative activity in the electoral sphere. Like Poland and Russia, Ukraine adopted new electoral laws for each election after 1989, and each law was preceded by lengthy debates reflecting many basic issues of post-communist change. Principal among them was the proper relationship between economic and political structures, which manifested itself in terms of the right of various types of groups to nominate candidates for election. The main struggle of Ukraine's pro-reform forces during this period was to establish the legitimacy of political parties in a multi-party context and to seek party monopoly over political mobilization. Groups associated with the former *nomenklatura* in the first instance, and latterly with the presidential system, fought to maintain the power of administrative structures tied to the executive branch and to state-owned industries. They steadfastly opposed such innovations as the nomination and election of parliamentary deputies from party lists and the inclusion of party representatives on electoral commissions.

Despite the power of bureaucrats and members of the former *nomenklatura*, the Ukrainian electoral system became considerably more 'party friendly' over the period in question, largely as a result of a shift in the stance of the major left-wing political organizations from supporting administrative elites to promoting the common interests of parties as institutions. As politicians gradually restructured their political support bases, they discovered the usefulness of parties, especially shady economic elites who found it convenient to be able to invent attractive party images to enhance their vote share.

There were four principal stages in the evolution of electoral system design in Ukraine, punctuated by the quadrennial elections to parliament: (1) pre-independence debates surrounding the new law for elections to the Ukrainian republican parliament of 1990; (2) the 1991–3 period of failed attempts to introduce significant changes to the Soviet-era election law in advance of the first post-Soviet parliamentary elections in 1994; (3) the 1994–7 period, in which parliament took stock of the multiple problems associated with the 1994 elections and adopted a semi-proportional law; (4) 1998–2001, when further major reforms were considered but rejected (see Table 8.1). These phases are distinct not only because each was dominated by the run-up to a different parliamentary election, but also because the constitutional situation in Ukraine changed from each period to the next, as did the party system.

There was nevertheless a notable continuity in the issues dominating all four debates over electoral reform. The most prominent issues in each case were those surrounding rights of contestation. A second area of concern was how to ensure the impartiality of electoral administration, where corruption was widely perceived to have hindered genuine competition.

Table 8.1 Main changes in the law on elections to the *Verkhovna Rada*

Election year	Electoral system type	District structure	Seat allocation formula	Threshold
1990	Semi-competitive two-round SMD	450 single-member districts	First round: absolute majority; second round: plurality	N/A
1994	Two-round SMD	450 single-member districts	First and second rounds: absolute majority	N/A
1998	Mixed (single-member plurality plus national list)	225 single-member districts plus 1 national district	SMDs: plurality; lists: largest remainders (Hare quota)	4%
2002	Mixed (single-member plurality; plus national list)	225 single-member districts plus 1 national district	SMDs: plurality; lists: largest remainders (Hare quota)	4%

The pre-independence period: elections before multi-party competition

Ukraine had meagre historical resources with which to develop democratic electoral institutions. It had experienced statehood only during brief and turbulent periods before gaining independence from the USSR in 1991, and Ukrainian elites played little role in developing electoral institutions before this time. Following the limited competition of the elections to the Soviet Congress of People's Deputies (CPD) in March 1989, the Ukrainian parliament began considering republic-level electoral legislation. Its first draft went through several versions and was published in the press on 6 August. The draft largely repeated the provisions of the CPD election law, with some minor modifications. It called for 25 per cent of deputies to be elected from social organizations and for a smaller working parliament chosen from among the ranks of those elected. In some respects this represented a liberalization: candidate-vetting meetings were not required, and the number of voters needed to nominate a candidate was reduced from 500 to 300. In other respects, however, the procedures were tightened; a new minimum (300 participants) was required for a workers' collective to nominate a candidate. The requirement that candidates must live or work in the district where they were nominated was also modified to make an exception for those whose work covered the district in question. This was widely perceived as a means of securing regional party and state leaders safe seats in remote and compliant rural areas. Finally, the draft banned the right to campaign for an election boycott, following the selective boycott called the previous March by the Ukrainian Helsinki Union.

Meanwhile, a group of the more radical deputies elected to the CPD in March 1989 had formed a Republican Deputies' Club which galvanized around the topic of electoral reform, criticizing the draft law and demanding removal of reserved seats for social organizations and the 'parliament-within-a-parliament' model.[1] They also called for removing candidates whose campaign platforms violated the Ukrainian constitution. In September the group proposed an alternative draft law. Spurred by this example, other groups in Ukraine put pressure on parliament (*Verkhovna Rada*) to change the law. Popular meetings endorsing electoral liberalization on 2 September attracted considerable support across Ukraine. The League of Young Communists (*Komsomol*) was also in the vanguard of those pushing for electoral reform, and it stated publicly that it would not take up the seats allocated to it in the draft law. At around this time the press published the results of an academic survey of popular opinion. A total of 59 per cent of respondents favoured a directly elected parliament (with 33 opposed), 53 per cent were against reserved seats for social organizations (27 for) and 72 per cent opposed nomination on the basis of workplace (as opposed to residence or work in the district). The survey also revealed a general distrust of electoral commissions; 78 per cent thought they should be elected at meetings of work collectives, and only 15 per cent thought commissions should decide whether to withdraw a candidate's nomination on the basis of the contents of his or her campaign platform.[2]

The groundswell of popular support for changes to the draft law undoubtedly influenced the thinking of the Ukrainian leadership. Events were moving fast. There was a danger that efforts to maintain control of the electoral process would backfire by provoking such wrath on the part of the electorate that even the carefully crafted control mechanisms detailed in the draft law would not prevent numerous radical reformers from being elected. The results of the 1989 CPD elections had demonstrated that a conservative majority was not sufficient to prevent an active radical minority from setting the agenda; this reflection undoubtedly gave the Ukrainian leaders pause for thought.

Three seemingly unconnected events intervened in quick succession to push the notoriously conservative Ukrainian party leaders to accept the need for further change. The first was the founding congress of the Popular Movement in Support for Perestroika – popularly known as *Rukh* ('movement'). The second event was the replacement of Brezhnev-era Ukrainian Party leader Volodymyr Shcherbyts'ky with the slightly less conservative Volodymyr Ivashko. The third event was a decision on 25 October by the CPD to allow the republics greater freedom to craft their own electoral systems. As in Russia, the final law eliminated seats for social organizations, but it went further still and provided for a directly elected parliament of 450 members. In March 1990 118 members of the hastily cobbled-together Democratic Bloc won seats; they were later joined by enough deputies to give the democratic opposition approximately one-quarter of the seats in parliament.

Electoral reform in the wake of independence, 1992–3: parties versus the 'party of power'

The legalization of alternative political parties in spring 1990 saw the registration of a plethora of new political organizations, mostly from the right-wing 'democratic' camp. But though there were over three dozen such parties by the time of the 1994 elections, most were little more than coteries of elites, with severely underdeveloped grassroots support bases and little ideological distinctiveness. Of the new parties, the main right-wing organization was Rukh, and the most vocal element of the centre was the Party of Democratic Rebirth (PDVU), formed mainly of communists-turned-democrats.

The configuration of parliamentary politics was unconducive to reform. Despite the large number of new reformist parties, parliament retained its conservative majority. However, the rapid disintegration of the Soviet centre provoked even obstinate pro-Soviet communists to adopt a more nationalist stance. In late 1991 the Soviet Union collapsed and Ukraine gained independence. The creation of the new state was validated in the December 1991 referendum by 90.3 per cent of the vote. President Leonid Kravchuk, elected the same day, was the former communist ideology chief, but – eager to defend the state which had honoured him with his new title – he rapidly embraced nationalism. The right at this point was punching above its numerical weight in parliament through enthusiasm and a sense that it had been vindicated by events.

Electoral reform began to be discussed in 1992 in the context of general debates about constitutional changes. The 1990 parliament was due to remain in power until 1995, but its legitimacy was undermined by the fact that it had been elected during the Soviet period, literally in a different country. There was therefore much talk of holding pre-term elections. This prospect (or possibility) gave added impetus to the speedy adoption of a new law, and several drafts were submitted to parliament. It was nevertheless nearly two years before a law was eventually passed, following a decision to call parliamentary elections for March 1994.

Several factors were relevant to understanding the immediate context of the law-drafting process; firstly, two years after independence the economy was in a tailspin, leading to considerable disillusionment with independence and nationalism. Secondly, the Communist party, banned in the wake of the Soviet break-up, was allowed to reform under a new name in October 1993. This was thus a time when the left was regrouping and reasserting itself. Thirdly, as we saw in Chapter 7, the left-dominated Russian Duma had only recently been forcibly dismantled and elections called for December 1993 under a mixed plurality–PR law effectively imposed by the 'reformist' Yeltsin.

Parliamentarians across the political spectrum accepted the desirability of a system of proportional representation. They were, however, divided over whether the introduction of PR should precede or follow party-system formation. The old guard on the left and among non-affiliated deputies tended to argue that Ukraine was not yet ready for PR because its parties were still so weak, while members of the new right-wing parties argued that PR was needed to strengthen parties as well as to structure parliament and enable it to form party-based governments.[3] There was also much talk of PR's ability to 'structure society' by encouraging the formation of political groups that could mobilize people along socio-economic lines.

In early 1993 the Rada received two drafts, one from the Party of Democratic Rebirth (based on a draft formulated by the Association of Young Ukrainian Political Scientists and Politicians) calling for half the deputies to be elected from single-member districts and half from party lists, and a fully proportional draft registered by Rukh.[4] A working group headed by independent deputy Anatolii Tkachuk was established that spring within the parliamentary Committee on Legislation and Legality. In the summer of 1993 the non-party deputy parliamentary speaker, Vasyl' Durdynets, proposed a further draft, with 100 deputies to be elected on party lists and the remainder by the majoritarian method. The Tkachuk group eventually put forward a bill for a mixed law which combined elements of the PDVU and Durdynets' drafts. Though the bill was discussed by the Rada, no consensus could be reached and it was held over until a final decision had been made to call pre-term elections.

Debate on an eight-point resolution on the basic provisions of the electoral law began on 7 October. Coincidentally or not, this was also the day after the introduction of the Russian mixed electoral system had been announced. Speaker Ivan Plyushch pre-empted direct discussion of the mixed versus majoritarian choice by assuming that the law would be a mixed one and urging the parliament to focus its attention on what he described as the 'quota' of deputies to be elected by proportional representation. Plyushch admitted openly that he preferred the mixed 350/100 version proposed by Durdynets, and he was keen to avoid passage of a fully majoritarian law, which he said would make the Rada look 'conservative'.[5] The new parties of the right and centre-right at this point rallied around the mixed law, while many Socialists, the (newly legalized) Communists and most unaffiliated deputies favoured maintaining the pure single-member district system. The introduction of party-list seats did not win the support of more than a third of the deputies present, and even a proposal that a clause be included to the effect that the elections would be held on a multi-party basis received only 164 votes.

The debate revealed clearly that the key question under discussion was the proper subjects of democratic elections, and that the PR versus majoritarian debate was construed in terms of the rights of independent candidates supported by traditional Soviet-era local power structures on the one hand and party-backed candidates on the other. Several right-wing members claimed that Ukraine must introduce party lists for the elections to be seen by western observers as having been conducted on a multi-party basis. Adherents of the majoritarian law, however, observed that single-member district elections can also be multi-party elections; they viewed innovations such as listing the candidate's party affiliation on the ballot and allowing parties to nominate candidates as being sufficient concessions to multipartism.

In this context the nomination process remained as important as – if not more important than – district design and seat allocation formulae. When asked rhetorically by a fellow committee member whether nomination rights or method of election was the more important question, Tkachuk replied unconditionally that 'the question of the nomination of candidates is surely the key to every electoral law'.[6] Throughout the course of the debate deputies at all points of the political spectrum echoed this view, repeatedly describing nomination procedures as the 'key' to the electoral law. Leftist and independent candidates were eager to retain the Soviet-era provision of nomination by work collectives and civil society organizations, whereas those associated with the new parties of the right wanted nomination rights restricted to political parties and groups of voters or candidates themselves.

The distinction between PR and majoritarianism was also viewed in terms of the corruptibility of the latter. The right saw the single-member system as a means for the old *nomenklatura* – the so-called 'party of power' – to maintain control of politics through their patronage networks and other local resources. A law which downplayed party affiliation had the added advantage of allowing the 'party of power' to win seats without having to resort overtly to a label designating a discredited ideology. The personalism this was seen to foster was associated by the right with lack of accountability. Speaker Plyushch stated baldly that 'Those who vote for the majority system are first and foremost those deputies who envisage that they will be able to solve the problems of their district in the same manner that they solved them previously, in other words by using the means of the state. We must not allow this mechanism of creating the basis for corruption to be imposed on the next Verkhovna Rada'.[7] In this context workplace-based nomination was an added means through which the old *nomenklatura* of the 'party of power' could maintain the political fabric of the communist period. The adherents of majoritarianism countered that party politics was also notoriously corrupt, and they several times referred to the recent Italian decision to move away from PR.

The Committee on Legislation and Legality revised the draft along fully majoritarian lines, and the full bill was considered by parliament on first reading (9 and 10 November). With time getting short, Plyushch was keen to push for a compromise solution. Though the issue of mixed versus majoritarian system had in theory already been decided, it was debated yet again after Communist faction leader Yevhen Marmazov indicated a willingness to allow 50 per cent of the seats to be elected by PR as an 'experiment', conceding that he understood the need to have a mixed system 'in future'.[8] This view was reinforced by Socialist party leader Oleksandr Moroz, who stated 'the necessity of a mixed electoral system'.[9] This was an about-face for the Socialist, who had only the previous month been insisting on nomination by work collectives only. Whether this change arose from behind-the-scenes bargaining or the altered positions of the Socialist party after the official lifting of the ban on the Communists is a moot point. But interventions by other members of left and right parties indicate that there were numerous divisions within partisan groups. Plyushch called for a rank-order vote on the different drafts under consideration, and the current majoritarian draft received the most votes (274), with the 350/100 variant coming a poor second (197) and the 50/50 mixed and fully PR drafts trailing at 82 and 84 votes respectively.

Prior to the second reading, the Legislation Committee again revised the draft law. The debate on second reading took place in an extended article-by-article discussion (17 and 18 November). Now the most contentious issues revolved around nomination procedures, including the right of work collectives to nominate candidates, controversially reintroduced to the bill by the Committee. Other issues included campaign finance provisions (the left wanted only state finance), and the composition of electoral commissions (the right wanted party representation). The bill was eventually passed by 245 to 8 in evident violation of the requirement for a constitutional majority, causing further disturbances in the parliament and again provoking the wrath of the right. The law was nevertheless signed by the president immediately and came into force on 27 November. Though the law differed from its predecessor on at least 50 counts, it largely preserved the Soviet-era system. The major changes included an absolute majority requirement for success in the *second* round of voting, procedures for political parties to nominate candidates and provisions for private campaign finance.

There are, however, indications that some aspects of the law were the unintended result of poor drafting in the rush to get it through parliament. The fifty-per-cent-plus-one majority requirement in the second round was apparently included by mistake.[10] The second alleged blunder concerns the onerous requirements for parties to nominate candidates. Secretary of the Central Election Commission Ihor Tsyluyko claimed in an interview that these requirements had been devised when the law was still a mixed one, and they were meant to apply to the nomination of entire lists. When the PR component of the law was removed, these provisions were simply left unchanged.[11]

Though the new democratic parties were unhappy with the outcome of these deliberations, contemporary survey research indicated that the electorate was not. A poll conducted in October 1993 found that whereas 43.6 per cent supported the majoritarian system, only 16.3 per cent supported PR and 13.3 per cent a mixed system. Furthermore, 51.5 per cent favoured the nomination of candidates through work collectives as against 25.1 per cent who preferred to have them nominated by political parties.[12] The people clearly remained to be convinced of the supposed benefits of the more 'democratic' electoral rules proposed by the new parties, and these parties largely failed to lead public opinion. Whatever the machinations in parliament, it seems that popular antipathy to parties in general was still high.

In the event, the hurdles for party nomination proved a serious barrier. A majority of candidates – 62.3 per cent – were nominated by groups of voters, 26.7 per cent by work collectives and only 11.0 per cent by parties.[13] Examination of the party affiliation of candidates as indicated on the ballot reveals that 27.3 per cent of candidates were members of parties,[14] which meant that most party affiliates chose nomination either as independents or by work collectives. Of those elected, however, fully half were party members. Whatever the true intentions of those supporting the law, its effect undeniably hindered the development of cohesive political parties. And though party-affiliated candidates did far better at the polls than independents, the many independent deputies in parliament often switched political allegiance, and with little to make them beholden to their chosen organization, party members frequently defected from their fellows.

From the point of view of effectiveness, the most problematic aspect of the election outcome was that only 338 of the seats were filled following the first two rounds of voting in March and April 1994. Of the elections declared invalid, 20 were the result of inadequate turnout in the second round and 91 the consequence of a failure on the part of either of the two candidates in the run-off to reach the 50 per cent mark.[15] There were subsequently 11 attempts to fill the vacant seats before parliament finally simply gave up in 1996, declaring a moratorium on new by-elections, though nearly one-tenth of seats remained vacant.[16]

What is most striking about the manoeuvrings over the new law is the degree to which levels of individual integration into organized parties proved more important in determining attitudes toward reform than ideology. Non-party members and members of small parties on both left and right tended to support the single-member system and workplace-based nomination, while the largest parties – Rukh, the PDVU and the Socialists – supported at least an element of PR and nomination by parties. This divide clearly reflected the varying nature of the electoral support bases of the individual deputies as much as it did the electoral prospects of the parties as organizations. It is noteworthy that there was disagreement within the large parties of the left, the Communists and Socialists, with the leaders being far more supportive of party lists than those further down in the party, who would most likely not benefit from them. The old guard of the *nomenklatura* who had not linked themselves with any of the post-1991 parties had an interest in promoting electoral institutions that would allow them to capitalize on the local social networks which were their main political resource.

1994–98: the drive to institutionalize political parties

Though the process of revising the electoral law in 1993 had seemed lengthy at the time, subsequent efforts spanned far greater periods and involved far more debate. Many had thought the passage of a new post-Soviet constitution in 1996 would put an end to the wrangling over the powers of the respective institutions of the state. Yet the tussle continued, and the increased powers allocated to the president under the new constitution made the chief executive a central player in the electoral reform process. In the immediate aftermath of the 1994 elections, attention was concentrated on improving electoral institutions to make them more efficient and effective. The failure of the 1993 law to accomplish the minimum required of an election law – to elect a parliament – resulted in a considerable amount of hand-wringing and mutual recrimination among the Kiev elite. Nevertheless, the urgent need for a new Ukrainian constitution caused the electoral legislative agenda to be put on hold and prevented a new law from being passed until

September 1997, again only shortly before elections were due to be held the following March. And again the new law suffered from considerable technical difficulties and was subject to extensive legal intervention, making the 1998 elections hardly more successful in technical terms than those of 1994. Nevertheless, the law passed in 1997 did herald a move toward serious electoral reform. It mandated that half of the seats of parliament be allocated proportionally on the basis of national lists, and it removed the contentious absolute majority turnout and success requirements which had dogged the 1994 elections. With these changes Ukraine brought its electoral legislation into line with that of other states in the region.

Following the 1994 elections, western advisers advocated a switch to a mixed system,[17] and there was widespread recognition within the Ukrainian elite that the electoral system needed to be radically overhauled.[18] A number of factors combined to make reform a more attractive option at this point. Firstly, the new political parties had received a bitter lesson in the importance of electoral system design in 1994. This included the left-wing Socialists and the Rural Party, which had both performed far worse than expected. The Communists, for their part, could look to the Russian 1993 results, in which the Communist Party of the Russian Federation had won twice as many seats on the proportional list part of the ballot as they had in single-member districts. The division between party deputies and independents sharpened as the left-wing Communists and Socialists saw that, as parties, they had common interests with the new political organizations of the right. It was also becoming clear that the large number of independent candidates and the high degree of dispersal of seats among 14 parties was making it extremely difficult for the parliament to pass legislation. There was thus a consensus among party leaders across the political spectrum that a move toward PR was desirable in order to help structure the Ukrainian political scene and enable more effective decision-making.[19]

It is interesting to note that, as in Russia, proportional representation was seen by these politicians as the system most likely to generate accountable majority government, whereas single-member district elections were associated with fragmentation. Though this may seem strange to comparative students of electoral systems, it made sense in the post-Soviet context, where party-list voting combined with a relatively high threshold of representation worked as an engine of party consolidation. Since drafting the previous electoral law Ukrainian legislators had witnessed two Russian elections in which there had been a stark contrast between the party fragmentation resulting from single-member seat elections and the magnification of large-party strength that had been the outcome of list voting.

With an increasingly confrontational president having been elected in 1994, there was also added urgency for the parliament to enhance its decision-making capacity; generating a more structured parliament was viewed as a means for the Rada to increase its power and legitimacy vis-à-vis the president. Referring to the upcoming debate on the constitution, the Socialist speaker, Oleksandr Moroz, argued that 'if we record [our preference for] a mixed system today, there will be a political majority in parliament, and that means that it will not be possible to write into the constitution that the Cabinet of Ministers will be formed without [the approval of] the Rada'.[20] Whatever we may think of the logic of this argument, it demonstrates that the parliamentary leadership perceived electoral reform not only in terms of their party personal and party political interests, but also in terms of their institutional interests as parliamentarians. In effect, as in Poland in 1991, institutional interests now took precedence over partisan differences as the institution of parliament came under threat. President Kuchma was not a member of any party, though he was supported by a range of small centrist parties and independent deputies. He was wary of increased party organization by either his left-wing or his right-wing rivals. He therefore opposed a proportional law, especially one with a threshold that would exclude his centrist allies and magnify the seat share of the large parties. Critics of PR argued against list voting, lest it generate a 'monopoly' on the political process – an echo of criticism of party monopoly during the communist period.[21]

A working group on the electoral law was set up under the auspices of the parliamentary committee on Legal Policy and Judicial Reform. The group was headed by Oleksandr Lavrynovych, deputy leader of Rukh, member of the Central Election Commission (CEC) between 1990 and 1993, and acting head of the CEC between November 1992 and November 1993. The working group also included two representatives of the International Foundation for Electoral Systems.

Agreement on the desirability of a mixed system was formalized in the 'Constitutional Accord' between the president and the parliament on 7 June, which called for a mixed law along with a draft of other institutional structures designed to serve Ukraine as a 'little constitution' until a new fundamental law was passed. In July 1995 the working group finalized its draft,[22] which called for 50 per cent (225) of the seats in parliament to be elected in single-member districts according to a plurality rule and with no turnout requirement. The other 225 seats were to be elected from national party lists according to proportional representation with a 3 per cent threshold. The draft also made it considerably easier for parties to nominate candidates for single-member seats, abolished nomination by work collectives, lowered the number of signatures for nomination candidates by groups of voters to 200, and allowed 'self-nomination'. Regulations on private financing remained much the same as they had been in the 1993 law, but with new requirements for disclosure of income. The CEC members were now to be nominated by the president for six-year terms and confirmed by parliament. These provisions were mostly the same as those eventually adopted in 1997, though there was considerable debate and redrafting over the course of the intervening two and a half years.

The bill was presented to the Rada on 6 October. The main issues dominating the debate at this stage included the choice between national and regional lists, the list threshold, the basis on which single-member district seats would be allocated (relative or absolute majority), mode of nomination, turnout requirements and the composition of electoral commissions.[23] The bill was passed on its first reading on 18 November, with a second reading scheduled for March 1996. But the constitution took precedence at this point. The Presidium of the Rada felt it better to wait until after that had been passed before moving on to legislation with constitutional implications, and the bill was shelved.

Though there was some discussion of whether to include the basic shape of the electoral system in the constitution itself, this did not happen. The document approved in June 1996 states only that elections are 'held on the basis of universal, equal and direct suffrage by secret ballot' and that 'voters are guaranteed free expression of their will' (Article 71). As in Poland after 1997, the new constitution altered the legal infrastructure within which elections took place in such a way as to necessitate numerous minor legislative changes. This meant that elections could not be conducted on the basis of the existing law and further work on the proposed bill was necessary prior to the elections due in March 1998.

On 14 November 1996 the Rada considered five versions of the law: the official text drawn up by the parliamentary working group; a similar draft proposed by Communist Oleksandr Steshenko; a pure proportional law with a 3 per cent threshold drafted by a range of small parties from across the political spectrum; and two slightly different mixed laws put forward by members of the centrist Popular Democratic Party (NDP). Much of the discussion focused on which types of electoral institution would be most susceptible to corruption and abuse. The main party representatives argued that single-member districts could easily be bought by local notables, citing instances from the most recent parliamentary and local elections. Opponents of PR argued that it was just as easy to 'buy' an entire party behind which 'shady capital' could then hide. The most frequent example given by these speakers was again Italy, where there had been a popular backlash against PR due to its alleged link to corrupt politics. Nomination rights also figured as a prominent topic of debate. Nomination by workers' collectives was supported half-heartedly by the Communists and fervently by the far-left Progressive Socialists but vehemently opposed by the right. The Socialists took the pragmatic position that the relative paucity of nominees from collectives in 1993 demonstrated that this mechanism was a thing of the past. More popular among centrist deputies were proposals that civil society organizations be allowed to nominate candidates.[24] The Steshenko draft won the most votes and was again sent to the working group for further consideration in the spring of 1997. With the support of both the left and the right, the resultant draft, which stipulated a mixed system with one PR district and a 4 per cent threshold, was passed on first reading on 5 March 1997.

At this point opposition began to mount as the political configuration of parliament shifted in favour of groups which supported the president. Passage on second reading was consequently difficult, due to the blocking tactics by centrist parties and independents allied with the president. As we might expect from considerations of interest, the large parties of the left and the right, Rukh and the Communists, both preferred a higher threshold of, say, 5 per cent, whereas the smaller parties, mostly clustered in the centre of the political spectrum, were split between wanting a mixed law with a low threshold and a purely majoritarian law. When it became obvious that a threshold of 1 or 2 per cent was not going to pass, support rose among the centrists for a law with a larger component of single-member seats. The second reading had failed nine times by late August. At this point President Kuchma expressed his preference for a fully single-member system based on the existing law.[25] NDP members Roman Bezsmertnyi (official representative of the president in parliament) and Mykhailo Syrota (leader of the Constitutional Centre faction which supported the president) submitted a 75 per cent single-member system for consideration.

The tension between the president and the main parties in parliament intensified. Kuchma suggested that the adoption of a mixed system would be conditional on passage of his contentious reform budget, whereupon the Committee on Legal Policy initiated an impeachment procedure against the president in order to try to get him to change his position. When the law was finally passed on 24 September amid growing anti-presidential sentiment, Kuchma refused to sign it and instead proposed 15 amendments. Parliament accepted 12, but rejected the proposal for a two-round system for the single-member district elections. Though the president toyed with vetoing the law, he finally signed it on 22 October.[26]

The resulting law was far from satisfactory, and the electoral process was marked by legal ambiguities and challenges; these threatened to undermine its legitimacy and resulted once again in considerable delays in finalizing the results. In late 1997 the Constitutional Court considered two separate appeals by 109 deputies, lawyers and political advisers as to the constitutionality of the law, in particular the provision that candidates be allowed to stand both on party lists and in single-member districts. While the Court was considering the appeals, the Rada hastily made three minor amendments to the law in December.[27] Finally in February, when the campaign was in full swing, the Constitutional Court delivered a scathing ruling, declaring the law unconstitutional on more than forty counts, including the allowance of double candidacies. At the same time, however, the Court decided it was too late in the current campaign for changes to the law. It ruled that the elections could go ahead regardless, provided minor changes were made to the regulations governing electoral commissions.[28] The majority of this legal quibbling revolved around relatively minor issues; still it cast a shadow over the legal status of the law throughout the electoral process and left some doubt as to the constitutional legitimacy of the parliament.[29]

As in 1993, the mass public was not actively involved in deliberations over the new electoral law, but there is evidence that the need for reform was gaining popular support. When asked immediately prior to the March 1998 elections 'Do you think (the new) electoral system will be more or less democratic than the old one?', 33.4 per cent of respondents in 25 representative electoral districts throughout Ukraine replied that it would make no difference, and 34.1 per cent either 'didn't know' or declined to answer the question. Only 8.8 per cent viewed the new system as less democratic than the old, however, and 23.7 per cent thought it would be more democratic.[30] Electoral reform was clearly not an issue that polarized the mass public at this point, but among the minority who were willing to express a view on the topic, two and a half times as many favoured the new law as opposed it. Again, Ukrainian law-makers appear to have been legislating in line with popular opinion.

Overall there is little evidence that PR had a significant impact on the basic partisan balance in parliament between left and right.[31] It did, however, benefit centrist parties (which had been hesitant to adopt it): four of the eight parties that crossed the threshold were from this portion of the political spectrum. It also served to give parties a greater role in parliamentary deliberations and, at least for a time, to give parliament a more clear-cut structure.

1998–2001: parties versus the president

Following the 1998 elections, feeling grew among Ukraine's parties that greater proportionality would be desirable. This was partly because there were now 225 deputies who had been elected through party lists, and also because the 1998 election had demonstrated that, contrary to expectations, centrist parties could do quite well out of a proportional system. The centrist sector of the political spectrum had previously been dominated by independents and those with weak party attachments, but the demonstrated ability of centrist parties to pull list votes altered perceptions of electoral possibilities. Moreover, the fragmenting tendency of the single-member system became even more evident as representatives of 22 parties were elected through this mechanism as opposed to only eight parties from the list portion of the ballot. The protracted debate that ensued between the spring of 1998 and the eventual adoption of a new election law in October 2001 was instructive in its revelations about the development of three of the fledgling state's new institutions: the parliament, the presidency and the party system.

It was becoming increasingly clear that as the party system became stronger, it was posing a threat to the presidency of Leonid Kuchma. Kuchma initially gave his tentative support to the adoption of a proportional law, evidently in the belief that it would generate a parliamentary majority with which he could work.[32] He in any case hoped to bring about constitutional amendments to create a bicameral parliament with an upper chamber over which he hoped to have more control. In early 2001 head of the Presidential Administration, Volodymyr Lytvyn, and the president's representative in parliament Roman Bezsmertnyi, were still talking of the conditions under which a fully proportional system might be introduced.[33] Yet when opposition to his policies began to mount and when it became increasingly clear that the constitutional changes would not be realized, Kuchma made strenuous – and ultimately successful efforts – to retain the basic principles of the mixed system currently in force.

During the period following the 1998 polls most of the main parties declared their preference for a fully proportional law. Oleksandr Lavrynovych of Rukh favoured exploring variations of PR, including regional districts and preferential voting.[34] Deputy leader of the centrist Hromada party (later leader of the Fatherland party) Julia Tymoshenko also voiced her party's support for full PR on the grounds that single-member districts are 'bought', whereas proportional representation generates real competition among parties.[35]

Because the 1998 law on elections had been ruled unconstitutional by the Constitutional Court, the passage of a new law was once again an imperative rather than a choice. As during the period following the 1994 elections, much criticism of the existing electoral law focused on its failure to serve its primary function of electing a parliament in an orderly fashion.[36] The drawn-out legal challenge to both the 1997 law and the electoral process grounded in it generated a number of procedural recommendations from legal and electoral specialists. The Central Election Commission prepared a draft based on a series of technical changes to bring the law into line with the Constitutional Court's ruling and to address several of the criticisms levelled at electoral administrative procedures by international bodies such as the Council of Europe and the OSCE.[37]

Several other new drafts were also registered for consideration by the Rada in October 1998. The Committee on State-building and Local Government made a decision to bring the electoral law to a plenary session in June 1999, taking as its bill a fully proportional draft developed by Communist party members Heorhii Ponomarkenko and Anatolii Peihaleinen together with presidential representative Bezsmertnyi of the centrist Popular Democratic Party. The draft called for a fully proportional system in a single state-wide district. It also reflected greater attention to procedural aspects of the electoral process. Amid widespread fears of malfeasance, administrative issues took on increased significance. Allegations of fraud in both the presidential elections of 1999 and a referendum on constitutional changes held at the prompting of the president in April 2000 made legislators keen to reinforce the law with measures to prevent the abuse of 'administrative resources'.

Opponents of the bill, who favoured retention of the existing mixed system, were mainly members of centrist factions allied with the president – Working Ukraine, Rebirth of the Regions, Solidarity and the Social Democratic Party (united), only one of which (the Social Democrats) had been formed on the basis of a party that had crossed the 4 per cent threshold in 1998. On 18 November 1999 the Rada adopted the PR draft on the first reading, at the same time rejecting alternative proposals. At this point the bill languished for over a year; it was finally passed on second reading in January 2001.

Over the course of the following nine months President Kuchma vetoed the law five times before a semi-proportional law similar to the existing law was finally agreed on 30 October, once again just in time to begin preparations for the March 2002 elections. The first presidential veto, delivered as late as possible on 19 February, was accompanied by a nine-page document justifying the president's decision on the grounds that the draft violated the Ukrainian constitution. The gist of the argument was that the law gave undue powers to political parties by giving them sole right of nomination and enhanced powers over aspects of electoral administration.[38] Critics of the president argued that the real reason for his veto was the fact that the PR law limited the opportunity of regional governors and local political bosses loyal to the president to influence the electoral process through the deployment (and abuse) of state resources.[39] The Rada made several revisions to the bill without altering its underlying structure, but the new version too succumbed to a presidential veto which parliament was unable to override. In June the Rada passed a draft based on a 75 per cent PR, 25 per cent single-member split (335 seats to 115). This too was rejected by Kuchma, as was a slightly amended version passed the following week. The fourth veto – dubbed the 'Anti-Party Manifesto' by analysts critical of the president[40] – was issued on 14 August but without proposing any changes. The main bone of contention remained the relative proportion of single-member and list seats; the president let it be known that he would not accept any bill that provided for fewer than 50 per cent single-member districts.

Time was fast running out, and any reforms were seen as preferable to conducting the elections on the basis of the existing law (which had in any case been judged unconstitutional). After the Rada again tried unsuccessfully to override Kuchma's veto, the pro-PR groups saw that they were unlikely to gather the necessary two-thirds majority to increase the proportion of PR seats. They agreed (230 to 113) to a revised version of the bill maintaining the 50/50 split between single-member and list seats in order to guarantee that reforms of electoral administration would be enacted. These included the inclusion of party representatives on electoral commissions and tighter campaign finance regulations, the centralized printing of ballots and the mandatory distribution of electoral results to observers at polling-station level.

On 4 October Kuchma unexpectedly vetoed the law for a fifth time, citing the length of the official campaign period (the bill stipulated 170 days, whereas his preference was for a 90-day campaign) and party control over the formation of electoral commissions. He also again suggested that non-party citizens have the right to nominate candidates and proposed that official observers be in charge of monitoring the electoral process. These were perceived as moves enabling him to gain leverage over that process through the mobilization of the extensive patronage-based grassroots support built up during his time in office. Had the full 170-day campaign period been agreed, preparations for the elections would have had to begin on 12 October, so one of Kuchma's key demands – the reduction of the campaign period – was bound at this point to be adopted.

A deal was thrashed out between president and a group of 11 right-wing and centrist factions on 17 October calling for a 90-day campaign period, the replacement of signature-collection by monetary deposits to secure candidate registration, and the right to participation in local election commissions of parties that currently had factions in parliament as well as those that had passed the 4 per cent list threshold at the previous elections (16 in total), with participation by other parties to be regulated by lot. In return the president agreed to withdraw his demand that the selection of domestic observers be regulated through an official process and include local government administrators, and the stipulation that only parties registered at least a year prior to the elections be allowed to participate. On 18 October the Rada passed a draft based on the agreement by 234 to 123; the opponents were made up largely of Communists, the Socialists and the Fatherland faction. Finally, on 30 October, Kuchma signed the law. At the same time he suggested further changes; these and other alterations were considered by the Rada, though only minor amendments were made.[41]

In sum, each modification made to the electoral bill during its tortuous birth between January and October 2001 brought it closer in form to the proposals of the president. Kuchma made full use of his strong bargaining position, content in the knowledge that his opponents would not be able to muster the necessary two-thirds majority to override his veto. His repeated vetoes served to delay the process until the last possible moment, when deputies were obliged to accede to his demands in exchange for minor improvements over the existing law. Criticism of parties and the powers given to them in the electoral process proved a convenient populist device through which Kuchma was able to exploit mistrust of organized politics.

Conclusion

The central place of political parties in competitive democratic politics was determined in most countries during the immediate post-communist transition. In Ukraine the proper role of parties was still being debated ten years after independence, and this debate was at the heart of deliberations over electoral reform. Each side in this debate accused the other of being a throwback to the *ancien régime*. For advocates of proportional representation, single-member districts were associated with the Soviet mechanism of mobilization and non-competitive politics, whereas for defenders of this system the supremacy of parties over politics harked back to the dominance of the CPSU in Soviet political life. Party leaders – especially the leaders of large parties – tended to argue for an electoral system that would make it possible to form an ideologically cohesive majority in parliament. This they saw as the likely result of proportional representation.

Other states in the region provided the main points of reference in discussions of electoral system design – especially Poland and Russia, with which Ukraine shares the greatest cultural and linguistic affinities. Though mention was made of Western European and North American countries during debates, there was often a sense that the political circumstances of post-communism meant that electoral laws would not function in the same way in Ukraine as they functioned in established democracies, and that Ukraine had different needs. In many senses this perceptual horizon limited the design elements that were on the menu in Ukraine. For example, the alternative vote system was never considered, despite the strong preference among many deputies to have both an absolute majority outcome and an electoral system capable of forming the entire parliament in a single day. Interestingly, a compensatory mixed system was also never seriously considered, despite Ukraine's proximity to Hungary, and despite the fact that German experts provided the Rada with advice. The Slavic parallel-mixed systems employed in Bulgaria, Russia, Lithuania and Croatia provided the most relevant examples for Ukrainian electoral system designers. As far as direct advice from foreign actors is concerned, expert advice sponsored by the Organization for Security and Cooperation in Europe, the International Foundation for Electoral Systems, the United States Agency for International Development, the National Democratic Institute, the Friedrich Ebert Stiftung and other organizations served mainly to improve the technical aspects of electoral administrative procedures.

Within the perceptual context established by electoral experience in Ukraine and elsewhere in the region, the dynamics of electoral reform were played out in terms of the changing interests of political actors. As parliamentarians became increasingly integrated into political parties, their perceptions of their interests began to reflect those of their parties. This rise in the prominence of parties in parliament was counterbalanced by the powers of patronage vested in the president and his administration. The ongoing conflict between these two types of power base resulted in a hybrid mixed electoral system which proved, as in Russia, resistant to change, despite the fact that it was the preferred option of very few. Electoral reform in Ukraine was thus caught up in larger questions of the nature of the new Ukrainian political system; at the same time evolving electoral institutions served to shape both actors and perceptions.

9
Conclusion: Embodying Democracy

The transition from communism to market democracy brought about a fundamental reconception of political representation, reflected in the wave of electoral reforms that swept the Central and Eastern European region during the early post-transition years. While the communist understanding of representation focused largely on the proportional inclusion of different sectors of society, this was transmuted in post-communist conceptions of democratic representation into a desire for fair competition among political parties. In electoral system terms, this conceptual shift was reflected in a move in institutional design principles from a commitment to demographic proportionality toward a widespread, if still not universal, belief in partisan proportionality.

None of the post-communist countries of Central Europe and the former Soviet Union democratized without some use of party lists, whether in mixed systems or through proportional representation for the lower or single chamber of its national legislature. Of the 2681 legislative seats in the eight states, 2055 – 76.65 per cent – were designed to be chosen by means of some form of proportional representation by the close of 2001. The average proportion of list seats in 18 post-communist Central and Eastern Europe states rose from 70 per cent at the start of the transition to 81 per cent ten years later (see Table 9.1).

Four of the eight states studied here initially adopted proportional representation for their sole or dominant chamber. The Czech Republic, Slovakia, Romania and Poland thus moved furthest from the majoritarian system of the communist period. Hungary adopted a mixed-linked and Russia and Bulgaria mixed-parallel systems, while Ukraine initially retained its single-member electoral law. The most radical changes following the first free elections occurred in Bulgaria, with the adoption of proportional representation, and Ukraine, which shifted to a mixed system. A strong impetus to majoritarianism in the Czech Republic and Romania found echoes in Poland but was nowhere to bear fruit. Hungary, Russia and Romania demonstrated marked stability, though Hungary joined Romania, Poland, the Czech Republic and Slovakia in adjusting its electoral threshold (see Table 9.1). Yet seat allocation formulae were not the only topic that occupied the minds of electoral engineers in the post-transition states, as each country reacted to institutional change according to the specific features of its own transition. In understanding electoral reform and the outcomes that resulted, it is therefore necessary to consider both the common characteristics of post-communism, as well as the idiosyncratic factors within each country that shaped the perceptions and goals of the actors involved. This final chapter draws together the strands of the analyses developed in the individual country studies in an effort to explain both the electoral reform process and its outcomes.

Table 9.1 Electoral laws in post-communist Europe: patterns in variation among regions and over time

Country	First electoral law used for fully-competitive multi-party elections	Electoral law as of 31 January 2002
Poland	PR	PR
Hungary	**Mixed, 54% PR**	**Mixed, 54% PR**
Czech Republic	PR	PR
Slovakia	PR	PR
Romania	PR	PR
Bulgaria	**Mixed, 50% PR**	PR
Russia	**Mixed, 50% PR**	**Mixed, 50% PR**
Ukraine	SMD	**Mixed, 50% PR**
Albania	SMD	Mixed, 26% PR
Bosnia	PR	PR
Croatia	Mixed, 54% PR	PR
Estonia	PR	PR
Latvia	PR	PR
Lithuania	Mixed, 50% PR	Mixed, 50% PR
Macedonia	SMD	Mixed, 29% PR
Moldova	PR	PR
Slovenia	PR	PR
Yugoslavia	PR	PR
Average proportion of list PR seats	70% **(69%)**	81% **(82%)**

Characterizing the process of post-communist electoral reform

Understanding the electoral reform process in the post-communist setting is key to an appreciation of what makes that setting unique and of how the context of post-communism affected electoral outcomes. It is also of interest in and of itself. There were substantial variations in the electoral reform dynamics among these eight countries, reflecting the emergence of political patterns that varied considerably in terms of stability, consensus and the potential for further democratic reform. Of interest is how we may characterize these differences and what role they played in structuring the process of institutional design.

A second relevant question concerns variations in the extent of reform among our eight cases. We argued in the introduction that useful distinctions might be made between the reasons for change at the outset, the reasons why change took specific forms, and why systems persisted or did not. Why did some systems become locked in at an early stage while others remained in flux?

The zero-stage reform process

At the initial 'zero-stage', the post-communist electoral design process was characterized by the decision-making fora in which it took place, by the major actors involved, and by the issues that formed the centre of debate. This was the period when elites embraced, at least formally, the democratic *Zeitgeist* and embarked on the new state-building project of political transformation.

The decision-making fora

One of the key features of the zero-stage electoral reforms was the fact that most of the 'founding' electoral systems were chosen through extra-constitutional means. The initial electoral laws were shaped within three distinct institutional contexts: round-table discussions between ruling communist elites and opposition forces (Hungary and Bulgaria); informal discussions resulting in electoral legislation by decree (Romania and Russia); and ordinary parliamentary debates (Czechoslovakia, Ukraine and Poland in 1991).

The extra-constitutional round-table was the modal design forum among the countries examined here (though not the modal forum within a wider set of post-communist states). The round-table format used in Poland proved a useful device readily adopted elsewhere in Central Europe. However, Poland was exceptional in that the Round Table did not aim to generate a law for fully competitive elections. The Polish Round Table was the analogue of elite decisions in the Soviet Union in 1989 and 1990 to permit more extensive political competition within the framework of socialist pluralism. In both Hungary and Bulgaria, however, the Round Tables were genuine negotiating arenas whose brief was (among other things) to provide an electoral law ensuring free, competitive elections; and in both cases the (ex)communists began the negotiations from a position of dominance. In Hungary, however, the course of the round-table negotiations was characterized by a shift in the relative strength of the bargainers from the MSzMP to the opposition, which placed its own stamp firmly on the outcome. Moreover, the requirement for legal ratification also gave scope to parliament, increasing the proportion of single-member districts agreed at the Round Table in accord with its own strong preference for personal territorial representation. In Bulgaria, where the opposition was new and inchoate, the Communists (soon renamed the Socialist Party) were in a position of overwhelming dominance; but paradoxically, the opposition gained strength from its weakness. Needed by the communists as an electoral competitor, the opposition effectively threatened to boycott the elections and won considerable concessions as a result.

The initial electoral laws adopted in Romania and Russia were instituted by decree following violent confrontations, though under rather different circumstances in the two cases. In Romania the character of the Ceauşescu regime continued to make itself felt in the role of the (ex)communist-dominated Council of the National Salvation Front. Although the composition of both the Council and the Provisional Assembly was more heterogeneous than is often thought, the lack of organized opposition prior to December 1989 meant the absence of a convincing interlocutor for the Front. The Front remained the dominant, if not altogether unified, political actor. It withdrew from its original preference for a two-round majoritarian system and a contingent of non-elected members because of criticism, both in the press and from the newly emerging proto-parties. As in Bulgaria, the FSN needed to ensure parliamentary representation for the opposition to confirm Romania's new democratic credentials. However, internal divisions, inexperience and a broad lack of knowledge of electoral systems also made the persuasiveness of individuals important, above all Ion Iliescu but also the Liberal leader Câmpeanu.

Both Russia and Ukraine shared common problems of embarking on independent statehood with the inherited structures of the late-Soviet regime largely intact. Although the Soviet republic elections of 1990 allowed more scope for political competition than hitherto, communists of various shades dominated the republican parliaments, transmuted in late 1991 into the parliaments of independent Russia and Ukraine respectively. But in Russia, unlike in Ukraine, confrontation between the executive and legislative branches of power led to an executive coup, during which President Boris Yeltsin dissolved the parliament and called for elections. The provisions governing these elections were established in a series of decrees reflecting continuing deliberations among his entourage of advisers.

Parliament served as the main forum for deliberation in the other cases (as it did in most of the post-communist cases not studied in this volume). Czechoslovakia was, however, something of a hybrid case. Although the Round Table device was used here, it did not provide a genuine negotiating forum. The decision to opt for proportional representation was effectively taken by an inner core of the dominant opposition organization, Civic Forum/Public against Violence. As in Bulgaria, the strongest political force (here the opposition rather than the incumbents) aimed at not only a 'fair' system embodying pluralist principles of representation, but one in which responsibility for future difficulties would be shared. Consultations with other political parties in two special round-table discussions in January 1990 were unproblematic. Firstly, PR suited small and new parties and secondly – as elsewhere – the electoral law was viewed as a provisional one for the first free elections. The new law could also claim historical legitimacy, with its basis in the law of 1946.

In Ukraine, by contrast, the old guard retained its dominance, albeit with a new gloss of nationalist rhetoric following the failed August coup in the USSR. When Kravchuk was elected Ukrainian president in December 1991, he was determined to defend the new state, but he had difficulty assuaging the multiple interests that threatened it. As the economy deteriorated, neither parliament nor the president pressed for speedy elections. Ukraine was therefore distinctive in that a still-conservative and rather fluid parliament was the forum in which was decided the nature of the law governing its first free, fully competitive elections, and in largely retaining the old late-Soviet law. The process was marred, however, by ambiguity as to the proper procedure for passing the law, with a number of law-makers crying foul when the law was passed by an absolute rather than the required super-majority.

Although Poland had been the first to inaugurate the transformation of the communist system, this in itself delayed the process of determining a fully democratic electoral law. Despite the skewed composition of the Sejm in favour of the communists and other establishment parties, the Round Table parliament (June 1989–October 1991) was fully committed to electoral reform, but new legislation had to compete for parliamentary time with a panoply of other system-transforming legislative measures. It was this parliament that provided the chief decision-making forum, and the architects of electoral reform had the full benefit of the parliamentary infrastructure for their ground-laying work through the committee system. Rapidly, however, the Sejm found itself locked in battle with President Lech Wałęsa, who was determined to impose his own variant of the electoral law. The Sejm won the ensuing institutional battle at the price of a tolerable, but unsatisfying compromise.

The diversity of the crucibles in which the founding electoral laws took shape attests to the importance of transition-related factors at this stage of the reform trajectory. Country-specific features loomed large in this domain, though events in the leaders – Poland and Hungary – were watched closely by those who followed. Democracy was everywhere on the agenda, but the nature, experience and short-term interests of key actors were far from identical.

The decision-makers

Two attributes of the decision-makers involved in electoral reform stand out: firstly, they were heterogeneous, and secondly, they were shaped as actors by the very laws they constructed. Political parties were initially inchoate in most cases, as communism had remained hostile to pluralism until the bitter end, and elections played an important role in promoting party development.

The actors involved in reforming electoral systems were heterogeneous in the sense that the allegiance of individuals to collective political organizations was neither uniform nor consistent. Even within the same state at the same time, some parties were coherent enough to function as unitary actors (especially the communist successor parties), whereas other parties were loosely organized groups with little coercive power over their members, and many politicians acted largely on their own. In some cases institutions also functioned as actors when individuals perceived their interests as members of parliament or as allies of the president as more important than incipient partisan affiliation. Support for the president was particularly important in the two countries with the strongest presidents, namely Russia and Ukraine; but it was also a factor for a brief period in Poland.

The heterogeneity of the decision-makers involved in electoral-system design debates contributed to the formative character of that process. This meant that actors (and by definition the preferences of those actors) were endogenous, and also that the factors and forces relevant to the decision calculus varied over the course of the period under investigation. During the founding period actors were often neither stable nor coherent; allegiances of individuals to particular party organizations tended to be conditional and contingent. But as time wore on, many political parties became more well-defined political actors, some demonstrating considerable cohesion and discipline and clearly responding to the incentives of the electoral system. At the same time, electoral laws contributed to stabilization by presenting barriers to entry and reinforcing the cartel of victors, though they did not necessarily inhibit party tourism *within* the cartel. As a result, new parties continued to emerge largely through splits and mergers among parliamentary parties. The reach of the electoral system's opportunity structure was therefore limited, and the occasional breakthrough (such as Simeon's movement in Bulgaria and Self-Defence in Poland in 2001) was still easier than in 'mature' democracies. The shaping of electoral laws and the shaping of political parties were thus interlinked processes that exhibited reciprocal causal interaction but not causal determinism.

Interestingly, the endogeneity of actor formation was a focus of debate in many of the countries studied here. In Russia and Ukraine, the effect of the electoral law on party development was a major consideration in discussions of the respective laws. In Czechoslovakia the strengthening of parties was the concern that set the main parties against President Havel's proposal for the supplementary vote in 1991. President Wałęsa favoured closed lists to promote party development in Poland. This demonstrates that actors had some understanding of the *general* consequences of electoral systems vis-à-vis party system development. Yet they were often mistaken when it came to the specifics of how laws would affect individual political groups and this hampered their ability to craft electoral institutions to suit their immediate political ends. The danger of selective party promotion is that by trying to help certain parties, the electoral system might inadvertently help others. Czechoslovak politicians discovered this in 1992, when the various thresholds meant to keep out anti-federal parties instead disqualified a range of pro-federal, liberal micro-parties, and in 1993 the success of Zhirinovskii's nationalists confounded Russia's electoral architects.

The issues

In Hungary, Czechoslovakia, Romania and Bulgaria in 1990, in Poland in 1991 and in Russia and Ukraine in 1993 the basic architecture of the electoral system formed the main issue of contention. In Hungary the principle of a mixed system was accepted early on in the negotiations, but the ruling MSzMP initially favoured a far stronger single-member element (over 80 per cent) than the opposition, which endorsed a fifty-fifty split as part of its own internal compromise. In Czechoslovakia the arguments took place largely within Civic Forum/Public against Violence, with minority but vocal advocacy of a majoritarian system. In Bulgaria the BSP favoured a parallel-mixed system with a preponderance of the single-member element (175/75), while the opposition SDS bargained for a larger number of PR seats. The biggest shift came in Romania, where the dominant FSN preferred a majoritarian system but agreed to proportional representation, favoured by the resurgent but weak historic parties, to ensure its own legitimacy and that of the election. In Poland the main divisions were between those who favoured a mixed system (whether linked or parallel) and those endorsing proportional representation. The president held both views: he supported a parallel-mixed system, but moved rapidly to support PR.

Consciousness of systemic factors – notably questions of legitimacy, the quality of representation and how far the system should promote the development of political parties – was everywhere apparent. In a climate of suspicion, if not hostility to 'party', where new parties were weak and largely unknown, this was not a trivial concern. Those who argued that voters should have a personal choice of deputy through single-member districts were not necessarily articulating naked self-interest. A stress on the quality of representation, part of the ideology of Soviet-style 'socialist democracy', found strong echoes in this context, not solely (and not always) among communists and their successors. Within the opposition movement Civic Forum in the Czech Lands prominent voices advocated a single-member system to provide greater opportunities for independents and many saw PR as but a temporary expedient. In Ukraine stances were reversed, with PR seen by the left and the moveable 'swamp' of deputies as desirable in the future when parties were more developed. New liberal parties in Poland and Hungary, the Democratic Union and the Alliance of Free Democrats, endorsed the mixed system as the best means of providing personal representation while also fostering the development of political parties.

The issues specific to subsequent debates depended partly on mutual assessments of final negotiating positions, partly on trade-offs over other institutional disputes, partly on the degree of consensus. In Romania, Bulgaria and Ukraine debates also displayed a sensitivity to the perceptions of the international community, including those of future election observers. These three countries, along with Russia, were most explicitly concerned with the legitimacy of the system, including issues of corruption and electoral administration.

In Hungary after broad agreement was reached on a mixed system, compromises were piecemeal and cumulative. The Socialist Workers' Party accepted a fifty-fifty split of single-member and PR seats as it saw its own support eroding rapidly, but its addition of a third tier of national compensation seats was gained at the cost of a regional basis for the initial PR allocation. The issue of second-round entrants in single-member contests became enormously contentious, however, as the MSzMP feared huge losses in two-candidate run-offs. In the end the opposition finally acknowledged that no compromise could be extracted, but in turn it gained concessions on aggregating both unused list and losing first-round single-member votes for national tier allocation.

In Romania controversies over whether to define the system as 'multi-party' or 'pluralist', the restoration of interwar provisions for non-elected senators and distinctive proposals for minority representation found few echoes elsewhere, though the Hungarian parliament also raised issues of minority and church representation. In Ukraine traditional workplace-based nomination remained one of the most contentious elements of electoral reform. This was clearly linked to the power bases of the old but still dominant *nomenklatura*. In Poland this issue was less prominent, and it was the Solidarity trade union that was most concerned to retain the right to put up candidates: Solidarity was strong enough to keep the right of nomination by social organizations intact until the constitutional settlement of 1997.

In Czechoslovakia and Bulgaria major second-order disputes were conspicuous by their absence, and once they had agreed to PR and a mixed system respectively, other issues were easily settled. In the Czechoslovak case, using the 1946 law as a basis for discussion provided an easy route to agreement, given the need for speedy passage of a new law. In Bulgaria and Ukraine timing of elections was also a factor, and in Poland too the need to comply with the 1991 election timetable finally secured sufficient parliamentary unity to override the second presidential veto of the electoral law.

The first electoral reform experiences in the post-communist states were characterized by variety in decision-making fora, in the range of relevant actors and in the issues that dominated debates. The circumstances under which communism had collapsed were crucial in structuring the dynamics of elite interactions, and conjunctural factors thus played a major role in shaping the institutional design process.

Post-zero-stage: change within a new political system

Our cases provide limited evidence for the notion that, once in place, electoral systems become part of a set of self-reinforcing institutional structures. Virtually all of the founding electoral systems were viewed as transitional by their framers, yet subsequent changes were often less extensive than had been expected. Those countries that made the most radical shift at the outset, that is to proportional representation, subsequently retained it (if not without challenge). This applied also to the Czech Republic and Slovakia, whose republican parliaments – now the parliaments of independent states – had been elected by PR in the second free Czechoslovak elections of 1992. Poland and Romania maintained proportional representation. Russia and Hungary also retained their mixed systems. This relative stasis is perhaps all the more surprising given the rapid changes taking place in other aspects of the institutional architecture of the states in question. This meant that there were in many cases formal requirements for change, because the initial law had been passed by decree (Romania and Russia), because the body elected in the founding election was a temporary one (Bulgaria), because of changes to the constitution (Poland and Ukraine), or because of constitutional court judgements (the Czech Republic and Ukraine). These requirements had an 'unlocking' effect, yet the alterations thereby generated were not in all cases extensive.

In two countries, Bulgaria and Ukraine, the type of system did change radically. The Bulgarian round-table negotiators were explicitly negotiating a provisional electoral law; but the continuing dominance of the BSP raises the question of why change took place when the decision-making arena shifted to parliament. In fact the shift from a mixed parallel system to closed-list proportional representation was unproblematic. Allegations of irregularities in 1990 led to a concern to ensure clean elections. Single-member constituencies were believed to be part of the problem, and the Union of Democratic Forces (SDS) rejected them decisively, threatening to boycott elections if they were retained. The unity of the SDS was fraying badly, so protestations of principle also served their own interests. At the same time the BSP leadership no longer held the presidency, which it had yielded to SDS leader Zhelyu Zhelev after the discrediting of President Mladenov. The 'hungry winter' of 1990–1 and continuing economic deterioration undermined the BSP's claim to competence. Proportional representation looked attractive, enabling a party to win seats commensurate with support, while closed lists would undermine the entrenched power of local *apparatchiki*. Two major actors with congruent interests led to early agreement, but not enduring consensus, for the BSP reasserted its mixed-system preference in 1994.

In Ukraine the shift to a mixed system in 1997 was prompted by a similar move in Russia, which showed a hitherto recalcitrant left that it could benefit from proportional representation. Two further factors contributed to the change: the growing organizational strength of parties within parliamentary structures and a near-universal perception that the single-member system employed in 1994 had failed to serve the new state's needs. Thus in both Bulgaria and Ukraine single-member districts were associated with the discredited socialist system and their removal/reduction was seen as a victory for the 'democratic' right. In both cases also the (ex-)communist left agreed to an increase or introduction of list seats when experience demonstrated that it would not hurt them electorally.

However, the balance sheet of two changed systems and six intact by 2001 certainly overestimates the extent to which electoral systems had begun to be locked in. It also raises the question of what types of changes should be regarded as significant, not least because the differences between types of systems are far from absolute. Even the time-honoured dichotomy between majoritarian and proportional systems depends crucially on district magnitude, legal thresholds, allocation formulae and type of ballot structure.[1]

Three situations pertained in the six countries which maintained the basic shape of their electoral laws. Firstly, there was one case (Hungary) where change was absent because there was no realistic chance of achieving it, despite a general air of dissatisfaction in many circles: Hungary still had no final constitutional settlement, and many proposals were mooted for further institutional development, such as a second chamber or a smaller parliament, with potential implications for electoral reform. Secondly, there were cases where significant change was desired by many, but not sufficiently many to bring it about; tinkering with elements of the existing system was the most that could be achieved given the constellation of political forces (the Czech Republic to 2002, Slovakia, Romania and Russia). Thirdly, there were two cases where considerable change was wrought within the confines of the basic electoral architecture (Poland in 1993 and 2001 and the Czech Republic in 2002).

Lack of impetus to change is easier to identify, if not necessarily to explain. All countries faced problems arising from inadequate drafting of laws. This was a universal feature of the transition process, with complex legislation requiring subsequent amendment to remedy technical inadequacies or to remove inadvertent gaps and 'accidental' provisions. Leaving these aside, both Hungary and Russia maintained their new electoral laws virtually intact. Though Hungary raised its threshold by 1 per cent, the complex round-table law remained in all its glorious complexity. One reason stemmed from the need to mobilize a two-thirds parliamentary majority for electoral reform, thus preventing even the strongest single party from imposing change. Moreover, even when the two Hungarian governing parties agreed to increased PR thresholds for electorally allied parties in an effort to damage their opponents, the latter simply bypassed the new provisions. Another explanation lies in the lack of political problems that could (with some plausibility) be 'fixed' by changes in the electoral system: in particular, Hungarian parliaments and governments served their full terms, despite numerous intra-coalition tensions and party splintering. Thirdly, although the system was arcane and unpredictable in many respects, tampering with complex, interrelated elements was equally likely to generate unpredictable outcomes. Finally, both elites and parties appeared to 'learn' and display adaptive behaviour, with successive elections creating a sense of familiarity and thus conveying a legitimacy upon this strange creation.[2] Some elements clearly suited the stronger political parties; the mixture of single-member and PR districts itself created opportunities for different candidate-selection strategies, with the safeguard (for parties) of the national list.

In Russia the design of the mixed system was the product of lengthy debate among a narrow group of presidential advisers. But following the 1993 elections, President Yeltsin fought a losing battle to increase the proportion of single-member districts in the Duma in order to capitalize on the local support bases he had built up through patronage. As in Ukraine, organized political parties were perceived to be a threat by the non-partisan president, and a reduction in the PR component of the electoral system was seen as the most effective way of preventing parties from growing in strength. But Yeltsin never managed to convince the party-dominated Duma, and post-1993 changes to the electoral law were mainly confined to a minor increase in regional identity on the party lists and reform of campaign finance regulation.

In Romania too only thresholds changed, albeit more substantially than in Hungary: first to 3 per cent in 1992, then by government decree just before the 2000 elections to 5 per cent for parties and 8–10 per cent for alliances. Electoral reform was indeed desired by many, not least the remnants of the old guard who hankered for a return to communist-style representation through single-member districts. However, change remained hampered by the persistence of features characterizing the earliest stages of democratic transition: conflicts of jurisdiction, magnified by the comparable, duplicating powers of the Senate and the Chamber of Deputies; fluid parties, with perennial splits and mergers and fluctuations in electoral support; conflicts between individual and party preferences; and concerns with legitimacy. It was not until 2001 that a rather improbable, and not necessarily enduring, consensus appeared to emerge, with the minority government finding support for majoritarianism among those who aspired to be the second party of the putative two-party system that would develop as a result. Indeed, the Romanian case highlights the common if misguided tendency to seek solutions to perceived political problems through changes in the electoral law.

In Romania the main problem was deemed to be failings in the 'quality of representation'. In both the Czech Republic and Slovakia key actors also desired fundamental change, but they failed to achieve the less proportional regime sought allegedly to resolve problems of government formation. In each case the strongest party sought changes to further strengthen its position with a push to majoritarianism, also presented here as a response to a major dysfunction of the existing system. In the Czech Republic the ODS found a (semi-)willing partner in the Social Democrats, while in Slovakia the Movement for Democratic Slovakia (HZDS) had no such ally. Mečiar, the most popular Slovak politician, already advocated a majoritarian (failing that a mixed) system in 1995 on the grounds that the 5 per cent threshold was not enough to ensure a 'manageable' number of parties. However, his small coalition partners were understandably resistant, so Mečiar demonstrated his opportunism by increasing proportionality with the institution of a single national district, while seeking to penalize his opponents with the application of the 5 per cent threshold to each party within an electoral alliance. As in Hungary, parties seeking alliance responded by making the (individual party) threshold redundant, when they formally constituted themselves as unified entities rather than electoral coalitions. After 1998 the controversial threshold provision was revoked but continuing debate over the shape of electoral districts left the single national district intact.

In the Czech Republic major elements of the largest party to 1998, the ODS, had initially preferred a majoritarian system, along with many other actors for whom PR was seen as second best in the longer term. In 1995 ODS leader Klaus still seemed content, having won in 1990 (as Civic Forum) and in 1992. He changed his tune following his failure to form a majority government after the 1996 election, and subsequently reached agreement with the (similarly minority) new governing party, the Social Democrats, in the 'historic compromise' of 1998. The changes were presented as a means of dealing with a putative consequence of the electoral system, namely difficulties of coalition-building. They represented rather transparent efforts to limit competition and strengthen the then two largest parties, namely themselves. In the Czech case, however, a major institutional constraint existed in the constitutional requirement for proportional representation. Given this, proponents of change adjusted district magnitude, quotas and thresholds, only to be scuppered by the Constitutional Court's judgement that the cumulative impact of the measures would not accord with the requirement for proportionality. The resulting law of 2002 also altered all three of these elements, as the looming election drove the Senate to concede new provisions.

Poland provided the case of most frequent change of the electoral system within the broad PR framework. There was little sign of institutional inertia; indeed all basic elements of the electoral system were contested throughout the decade, and in 1993 and 2001 significant changes occurred in thresholds, electoral formulae and district magnitude. Changes in the nature and relative strengths of the actors account for these changes, but perceptions of systemic requirements also played a role. The crucial problem in 1991–3 was seen as government formation in the context of a highly fragmented parliament. Unlike the Czech Republic, this was a genuine problem, but arguments about systemic needs dovetailed neatly with the interests of the larger parties. However, these failed to generate the anticipated political alliances, and their cumulative impact gave an unexpectedly large seat premium to the victors in the 1993 election. In 2001 the perceived problem was political rather than structural, namely the overwhelming lead in all opinion polls of the social democrats over all other contenders. The SLD's opponents were able to unite on measures that undermined it, while simultaneously seeking (but largely failing) to improve their own electoral prospects. One element of the electoral law that remained constant was the open list, designed to give voters the choice of an individual in the context of little known parties. Voters made full use of the opportunity, and public opinion was notable in maintaining it, despite a general party preference for a closed-list system.

Though debates over post-founding reforms were conducted largely by those parliamentarians most affected by them, a variety of other institutions also served as active players. This depended in great measure on the constitutional structure of the state and on the proclivity of potential veto players to involve themselves in the process of electoral reform. All eight states considered here have constitutional courts that could in theory have become involved in disputes over the electoral law, so long as there were dissatisfied parties seeking constitutional sanction of their views. Russia and Ukraine have strong executive presidents who intervened in matters of electoral reform, with the Ukrainian president Kuchma holding the record for the number of successive vetoes imposed on electoral legislation. The Romanian and Polish presidents also possess considerable powers, while in the Czech Republic, Slovakia, Hungary and Bulgaria presidents are generally weak. Finally, four of the eight cases have bicameral legislatures with upper houses that could involve themselves in debates over the laws governing the composition of their lower counterparts. The Romanian Senate was active, and the Czech Senate became more involved after 2000, when the balance of power shifted to the non-Klaus opposition and the chamber was used as a springboard for counter-initiatives. The reduction of the Senate's powers in Poland rendered it less able to play a role, though it was active at the outset and continued to offer amendments to each law passed by the Sejm. Elsewhere upper chambers rarely showed any great interest in how lower chambers are elected.

Constitutional courts involved themselves in electoral matters in four cases (the Czech Republic, Slovakia, Russia and Ukraine), while most presidents – executive and non-executive – played some role in legislative electoral debates (the exception being Hungary). Unlike in Poland and Romania, in Russia and Ukraine active presidents invariably came down on at least one occasion on the side of an increase in the proportion of single-member seats in an effort to weaken the grip of parliamentary parties on politics. All in all, the extent of reform appears to be strongly linked to idiosyncratic aspects of the political processes in different countries.

Explaining reform outcomes

We have found that post-communist electoral system design was an iterative, recursive process that both formed political actors and was formed by them. It is thus instructive to consider reform outcomes from both diachronic and synchronic perspectives.

Trends over time

Participants in electoral reform processes were conscious from the start of setting out to construct a legitimate democratic political system.

The most widespread common response was the initial openness of the system. Among the countries considered here, initial limits to party registration and candidature were generally very permissive and often made provisions for multiple channels of access, if not by means of a formal mixed system then by giving nomination rights to different types of organization (see Table 9.2). Low entry barriers, with concomitant free media access, were a sign of democratic credibility.

Table 9.2 Nomination requirements: variations over time

Country	First post-communist legislation		Legislation as of January 2002	
	Who has right of nomination?	*Requirements for nomination*	*Who has right of nomination?*	*Requirements for nomination*
Poland	Parties, political and social organizations, and electors	*District level*: 5000 signatures *Nat. level*: candidates in at least 5 districts	Parties, including coalitions, electors and minority organizations	3000 signatures
Hungary	*SM*: parties, social organizations, coalitions, and electors *MM*: parties and coalitions	*SM*: 750 signatures *NL*: candidates in at least 7 districts	*SM*: parties, social organizations, coalitions, and electors *MM*: parties and coalitions	*SM*: 750 signatures *NL*: candidates in at least 7 districts
Czech Republic	Parties and coalitions	Party must have 10,000 members and/or signatures	Parties and coalitions	Monetary deposit
Slovakia	Parties and coalitions	Party must have 10,000 members and/or signatures	Parties and coalitions	Party must have 10,000 members and/or signatures
Romania	Parties, political groupings and electors	251 members required for registering a party Independents: 251 signatures	Parties, political groupings, alliances and electors	10,000 members required for registering a party Independents: signatures of 0.5% of the electorate in the district
Bulgaria	Parties, social organizations, coalitions and electors	Independents: 500 signatures	Parties, coalitions and electors	Independents: 1100 to 2000 signatures, depending on the district size

Table 9.2   (*continued*)

Country	First post-communist legislation		Legislation as of January 2002	
	Who has right of nomination?	*Requirements for nomination*	*Who has right of nomination?*	*Requirements for nomination*
Russia	*SM*: parties, movements, coalitions and electors *MM*: parties, movements and coalitions	*SM*: signatures of 2% of electorate *MM*: 200,000 signatures	*SM*: parties, movements, coalitions and electors *MM*: parties, movements and coalitions	*SM*: signatures of 1% of electorate (*or* deposit for parties) *MM*: 200,000 signatures *or* deposit and minimum 46 branches of at least 100 members each
Ukraine	Parties and coalitions, social organizations, work collectives, educational institutions, military units and electors	300 signatures, and for parties: approval of 2/3 of branch members or conference delegates, min. 50	*SM*: parties, coalitions and electors *MM*: parties and coalitions	*SM & MM*: monetary deposit

SM: single member. *MM:* multimember
Source: Database on Central and Eastern European Elections at <www.essex.ac.uk/elections>.

Over time there was an increase in barriers to entry for newcomers and advantages to existing political actors which worked to entrench their positions. These did not necessarily take the form of more stringent nominating requirements, although this occurred in some countries. The range of organizations with right of nomination was restricted in Poland, Bulgaria, Russia[3] and Ukraine, and nowhere was it expanded. There were also moves in the Czech Republic, Russia and Ukraine to substitute in place of signatures the requirement for a monetary deposit to secure candidate nomination. Though this change in most cases reflected the logistical exigencies of electoral administration, it also benefited larger political organizations for which the deposit would not represent an overwhelming burden.

Changes in thresholds were another mechanism used to restrict entry (see Table 9.3). There was a rise in the average level lower-tier threshold for single parties from 3.29 per cent in the seven countries with list voting in their founding elections to 4.75 per cent at the close of 2001.

Table 9.3   Constituency design and seat allocation formulae: variations over time

Country	First post-communist legislation			Legislation as of February 2002		
	Size of chamber	Number of districts (lower + upper tiers)	Threshold	Size of chamber	Number of districts (lower + upper tiers)	Threshold
Poland	460	37 + 1	5% for a national list	460	41	5% for a party and 8% for a coalition
Hungary	386	176 + 20 + 1	4%	386	176 + 20 + 1	5%
Czech Republic	200	8	5%	200	14	5% for a party; 10% (alliances of two); 15% (alliances of three); 20% (alliances of four or more)
Slovakia	150	4	3%	150	1	5% for a party, 7% (2–3 parties), 10% (4+ parties)
Romania	387 (+ 9 minority deputies)	41 + 1	None	327 (+ 18 minority deputies)	42 + 1	5% (+ 3% for the second party in a coalition and 1% for each additional party, to a maximum of 10%)
Bulgaria	400	200 + 28	4%	240	31*	4%
Russia	450	225 + 1	5%	450	225 + 1	5%
Ukraine	450	450	N/A	450	225 + 1	4%

*Seat distribution among parties is calculated at the national level.
Source: Database on Central and Eastern European Elections at <www.essex.ac.uk/elections>.

Indeed, when Central and Eastern European states sought to regulate party system size, they usually did so by manipulating thresholds rather than through fiddling with district magnitude. District magnitude can often be more difficult to alter due to the relationship between electoral districts and units of territorial administration.[4] Moreover, changing thresholds forestalls intense conflict as deputies normally battle vigorously for constituencies where they have developed links with local structures.

Such inter-party collusion is not unique to Central and Eastern Europe, yet the region is notable for the rapidity with which restrictions were imposed. As noted above, evidence from the country studies suggests that in many cases these changes were intentionally designed to entrench those political organizations that had succeeded in the initial elections so as to 'strengthen' the party system. In short, electoral reform in the post-communist countries went hand in hand with party system development. Elections, especially those conducted under proportional laws, were a major motor of party development. They were not sufficient to this end, as financing, leadership, personal feuds and even spells in opposition also played vital roles in developing parties. Nonetheless, elections provided a party-mobilizing mechanism. It is not surprising therefore that as parties gained in organizational strength, they introduced measures to further enhance their powers.

Accounting for variations

The overall explanatory model that emerges from this volume is that of a three-stage process of contextualized strategic choice. First, options under consideration were shaped by existing models viewed as relevant by those involved in the reform process. Then perceptions of those options were shaped by the political context, aims and perceptions of the suitability of different institutions to achieve those aims. Finally, disagreements were adjudicated through strategic bargaining among actors who were, as we have seen, often heterogeneous.

Models

At the start of this volume we predicted that historical domestic models would be relevant if a state had a positive electoral experience in the not-too-distant past, especially if there was an urgent need for an electoral law to be adopted. The country studies suggest that, as predicted, historical experience was reflected where there was a usable past and law-makers were under acute time-pressure, as in Czechoslovakia. There were virtually no references to historical precedents during debates over successive electoral laws in Russia and Ukraine, where the majoritarian Soviet model appears to have been the only relevant one in this context. In other contexts historical influences surfaced in unusual ways, such as Bulgaria's stubborn adherence to its costly system of coloured ballots, despite much international pressure for their abolition.

As far as foreign models are concerned, there appears to have been more intra-regional influence than direct influence from models in Western Europe or elsewhere. The German example appeared in Polish, Hungarian and Russian debates but its subtleties were not always appreciated. The Hungarian elections of 1990 provided other states in the region with examples of all three main electoral system types being considered: single-member, proportional and mixed systems. As electoral events unfolded, many institutional engineers kept a close eye on their neighbours. Bulgaria pioneered the parallel-mixed system subsequently adopted elsewhere but there is little evidence of direct Bulgarian influence. Russian influence, however, did appear to affect the debates in Ukraine when it adopted a mixed parallel system. Where foreign models were influential, they were rarely adopted wholesale, but were adapted and transformed through the bargaining process, such that they often had very different effects. Indeed, the role of unintended consequences looms large in our analysis.

Context

The post-communist context was at the outset one of considerable if far from complete uncertainty. Uncertainty proved to be a factor shaping not only the choices made but also their timing. In all cases save the Czechoslovak and Russian, communists or their successors played a significant role in the negotiations, and uncertainty was unevenly distributed. In Bulgaria and Romania the Bulgarian Socialist Party and the (effective but unacknowledged successor) National Salvation Front had good reason to assume an electoral advantage, given the weakness, inexperience and fragmentation of the opposition and the brevity of the opposition's public exposure; this made speedy elections and rapid agreement a priority. In Hungary, where the ruling MSzMP was initially sure of its own continued political dominance, that confidence yielded to anxiety during the lengthy negotiating process, and the MSzMP shifted its stance accordingly. The Polish Social Democrats (SdRP from January 1990) remained the largest single element in the Sejm, but both they and the satellite-successor the Polish Peasant Party (PSL) had gained an appreciation of their rather weak immediate electoral prospects in the presidential elections of 1990. Of the emerging opposition forces, the Hungarian Democratic Forum (MDF) could – certainly by August 1989 – anticipate considerable electoral success. So too could Civic Forum in the Czech Lands and Public against Violence in Slovakia, where the acknowledged architects of the Velvet Revolution faced a myriad of untested resurgent, new and regional entities and the most discredited Communist Party in the region.

The perceived need for legitimacy and party system development generated consensus on many issues of electoral reform. Democracy was viewed as a collective good, and electoral systems outcomes reflected perceptions about the institutional manifestations of democracy. Neutral, transparent and efficient electoral administration, the fair distribution of seats among political contenders and the development of strong parties in a stable, moderate-sized party system were all seen as desirable aims by the vast majority of those involved in the process. They were also, at the outset at least, seen as outcomes yet to be achieved, and therefore as ends to be reached by means of electoral system design. As we have seen, such perceptions had strong formative effects on the evolution of electoral laws in the region and they account in part for the common features of these laws.

Strategic choice

A feature common to electoral reform in all the states considered here is the lack of extensive popular involvement. Provided the electoral system is of little interest to ordinary voters (as is normally the case), the process of electoral system design is relatively isolated from the pressures that often attend public decision-making. This isolation had at least two important consequences. Firstly, it released legislators from the necessity of behaving in such a way that would win public approval, leaving them to pursue their personal interests without fear of bad publicity (especially since their personal career interests were likely to be intimately related to the outcome). Secondly, with few highly emotive issues at stake and little potential for grandstanding and posturing, legislators appeared more inclined to compromise. These two factors both increased the likelihood that the electoral process was the result of bargaining among legislators.

Many standpoints could of course be viewed as interest-based, but the interests of institutions (notably presidents and parliaments) were not always easily separable from the interests of political parties or individuals, while arguments couched in general sociotropic terms often coincided with the interests of the parties, groups or individuals espousing them. In some cases debates in the electoral arena were part of the overall bargaining process over new institutional structures. In Bulgaria the Union of Democratic Forces (SDS) agreed to a variant of the mixed system proposed by the BCP/BSP in exchange for the convening of a constituent assembly instead of an ordinary parliament. Models that suggest a narrow agenda and impute uniform motivations and interests may predict the 'right' answer for the wrong reasons. In most cases collective actors were far from the unified bodies of many rational choice approaches.

Thus explanations in terms of narrow partisan interests explain at once too little and too much. They explain too little because many of the goals of electoral system designers were collective goals: legitimation, the development of an electoral infrastructure that functioned efficiently from a technical point of view and a competitive multi-party system. This last goal provides the key to why narrow partisan interests explain too much, in that they assume cohesive parties when none exist and where individuals may be more oriented toward their personal interests or indeed toward the interests of institutions they seek to defend.

Moreover, self-interested behaviour is not always only about maximizing seats in parliament. Cohesive parties may be able to afford to eschew narrow seat-maximizing strategies in favour of a strategy that will enable them to have a better chance of winning the following elections. This was the case, for example, in Bulgaria and in the Czech Republic, where strong parties favoured electoral systems that they believed would oblige them to enter into coalition, which in turn would allow them to spread the blame for transition-related economic austerity measures. Similarly, qualitative goals may in some cases override quantitative concerns. Bulgaria and Romania are cases where the desire of the ex-communists for legitimacy made them accept a system that was suboptimal in seat-maximizing terms.

The uncertainty characteristic of the post-communist context meant that there was in the initial stage a large gap between perceived and actual interests as indicated by electoral outcomes. This led to many unintended and unexpected outcomes, but it may also have led to more decisions in the interest of the collective good.[5] Uncertainty was severe for new political groups facing early elections with a paucity of organizational and financial resources and lack of name recognition, especially in rural areas. Delayed elections did not necessarily provide a more predictable environment, however. In Poland the number of potential political challengers grew steadily in 1991 as Solidarity disintegrated and new hopefuls appeared. In Russia uncertainties were magnified for all competitors by the plethora of emergency measures linked to the crisis of September 1993. In Ukraine the inconsistent, incoherent institutional relationships inherited from the Soviet regime, the lack of a structured parliament, the strong linkages between elements of the old elite and their local power centres, the re-emergence of the Communist Party after a period of illegality – all provided a context of uncertainty that favoured the conservative option. The Ukrainian parliament was dominated by representatives of the old regime, hesitant and ill informed about electoral systems. This contrasted with the situation in Poland, which was superficially similar: a parliament elected with limited competition dominated by the old establishment. In Poland the old elites made an early commitment to democracy, and the system there had been sufficiently open to provide a familiarity with the implications of change, elites already benefiting from the early introduction of market mechanisms, and scholars knowledgeable about a variety of constitutional and electoral mechanisms.

In other cases uncertainty was compounded by profound ignorance of the likely implications of diverse electoral arrangements. This was particularly evident in Romania, where the closed nature of the communist regime left its mark. There was no pool of available expertise among academics or political parties, no influx of willing foreign advisers and indeed no evidence of a desire to learn. Foreign exemplars were evoked but often misconstrued.

Following the initial tests of electoral strength, parties and other electoral actors had far better grounds on which to base strategic calculations. At the same time, they had less cause to be concerned about demonstrating their democratic credentials. Finally, the newly elected parliaments often proved effective devices for forging party identities. At this stage parties came to be the dominant actors in bargaining over institutional reform. It is interesting to note that strong parties proved particularly susceptible to the apparent charms of majoritarianism as a means of fostering political dualism – ODS in the Czech Republic, Solidarity (AWS) in Poland, Fidesz in Hungary. Such considerations were not absent from the perspectives of social democrats in Romania and the Czech Republic either. The lessons of Ukraine, where single-member districts maximized the survival of local politics, were apparently lost on its neighbours. However, in Poland the social democrats resisted such temptations, preferring adjustments that favoured larger parties within the PR framework. The continuing need to assert their democratic credentials remained stronger than the perceived attractions of majoritarianism.

The gist of the argument presented in Chapter 1 is that in considering electoral system design, political parties will seek both to maximize their seat share and to minimize their potential loss. This will tend to lead them to adopt proportional representation over majoritarian systems, as the former lead to greater predictability in outcomes, which are less costly. Though Hungary was an exception to this rule, it was Hungarian Socialist György Fejti who summed up this approach best when he declared that his party had adopted 'the principle of the smallest risk' (see Chapter 3 above). Following poor performances in founding elections, many opposition parties across the region assumed the same attitude. In various ways electoral system designers sought to spread their potential losses in order to be sure of keeping in the electoral game. Those that had greater confidence in their short-term survivability could afford to play a longer game and think in terms of the overall shape of the political system they were crafting.

Yet it is noteworthy that debates over the underlying principles of system design were not in all cases ones in which the strong favoured majoritarian solutions and the weak advocated proportionality. The foregoing analyses have demonstrated that for electoral reform, the three most relevant characteristics of the initial post-communist transition context were institutional flux, poorly formed and/or heterogeneous actors and high uncertainty. All of these decreased over time, and party interest came to dominate the decision-making process in most cases as parties became stronger and had a better sense of their own interests. At the same time founding elections demonstrated the democratic credentials of states sufficiently for legitimacy to be less of a concern as time wore on.

Electoral system design was accurately viewed by many involved as indirect party system engineering, though in most cases they had an exaggerated belief in their ability to shape the party system. As parties found their place in the political system their perspectives changed, but there remained a strong sense in the rhetoric of reform that the shape of electoral institutions ought to be guided by the demands of the transition. As far as we can tell, this commitment to steering the developing political system in the right direction was genuinely shared by many of the electoral system designers and the goal of maximizing the collective good represented an important supplement to considerations of personal and party-based interest.

Conclusion

Electoral systems during the first decade of post-communist political transformation were shaped by three embedded sets of factors: existing models delineated the range of alternatives considered, contextual factors shaped perceptions of those options by actors, and strategic bargaining determined outcomes within these parameters. Over the course of this ten-year period politicians in the post-communist states learned a great deal about electoral systems. The learning process both enabled them to engage in increasingly strategic behaviour and at the same time it widened the range of design elements that were seriously considered. The electoral systems that emerged from ten years of reform were in most cases a good deal more complex than those used for the first post-communist elections in these countries. And though outside agencies were certainly useful sources of information and expectations, the bulk of the learning was the result of domestic experience, with regional models playing a secondary role.

It is still too early to tell how many of the Central and Eastern European electoral systems have reached a state of equilibrium (or whether indeed they will). There may well be surprises in store if pro-majoritarian factions in any of these states are able to buck the trend toward increasing proportional list voting. Certainly in Poland and Romania electoral reform remained on the agenda. But the first ten years of post-transition electoral system change provided ample evidence of the complexity of institutional design processes and the diversity of factors that are relevant in even a relatively narrow set of similar cases. At the same time we have identified a number of general patterns which characterized the interwoven process of electoral system and party system development in a post-transition context.

Notes

1 Explaining the Design and Redesign of Electoral Systems

1. Dieter Nohlen, 'Changes and Choices in Electoral Systems', in Arend Lijphart and Bernard Grofman (eds), *Choosing an Electoral System: Issues and Alternatives* (New York: Praeger, 1994), p. 218.
2. Josep Colomer, 'Strategies and Outcomes in Eastern Europe', *Journal of Democracy*, vol. 6, no. 2 (1995), p. 84.
3. Karl Marx, *The Civil War in France*, in Robert C. Tucker (ed.), *The Marx-Engels Reader* (New York: W. W. Norton, 1972), p. 554.
4. V. I. Lenin, *The State and Revolution* (London: Penguin, 1992), pp. 38–43.
5. Oliver H. Radkey, *Russia Goes to the Polls: The Election to the All-Russian Constituent Assembly, 1917* (Ithaca, NY and London: Cornell University Press, 1990).
6. J. Arch Getty, 'State and Society under Stalin: Constitutions and Elections in the 1930s', *Slavic Review*, vol. 50, no. 1 (1991), pp. 26–35.
7. This was a mark of the inferior status of the 'People's Republics', which had not yet reached the stage of building socialism and therefore retained vestiges of earlier class politics.
8. For an overview of communist-era electoral systems, see Robert K. Furtak (ed.), *Elections in Socialist States* (New York and London: Harvester Wheatsheaf, 1990).
9. On the USSR see L. G. Churchward, *Contemporary Soviet Government* (London: Routledge & Kegan Paul, 1968), p. 107.
10. R. J. Hill, 'Continuity and Change in USSR Supreme Soviet Elections', *British Journal of Political Science*, vol. 11, no. 1 (1972), pp. 47–67.
11. See W. Hahn, 'Electoral "Choice" in the Soviet Bloc', *Problems of Communism*, vol. 36, no. 2 (March–April 1987), pp. 29–39.
12. Alex Pravda, 'Elections in Communist Party States', in Guy Hermet, Richard Rose and Alain Rouquié (eds), *Elections without Choice* (London: Macmillan, 1978), pp. 186–92; Victor Zaslavsky and Robert J. Brym, 'The Function of Elections in the USSR', *Soviet Studies*, vol. 30, no. 3 (1978), pp. 362–71; Theodore H. Friedgut, *Political Participation in the USSR* (Princeton, NJ: Princeton University Press, 1979), pp. 137–44.
13. Ronald J. Hill, *Soviet Politics, Political Science, and Reform* (Oxford: Martin Robertson, 1980), chapter 2; Stephen White, 'Reforming the Electoral System', *Journal of Communist Studies*, vol. 4, no. 4 (1988), pp. 1–17.
14. J. Hahn, 'An Experiment in Competition: The 1987 Elections to the Local Soviets', *Slavic Review*, vol. 47, no. 3 (1988), pp. 434–47; White, 'Reforming the Electoral System', pp. 1–17.
15. Stephen White, 'The Elections to the USSR Congress of People's Deputies March 1989', *Electoral Studies*, vol. 9, no. 1 (1990), pp. 59–66; Michael Urban, *More Power to the Soviets: The Democratic Revolution in the USSR* (Aldershot: Edward Elgar, 1990); Peter Lentini, 'Reforming the Electoral System: The

1989 Elections to the USSR Congress of People's Deputies', *Journal of Communist Studies*, vol. 7, no. 1 (1991), pp. 69–94.

16. Arend Lijphart, 'Democratization and Constitutional Choices', *Journal of Theoretical Politics*, vol. 4, no. 2 (1992), pp. 208–9.

17. Stein Rokkan, *Citizens, Elections, Parties: Approaches to the Comparative Study of the Process of Development* (Oslo: Universitetsforlaget, 1970), pp. 148–72; Andrew McLaren Carstairs, *A Short History of Electoral Systems in Western Europe* (London: George Allen & Unwin, 1980), pp. 9–10; Charles Boix, 'Setting the Rules of the Game: The Choice of Electoral Systems in Advanced Democracies', *American Political Science Review*, vol. 93, no. 3 (1999), pp. 609–24.

18. In some cases minor changes were made to the provisions for absent voting and voting by special categories of people; see Sarah Birch, 'Elections and Representation in Post-Communist Eastern Europe', in Hans-Dieter Klingemann, Ekkehard Mochmann and Kenneth Newton (eds), *Elections in Central and Eastern Europe: The First Wave* (Berlin: Sigma, 2000), p. 21.

19. Aníbal Pérez-Liñan, 'Neoinstitutional Accounts of Voter Turnout: Moving beyond Industrial Democracies', *Electoral Studies*, vol. 20, no. 2 (2001), pp. 281–97.

20. Barbara Geddes, 'Initiation of New Democratic Institutions in Eastern Europe and Latin America', in Arend Lijphart and Carlos H. Waisman (eds), *Institutional Design in New Democracies: Eastern Europe and Latin America* (Boulder, CO: Westview, 1996), pp. 15–42; Thomas F. Remington and Steven Smith, 'Political Goals, Institutional Context, and the Choice of an Electoral System: The Russian Parliamentary Election Law', *American Journal of Political Science*, vol. 40, no. 4 (1996), pp. 1253–79.

21. Rein Taagepera and Matthew Soberg Shugart, *Seats and Votes: The Effects and Determinants of Electoral Systems* (New Haven, CT and London: Yale University Press, 1989), p. 4; Lijphart, 'Democratization and Constitutional Choices', pp. 218–19; David Brady and Jongryn Mo, 'Electoral Systems and Institutional Choice; A Case Study of the 1988 Korean Elections', *Comparative Political Studies*, vol. 24, no. 4 (1992), pp. 405–29.

22. Matthew Soberg Shugart, 'The Inverse Relationship Between Party Strength and Executive Strength: A Theory of Politicians' Constitutional Choices', *British Journal of Political Science*, vol. 28, no. 1 (1998), p. 27.

23. André Blais and Louis Massicotte, 'Electoral Formulas: A Macroscopic Perspective', *European Journal of Political Research*, vol. 32 (1997), p. 116.

24. On Czechoslovakia see Václav Beneš, 'Democracy and Its Problems: 1918–1920', in Victor S. Mamatey and Radomír Luža (eds), *A History of the Czechoslovak Republic 1918–1948* (Princeton, NJ: Princeton University Press, 1973), p. 66; on Poland see Andrzej Ajnenkiel, *Spór o model parlamentaryzmu polskiego do roku 1926* (Warsaw: Książka i Wiedza, 1972), pp. 179–83. The Piast Peasant Party in Poland opposed PR, partly because it would enable the representation of the minorities ('non-Poles').

25. R. J. Crampton, *Eastern Europe in the Twentieth Century* (London: Routledge, 1994), pp. 9–10.

26. Michael Bernhard, 'Institutional Choice after Communism: A Critique of Theory-Building in an Empirical Wasteland', *East European Politics and Societies*, vol. 14, no. 2 (2000), p. 328.

27. Joseph Rothschild, *East-Central Europe between the Two World Wars* (Seattle and London: University of Washington Press, 1974), p. 20.
28. Hoensch described the 1920 elections as 'free, because they were *mainly* conducted by secret ballot' (emphasis ours); Jörg Hoensch, *A History of Modern Hungary 1867–1994* (London: Longman, 1996), p. 101.
29. Mattei Dogan, 'Romania, 1919–1938', in Myron Weiner and Regun Ozbudun (eds), *Competitive Elections in Developing Countries* (Chapel Hill, NC: Duke University Press, 1987), pp. 369–89.
30. See Robert Lee Wolff, *The Balkans in Our Time* (Cambridge, MA: Harvard University Press, 1956), pp. 132–6; Rothschild, *East-Central Europe between the Two World Wars*, pp. 323–55.
31. See, for example, Antony Polonsky, *Politics in Independent Poland 1921–1939. The Crisis of Constitutional Government* (Oxford: Clarendon Press, 1972) and Edward D. Wynot, Jr, *Polish Politics in Transition. The Camp of National Unity and the Struggle for Power 1935–1939* (Athens: University of Georgia Press, 1974).
32. Henry Roberts, *Rumania. Political Problems of an Agrarian State* (New Haven, CT: Yale University Press, 1951), p. 131.
33. John T. Ishiyama, 'Transition Electoral Systems in Post-Communist Europe', *Political Science Quarterly*, vol. 112, no. 1 (1997), pp. 98–101.
34. W. J. M. Mackenzie, 'The Export of Electoral Systems', *Political Studies*, vol. 5, no. 3 (1957), p. 255.
35. Indeed, in Bosnia the electoral system was (initially) imposed by the Organization for Security and Cooperation in Europe.
36. Lijphart, 'Democratization and Constitutional Choices', p. 218.
37. Rokkan, *Citizens, Elections, Parties*.
38. Jean Stengers, 'Histoire de la législation électorale en Belgique', in Serge Noiret (ed.), *Political Strategies and Electoral Reforms: Origins of Voting Systems in Europe in the 19th and 20th Centuries* (Baden-Baden: Nomos, 1990), pp. 85–6.
39. Stephen Holmes, 'Designing Electoral Regimes', *East European Constitutional Review*, vol. 3, no. 2 (1994), p. 41.
40. See Andrew Reynolds and Ben Reilly (eds), *The International IDEA Handbook of Electoral System Design* (Stockholm: International IDEA, 1997), pp. 13–14.
41. Krenar Loloci, 'Electoral Law in Eastern Europe: Albania', *East European Constitutional Review*, spring (1994), p. 42.
42. Jon Elster, Claus Offe and Ulrich Preuss, *Institutional Design in Post-communist Societies: Rebuilding the Ship at Sea* (Cambridge: Cambridge University Press, 1998), pp. 111–12.
43. One problem with this typology is the multitude of exceptions to the general rule and the numerous contingent and contextual factors adduced to account for them, including, among others, the perceived desirability of establishing electoral rules that would lead to balanced, stable and/or compact party systems. Herbert Kitschelt, Zdenka Mansfeldova, Radoslaw Markowski and Gabor Toka, *Post-Communist Party Systems: Competition, Representation, and Inter-Party Competition* (Cambridge: Cambridge University Press, 1999), pp. 31–5, 105–10.
44. Jack H. Nagel, 'Reform is the Error Term: Explaining Stability and Change in Electoral Systems', paper presented at the First Conference of the European

Consortium for Political Research, University of Kent, Canterbury (6–8 September 2001).

45. Henry E. Brady and Cynthia S. Kaplan, 'Eastern Europe and the Former Soviet Union', in David Butler and Austin Ranney (eds), *Referendums Around the World: The Growing Use of Direct Democracy* (London: Macmillan, now Palgrave Macmillan, 1994), pp. 174–217.

46. See Michael Bernhard's trenchant attack on Josep Colomer for ignoring such factors; Bernhard, 'Institutional Choice after Communism', pp. 326–7.

47. For example, Rokkan, *Citizens, Elections, Parties*; Kathleen Bawn, 'The Logic of Institutional Preferences: German Electoral Law as a Social Choice Outcome', *American Journal of Political Science*, vol. 37, no. 4, (1993), pp. 965–89; Boix, 'Setting the Rules of the Game'; Patrick Dunleavy and Helen Margetts, 'Understanding the Dynamics of Electoral Reform', *International Political Science Review*, vol. 16, no. 1 (1995), pp. 9–29.

48. Richard Gunther, 'Electoral Laws, Party Systems, and Elites: The Case of Spain', *American Political Science Review*, vol. 83, no. 3 (1989), pp. 835–58; Brady and Mo, 'Electoral Systems and Institutional Choice', pp. 405–29.

49. Geddes, 'Initiation of New Democratic Institutions in Eastern Europe and Latin America', pp. 15–42; Krzysztof Jasiewicz, 'Elections and Voting Behaviour', in Stephen White, Judy Batt and Paul G. Lewis (eds), *Developments in Central and East European Politics* (Basingstoke: Macmillan, now Palgrave Macmillan, 1998), pp. 166–87; Kitschelt et al., pp. 32–4; Elster et al., p. 112.

50. Kenneth Benoit, 'A Theory of Electoral Systems', paper presented at the Re-Thinking Democracy in the New Millennium Conference, Houston, Texas (16–19 February 2000); Kenneth Benoit and John W. Schiemann, 'Institutional Choice in New Democracies', *Journal of Theoretical Politics*, vol. 13, no. 2 (2001), pp. 158–61; Kenneth Benoit and Jacqueline Hayden, 'Institutional Change and Persistence: The Origins and Evolution of Poland's Electoral System 1989–2001', paper presented at the ECPR general conference, Canterbury (6–8 September 2001), revised version of 15 October 2001, pp. 5–8.

51. Rokkan, *Citizens, Elections and Parties*; cf. Lijphart, 'Democratization and Constitutional Choices'; Boix, 'Setting the Rules of the Game'.

52. Geddes, 'Initiation of New Democratic Institutions ...'; Remington and Smith, 'Political Goals, Institutional Context, and the Choice of an Electoral System ...', pp. 1253–79; Shugart, 'The Inverse Relationship ...'

53. Kathleen Bawn, 'The Logic of Institutional Preferences ...', pp. 965–89.

54. See Remington and Smith and the various articles of Kenneth Benoit cited above.

55. He argues that if the old regime liberalized, and the transition was negotiated on conditions largely dictated by the incumbents, there will be a preference for weak political parties and strong presidents. This is because incumbents know that they will have a hard time persuading voters to support them nationally for policy reasons, and can only win support by using the patronage/corruption links that they have cultivated while in power. They will therefore want to focus on pandering to local interests while relying on a strong president to guide policy. If, on the other hand, the old regime liberalized but lost control of the process, with the opposition

becoming an equal partner, there will be an attempt to balance party strength and executive strength. If the old regime refused to liberalize and had to be forced out, with an interim government running the country until new elections, the opposition will impose proportional representation in the belief that this will promote clear party profiles; Shugart, 'The Inverse Relationship...', pp. 13–17.

56. Boix, 'Setting the Rules of the Game', p. 622; Josep Colomer, *Political Institutions: Democracy and Social Choice* (Oxford: Oxford University Press, 2001), p. 210 *et passim*.
57. Steven R. Reed and Michael F. Thies, 'The Causes of Electoral Reform in Japan', in Matthew Soberg Shugart and Martin P. Wattenburg (eds), *Mixed-Member Electoral Systems. The Best of Both Worlds?* (Oxford: Oxford University Press, 2001), pp. 380–403.
58. Dunleavy and Margetts, 'Understanding the Dynamics...', p. 20; Benoit, 'A Theory of Electoral Systems', pp. 31–2.
59. For an overview of the path dependency approach that informs this analysis, see James Mahoney, 'Path Dependence in Historical Sociology', *Theory and Society*, vol. 29 (2000), pp. 17–26.
60. Gerard Alexander, 'Institutions, Path Dependence and Democratic Consolidation', *Journal of Theoretical Politics*, vol. 13, no. 3 (2001), p. 261.
61. John M. Carey and Matthew Soberg Shugart, 'Incentives to Cultivate a Personal Vote: A Rank Ordering of Electoral Formulas', *Electoral Studies*, vol. 14, no. 4 (1995), pp. 417–39; see also Richard Katz, *A Theory of Parties and Electoral Systems* (Baltimore, MD: Johns Hopkins University Press, 1980).
62. Ronald Rogowski, 'Trade and the Variety of Democratic Institutions', *International Organization*, vol. 41 (1987), pp. 203–24; Matthew Soberg Shugart, 'Efficiency and Reform: A Theory of Electoral System Change in the Context of Economic Liberalization', paper prepared for delivery at the Annual Meeting of the American Political Science Association, Boston (3–6 September 1998).
63. See Boix, 'Setting the Rules of the Game...'
64. Benoit 'A Theory of Electoral Systems', p. 4; cf. George Tsebelis, *Nested Games: Rational Choice in Comparative Politics* (Berkeley: University of California Press, 1990), p. 104.

2 Poland: Experimenting with the Electoral System

1. *Rzeczpospolita*, 25 January 2001.
2. Arend Lijphart, *Electoral Systems and Party Systems. A Study of Twenty-Seven Democracies, 1945–1990* (Oxford: Oxford University Press, 1994), p. 93.
3. The State Electoral Commission interpreted Art. 101 §2 that 'Seats are allocated to particular all-Polish lists of candidates... after adding together the number of votes cast for district lists linked to a given all-Polish list of candidates...' to mean that only those districts where a party had a candidate from that district on its national list would qualify for an all-Polish allocation. Thus the Christian Democrats received no allocation, despite winning seats in five districts: the link had to be specific for each district. The Supreme Court rejected this interpretation, and the UD and KPN lost one deputy each to Christian Democracy (*Chrześcijańska Demokracja*).

The Constitutional Tribunal upheld the Electoral Commission, but there was no change in the Sejm, which confirmed the 'validity of the election of all deputies' in November 1992.

4. These were the United Peasant Party (ZSL), the Democratic Party (SD), and affiliated religious organizations.
5. Janusz Reykowski, 'Komentarz', *Studia Socjologiczne*, no. 2 (1997), pp. 42–4; see also the confidential report addressed to General Jaruzelski in May 1989 in Stanisław Perzkowski (ed.), *Tajne dokumenty Biura Politycznego i Sekretariatu KC. Ostatni rok władzy 1988–1989* (London: Aneks, 1994), pp. 372–5.
6. Małgorzata Dehnel-Szyc and Jadwiga Stachura, *Gry polityczne – Orientacje na dziś*, (Warsaw: Volumen, 1991), p. 36.
7. Jacek Raciborski, 'Wzory zachowań wyborczych a dawne modele wyborców' in L. Kolarska-Bobińska, P. Łukasiewicz and Z. W. Rykowski (eds), *Wyniki badań – wyniki wyborów 4 czerwca 1989 r.* (Warsaw: PTS, 1990), pp. 218–20.
8. Jacek Raciborski, *Polskie Wybory. Zachowanie wyborcze społeczeństwa polskiego 1989–1995* (Warsaw: Scholar, 1997), p. 20.
9. *Sprawozdanie stenograficzne z 33 posiedzenia Sejmu RP w dniach 21 i 22 czerwca 1990 r.* (The Official Record, Stenographic Reports of the Sejm, henceforth abbreviated as *Spraw. stenog*... followed by the date in English.)
10. *Komisja Konstytucyjna Biuletyn VIII* (Warsaw: Kancelaria Sejmu, 1990), pp. 17–19 (henceforth cited as *KK Biuletyn*).
11. *Druk Sejmowy* 1161.
12. Cited in Filip Gawra and M.D. Zdort, 'Egzotyczne koalicje', *Rzeczpospolita*, 3–4 July 1999.
13. *Trybuna Ludu*, 4 July 1989.
14. *Druk Sejmowy* 462.
15. *Druk Sejmowy* 522.
16. *Spraw. stenog. z 39 posiedzenia...* (20–21 September 1990); *Spraw. stenog. z 40 posiedzenia...* (27 September 1990); *Spraw. stenog. z 42 posiedzenia...* (25–26 October 1990).
17. *Spraw. stenog... z 42 posiedzenia...*
18. Sprawozdanie z 4 posiedzenia zespołu ds ordynacji wyborczej', *KK Biuletyn* XX, pp. 22–3; also 'Sprawozdanie z 5 posiedzenia...', pp. 23–5; and 'Sprawozdanie z 6 posiedzenia...', pp. 25–7.
19. 'Sprawozdanie z 5 posiedzenia...', p. 24.
20. 'Sprawozdanie z 7 posiedzenia zespołu...22/1', *KK Biuletyn* XXI, pp. 18–19, 'Sprawozdanie z 8 posiedzenia... 29/1', *KK Biuletyn* XXI, pp. 19–21, 'Sprawozdanie z 9 posiedzenia...5/2', *KK Biuletyn* XII, pp. 16–18.
21. 'Sprawozdanie z 9 posiedzenia...5/2', pp. 16–18.
22. 'Sprawozdanie z 15 posiedzenia zespołu...15/2', *KK Biuletyn* XXIII, pp. 3–5.
23. 'Sprawozdanie z 15 posiedzenia...', pp. 7–8.
24. *Druk Sejmowy* 770.
25. *Druk Sejmowy* 763.
26. *Druk Sejmowy* 770-A.
27. *Spraw. stenog. z 59 posiedzenia...* (10 May 1991).
28. Ryszard Mojak, *Instytucja prezydenta RP w okresie przekształceń ustrojowych* (Lublin: Uniwersytet Marii Curie-Skłodowskiej, 1995), pp. 211–12.
29. *Druk Sejmowy* 908. See also Kazimierz Groblewski, 'Prezydenckie weto dla ordynacji wyborczej', *Rzeczpospolita*, 11 June 1991.

30. The Commission's revised version is *Druk Sejmowy* 917A.
31. *Spraw. stenog. z 63 posiedzenia...* (15 June 1991).
32. *Spraw. stenog. z 64 posiedzenia...* (21 June 1991).
33. *Druk Sejmowy* 944; *Rzeczpospolita*, 27 June 1991.
34. *Spraw. stenog. z 65 posiedzenia...* (27–28 June 1991).
35. Mikołaj Kozakiewicz, *Byłem Marszałkiem Kontraktowego* (Warsaw: BGW, c. 1991), p. 55.
36. Kenneth Ka-Lok Chan, 'Idealism versus Realism in Institutional Choice: Explaining Electoral Reform in Poland', *West European Politics*, vol. 24, no. 3 (2001), pp. 74–5.
37. *Druk Sejmowy* 125.
38. *Spraw. stenogr. 18 posiedzenia...* (19–20 June 1992).
39. *Biuletyn z posiedzenia Komisji Nadzwyczajnej do rozpatrzenia projektu ustawy Ordynacja wyborcza do Sejmu RP*, Nr. 477/Ikad., 25 June 1992.
40. *Biuletyn... 661/Ikad.*, 22 September 1992.
41. *Biuletyn... 482/Ikad.*, 30 June 1992; *Biuletyn... 495/Ikad.*, 7 July 1992; *Biuletyn... 837/Ikad.*, 17 November 1992, *Biuletyn... 932/Ikad.*, 15 December 1992.
42. *Biuletyn... 495/Ikad.*, 7 July 1992; *Biuletyn... 528/Ikad.*, 14 July 1992.
43. *Druk Sejmowy* 757.
44. *Spraw. stenog. z 40 posiedzenia...* (18–20 March and 31 March 1993).
45. *Spraw. stenog. z 40 posiedzenia...*
46. *Druk Sejmowy* 757B.
47. The Senate debate is *Sprawozdanie stenograficzne z 40 posiedzenia Senatu RP w dniach 20 i 21 maja 1993 r.*
48. *Druk Sejmowy* 959.
49. *Spraw. stenog. z 45 posiedzenia...* (27–29 May 1993).
50. See *Druk Sejmowy* 1161, 2144, 2203, 2209, 2418, 2418-A and also the June debate in *Sprawoz. Stenog. z 110 posiedzenia...* (24–26 June 1997).
51. The drafts are in the parliamentary record as *Druk Sejmowy* 1229, amended as *Druk Sejmowy* 1229-A; *Druk Sejmowy* 1290; *Druk Sejmowy* 1390; *Druk Sejmowy* 1395 respectively.
52. The full title of this parliamentary committee was Komisja Nadzwyczajna do rozpatrzenia projektów ordynacji wyborczej do Senatu i do Sejmu oraz o zmianie ustawy o wyborze Prezydenta Rzeczypospolitej Polskiej (henceforth NOW). Its brief embraced eleven bills, including two from the Senate and proposals from parties and individual deputies on Senate, presidential and Sejm elections.
53. *Biuletyn z posiedzenia Komisji* 27/4/00 – NOW.
54. *Biuletyn z posiedzenia Komisji* 24/5/00 – NOW.
55. *Biuletyn z posiedzenia Komisji* 12/7/00 – NOW; *Biuletyn z posiedzenia Komisji* 13/7/00 – NOW.
56. *Sprawoz. stenog. z 85 posiedzenia..., cz. 1* (6 September 2000).
57. *Druk Sejmowy* 2023; *Druk Sejmowy* 2090; *Druk Sejmowy* 2091.
58. *Biuletyn z posiedzenia komisji* 14/9/00 – NOW.
59. PBS data in *Rzeczpospolita*, 17 November 2000.
60. *Rzeczpospolita*, 18–19 November 2000.
61. *Sprawoz. stenog. z 3 kadencji, 103 posiedzenia...* (7 March 2001).
62. The final NOW report and draft law are *Druk Sejmowy* 2599.

3   Hungary: the Politics of Negotiated Design

1. Barnabas Racz, 'Political Pluralisation in Hungary: the 1990 Elections', *Soviet Studies*, vol. 43, no. 1 (1991), p. 112; István Kukorelli, 'The Birth, Testing and Results of the 1989 Hungarian Electoral Law', *Soviet Studies*, vol. 43, no. 1 (1991), p. 146.

2. András Bozóki, 'Hungary's Road to Systemic Change: The Opposition Roundtable', *East European Politics and Society*, vol. 7, no. 2 (spring 1993), p. 301.

3. Gábor Tóka, 'Seats and Votes: Consequences of the Hungarian Electoral Law', in Gábor Tóka (ed.), *The 1990 Election to the Hungarian National Assembly. Analyses, Documents and Data* (Berlin: Sigma, 1995), p. 44.

4. John R. Hibbing and Samuel C. Patterson, 'A Democratic Legislature in the Making. The Historic Hungarian Elections of 1990', *Comparative Political Studies*, vol. 24, no. 4 (1992), p. 423.

5. Zoltán Kovács and Alan Dinsdale, 'Whither East European Democracies? The Geography of the 1994 Hungarian Parliamentary Election', *Political Geography*, vol. 17, no. 4 (1998), p. 440. Ishiyama refers to it as an 'Additional Member' system, but Hungary did not provide for additional members; John T. Ishiyama, 'Electoral Systems Experimentation in the New Eastern Europe: The Single Transferable Vote and the Additional Member System in Estonia and Hungary', *East European Quarterly*, vol. XXIX, no. 4 (1996), pp. 487–507.

6. William F. Robinson, *The Pattern of Reform in Hungary: A Political, Economic and Cultural Analysis* (London: Praeger, 1973), p. 208.

7. For details see Hans-Georg Heinrich, *Hungary, Politics and Economics* (London: Frances Pinter, 1986), p. 66.

8. Zoltan Barany, 'Elections in Hungary', in Robert Furtak (ed.), *Elections in Socialist States* (New York: Harvester Wheatsheaf, 1990), p. 73.

9. Barnabas Racz, 'Political Participation and Developed Socialism: the Hungarian Elections of 1985', *Soviet Studies*, vol. XXXIX, no. 1 (1987), pp. 40–62, especially pp. 42–5; Barany, 'Elections in Hungary', especially pp. 78–80.

10. Rudolf Tőkés, *Hungary's Negotiated Revolution. Economic Reform, Social Change and Political Succession* (Cambridge: Cambridge University Press, 1996), p. 268.

11. Barnabas Racz, 'The Parliamentary Infrastructure and Political Reforms in Hungary', *Soviet Studies*, vol. XLI, no. 1 (1989), pp. 39–66.

12. Tőkés, *Hungary's Negotiated Revolution*, pp. 196–200. Pozsgay's effective legitimization was important, because the participants needed to know that their meeting came into the 'tolerated' category of the 'three Ts' – *támogatott, tűrt, tiltott* (supported, tolerated, prohibited); we are indebted to Sándor Gallai for this point.

13. Kukorelli, 'The Birth, Testing and Results of the 1989 Hungarian Electoral Law', p. 138.

14. András Bozóki, 'Political Transition and Constitutional Change', in András Bozóki, András Körösenyi and George Schöpflin (eds), *Post-Communist Transition. Emerging Pluralism in Hungary* (London: Pinter Publishers, 1992), p. 63.

15. Tőkés, *Hungary's Negotiated Revolution*, p. 315.

16. Gábor Tóka, Interview with Zoltán Tóth, 19 November 2001.
17. Kukorelli, 'Birth, Testing, and Results...', p. 138.
18. On the expression of these literary and historical currents see George Schöpflin, 'Critical Currents in Hungary 1968–1978', in Rudolf Tőkés (ed.), *Opposition in Eastern Europe* (London: Macmillan, 1979), especially pp. 167–9.
19. László Lengyel, 'The Character of Political Parties in Hungary (Autumn 1989)', in András Bozóki, András Körösenyi and George Schöpflin (eds), *Post-Communist Transition. Emerging Pluralism in Hungary* (London: Pinter, 1992), p. 34.
20. Lengyel, 'The Character of Political Parties', p. 35.
21. Zoltán Bíró, a reform-communist member of the Forum's provisional presidium and Pozsgay's close associate, was expelled by the MSzMP for undermining party unity in May 1988.
22. Erzsébet Szalai, 'The Power Structure in Hungary after the Political Transition', in Christopher Bryant and Edmund Mokrzycki (eds), *The New Great Transformation?* (London: Routledge, 1994), p. 122.
23. The Forum, the Free Democrats and the Young Democrats all originally subscribed to principles of collective leadership, attributed by Punnett and Ilonszki to their 'social movement' origins; Malcolm Punnett and Gabriella Ilonszki, 'Leading Democracy: The Emergence of Party Leaders and Their Roles in the Hungarian Parties', *Journal of Communist Studies and Transition Politics*, vol. 10, no. 3, (1994), pp. 101–19.
24. András Bozóki and Gergely Karácsony, 'The Making of a Political Elite: Participants of the Hungarian Roundtable Talks in 1989', paper presented at the ECPR general conference, Canterbury, UK (6–8 September 2001), p. 17.
25. János Kis, 'Kőszeg visszanéz', Beszélő, July–August, 2000; web-version reference provided by Sándor Gallai.
26. Zsolt Enyedi, 'Organising a Subcultural Party in Eastern Europe: the Case of the Hungarian Christian Democrats', *Party Politics*, vol. 2, no. 3 (1996), p. 387.
27. Bozóki and Karácsony, p. 12.
28. Bozóki and Karácsony, p. 9.
29. Bozóki and Karácsony, p. 6.
30. Bozóki, 'Hungary's Road...', p. 282.
31. The BSZBT, the League of Independent Trade Unions and the Independent Lawyers' Forum were also excluded from the initial invitation, but belated invitations were issued to the BSZBT and the League.
32. Bozóki, 'Hungary's Road...', p. 285.
33. Benoit, 'Hungary's "Two-Vote" Electoral System', p. 167.
34. *Magyar Nemzet*, 5 June 1989.
35. Kukorelli, 'The Birth, Testing and Results of the 1989 Hungarian Electoral Law', p. 142.
36. Tőkés, *Hungary's Negotiated Revolution*, p. 343.
37. Bozóki and Karácsony, p. 37.
38. Tőkés, *Hungary's Negotiated Revolution*, p. 368.
39. See, for example, Tóka, 'Seats and Votes...', p. 45; Benoit, 'Hungary's "Two-Vote" Electoral System', p. 166; John W. Schiemann, 'Hedging against Uncertainty: Regime Change and the Origins of Hungary's Mixed-Member

System', in Matthew Soberg Shugart and Martin P. Wattenburg (eds), *Mixed-Member Electoral Systems. The Best of Both Worlds?* (Oxford: Oxford University Press, 2001), p. 241.

40. Lijphart appears to have confused the SzDSz's stance with that of the government when he argues that the Communists were too optimistic, holding out for a mixed but predominantly majoritarian system with 75 per cent in single-member districts and 25 per cent by PR; Arend Lijphart, 'Democratization and Constitutional Choices', *Journal of Theoretical Politics*, vol. 4, no. 2 (1992), p. 215. Ishiyama also mistakenly identifies the SzDSz as supporting proportional representation; Ishiyama, 'Electoral System Experimentation ...', p. 499.

41. Schiemann, 'Hedging against Uncertainty', p. 242.

42. Interview with Péter Tölgyessy, cited in Schiemann, 'Hedging against Uncertainty', p. 242.

43. Tőkés, *Hungary's Negotiated Revolution*, p. 339.

44. Schiemann, 'Hedging against Uncertainty', p. 242.

45. Hibbing and Patterson, 'A Democratic Legislature in the Making', p. 433.

46. Interview, cited in Schiemann, 'Hedging against Uncertainty', p. 244.

47. The People's Party did not gain seats in 1990, but the Christian Democrat and Smallholders' votes were concentrated; see András Körösényi, 'The Hungarian Parliamentary Elections, 1990', in András Bozóki, András Körösényi and George Schöpflin (eds), *Post-Communist Transition. Emerging Pluralism in Hungary* (London: Pinter, 1992), especially pp. 84–5; this pattern was repeated, especially for the Christian Democrats, in 1994; Kovács and Dinsdale, 'Whither East European Democracies?', pp. 445–7.

48. Even Hungarian scholars make mistakes on the complex interaction of the three elements. Körösényi states that second-round votes are transferred. András Körösényi, *Government and Politics in Hungary* (Budapest: Central European University Press, 1999), p. 119.

49. Schiemann, 'Hedging against Uncertainty', n. 25, p. 50; Tóka, Interview with Zoltán Tóth, 19 November 2001.

50. Tóka, 'Seats and Votes ...', p. 60.

51. Schiemann, 'Hedging against Uncertainty', pp. 50–1.

52. Csaba Kereszeti was its spokesman during the parliamentary debate, see *Országgyűlési Napló*, 61. ülése (19 October 1989).

53. For example, the Committee for Regional Development and the Environment favoured 188–116–70; the Culture Committee proposed 187–137–50. The Sports and Youth Committee wanted 'more' single-member districts. Deputies Pál Filló and Bertalan Südi proposed 203–101–70 and 300–0–74 respectively.

54. *Országgyűlési Napló*, 61. ülése (19 October 1989), p. 5035.

55. *Országgyűlési Napló*, 61. ülése (19 October 1989), pp. 5035–108; *Országgyűlési Napló*, 62. ülése (20 October 1989), pp. 5113–14.

56. Of course, for opposition forces parliament itself was no longer legitimate; see János Kis, 'Between Reform and Revolution: Three Hypotheses about the Nature of the Regime Change', in Béla Király and András Bozóki (eds), *Lawful Revolution in Hungary, 1989–94* (Highland Lakes, NJ: Atlantic Research and Publications, 1995), pp. 42–3.

57. Tóka, Interview with Zoltán Tóth.

58. *Országgyűlési Napló*, 62. ülése (20 October 1989), p. 5124.
59. *Országgyűlési Napló*, 62. ülése (20 October 1989), p. 5126.
60. Louis Massicote and André Blais, 'Mixed Electoral Systems: A Conceptual and Empirical Survey', *Electoral Studies*, vol. 18, no. 3 (1999), pp. 341–66.
61. For further details see Marina Popescu and Gábor Tóka, 'Districting and Redistricting in Eastern and Central Europe: Regulations and Practices', paper prepared for presentation at the conference on 'Redistricting from a Comparative Perspective' at the University of California at Irvine (6–8 December 2001), pp. 14–15.
62. Racz, 'Political Pluralisation ...', n. 13, p. 111.
63. On this and other issues of redistricting see Popescu and Tóka, 'Districting and Redistricting in Eastern and Central Europe'.
64. Bill Lomax, 'The 1998 Elections in Hungary: Third Time Lucky for the Young Democrats', *Journal of Communist Studies and Transition Politics*, vol. 15, no. 2 (1999), p. 117.
65. József Deák quoted in RFE/RL Newsline, vol. 5, no. 222, Part II (26 November 2001).
66. There is a useful summary of the provisions in Martin Kovats, 'The Roma and Minority Self-Government in Hungary', *Immigrants and Minorities*, vol. 15, no. 1 (1996), pp. 42–58.
67. David Stark and László Bruszt, *Postsocialist Pathways. Transforming Politics and Property in East Central Europe* (Cambridge: Cambridge University Press, 1998), p. 44.
68. Attila Ágh, 'Defeat and Success as Promoters of Party Change', *Party Politics*, vol. 3, no. 3 (1997), p. 429.
69. Tőkés, *Hungary's Negotiated Revolution*, p. 363.
70. Kenneth Benoit and John Schiemann, 'Institutional Choice in New Democracies. Bargaining over Hungary's 1989 Electoral Law', *Journal of Theoretical Politics*, vol. 13, no. 2 (2001), p. 170, table 5; Hibbing and Patterson's simulations for 1990 give somewhat different results; see Hibbing and Patterson, 'A Democratic Legislative in the Making', p. 450.
71. Different proportionality measures give very different results; but see Hibbing and Patterson, 'A Democratic Legislative in the Making', pp. 436–7; Benoit, 'Evaluating ...', p. 488, Tóka, 'Seats and Votes ...', pp. 63–5.
72. Attila Ágh and Sándor Kurtán, 'Parliamentary and Municipal Elections in 1998: A Comparative History of the Hungarian Elections in the Nineties', *Budapest Papers on Democratic Transition*, No. 235 (Budapest: Budapest University of Economics, 1999); Kenneth Benoit, 'Two Steps Forward, One Step Back: Electoral Coordination in the Hungarian Election of 1998', paper presented to the 2000 Annual Meeting of the American Political Science Association, Mariott Wardman Park (31 August–3 September 2000).
73. Gabriella Ilonszki, 'Legislative Recruitment: Personnel and Institutional Development in Hungary, 1990–94', in Gábor Tóka (ed.), *The 1990 Election to the Hungarian National Assembly. Analyses, Documents and Data* (Berlin: Sigma, 1995), pp. 98–100.
74. Tóka, 'Seats and Votes ...', p. 56
75. Benoit, 'Two Steps Forward ...', pp. 13–16.
76. Benoit, 'Two Steps Forward ...', pp. 18–19.
77. Tóka, Interview with Zoltán Tóth.

4   The Czech and Slovak Republics: the Surprising Resilience of Proportional Representation

1. This analysis is influenced by Kathleen Bawn, 'The Logic of Institutional Preferences: German Electoral Law as a Social Choice Outcome', *American Journal of Political Science*, vol. 37, no. 4 (1993), pp. 965–89, and Gerard Alexander, 'Institutions, Path Dependence and Democratic Consolidation', *Journal of Theoretical Politics*, vol. 13, no. 3 (2001), pp. 249–70.

2. Matthew Soberg Shugart, 'The Inverse Relationship Between Party Strength and Executive Strength: A Theory of Politicians' Constitutional Choices', *British Journal of Political Science*, vol. 28 (1998), pt. 1, pp. 13–17.

3. This view is acknowledged but not shared by Civic Forum leader Petr Kučera, in *Zápis ze snìmu Koordinačního centra Občanského fóra konaného dne 17.2.1990 od 10:00 do 16:00* (unpublished minutes), p. 13. The poll results were published in *Fórum*, no. 3, 14 February 1990, p. 2. Public against Violence initially did not even want to stand in the elections, so its internal deliberations were less concerned with the electoral system.

4. Josef Vavroušek, 'Volby do zákonodárných sborů', *Fórum*, no. 4, 21 February 1990, p. 1.

5. This argument was best expressed by Zdenìk Jičínský, chairman of Civic Forum's working party on electoral legislation, at the 6 January 1990 meeting of the movement's assembly; see *Zápis ze snìmu Občanského fóra 6. ledna 1990*, unpublished minutes, p. 5.

6. Jiří Suk, *Občanské fórum. Listopad-prosinec 1989. 2. díl – Dokumenty* (Brno: Doplnìk, 1998), p. 220. See also Petr Kopecký, *Parliaments in the Czech and Slovak Republics: Party competition and parliamentary institutionalization* (Aldershot: Ashgate, 2001), p. 27, and Dieter Nohlen and Mirjana Kasapovic, *Wahlsysteme und Systemwechsel in Osteuropa* (Opladen: Leske & Budrich, 1996), p. 149.

7. A. Slezáková, 'Občanské fórum dnes a zítra', *Lidová demokracie*, 12 January 1990, p. 3. Pithart used the same reasoning to persuade sceptics in the Civic Forum assembly on 6 January; see *Zápis ze snìmu Občanského fóra 6. ledna 1990*, p. 10.

8. Rudolf Zeman, 'První kroky k demokracii', *Lidové noviny*, 24 January 1990, p. 2.

9. As argued by Civic Forum leader Petr Kučera, in *Zápis ze snìmu Koordinačního centra Občanského fóra konaného dne 17.2.1990 od 10:00 do 16:00*, p. 13.

10. Jan Kavan, Jana Rendlova and Petr Uhl, 'Spory o volební systém', *Fórum*, no. 2, 7 February 1990, p. 7.

11. Josef Vavroušek, 'Návrh na rekonstrukci zákonodárných sborů', *Lidové noviny*, 20 January 1990, p. 2. Foreign advice was solicited but appears to have arrived only after Vavroušek had already sketched out his options: the National Democratic Institute for International Affairs provided a briefing for Civic Forum on 15 January 1990, with recommendations very similar to his. See Robin Carnahan and Judith Corley, 'Czechoslovakia', in Larry Garber and Eric Bjornlund (eds), *The New Democratic Frontier: A Country by Country Report on Elections in Central and Eastern Europe* (Washington, DC: National Democratic Institute for International Affairs, 1992), pp. 119–20.

12. Vavroušek, 'Volby do zákonodárných sborů', *Fórum*, no. 4, 21 February 1990, p. 1; *Zápis ze snìmu Koordinačního centra Občanského fóra dne 20. ledna 1990*, unpublished minutes, p. 2 (remarks by Petr Pithart).

13. Jiří Vyvadil, 'Naše zákony pro svobodné volby', *Svobodné slovo*, 10 January 1990, p. 1, and *Svobodné slovo*, 12 January 1990, p. 1, and 13 January 1990, p. 1. The Czechoslovak Socialist Party was the neutered remnant of the party associated with Edvard Beneš, president of the republic in 1935–8 and 1940–8. Its bid to revive practices from the Beneš era not only reflected a rational strategy to maximize the return on its electoral performance, but also suited its campaign to forge a new identity linked to democratic traditions and thereby overcome its image of a Communist stooge.

14. For the transcript of the debate on the 1946 bill, see Digitální knihovna Prozatimního NS RČS 1945–6. 46. schůze (10. dubna 1946), starting at <http://www.psp.cz/eknih/1945pns/stenprot/046schuz/s046001.htm>; on the motives behind the 1920 bill, see Václav Beneš, 'Democracy and Its Problems: 1918–1920', in Victor S. Mamatey and Radomír Luža (eds), *A History of the Czechoslovak Republic 1918–1948* (Princeton, NJ: Princeton University Press, 1973), p. 66, and Eva Broklová, *Československá demokracie: Politický systém ČSR 1918–1938* (Prague: SLON, 1992), p. 80. Another immediate factor in PR's favour in 1920 was the popularity of the social democrats, which other parties did not want to see elevated to an outright majority.

15. For more detail, see Frank Dinka and Max J. Skidmore, 'The Functions of Communist One-Party Elections: The Case of Czechoslovakia, 1971', *Political Science Quarterly*, vol. 88, no. 3 (1973), pp. 395–422.

16. An identical threshold was applied in elections to the Czech Republic's legislature, but at first the Slovak legislature required only 3 per cent, to ensure places for the Hungarian minority and the small but symbolically important Democratic Party (which in committee had itself argued for 5 per cent!). It was raised to 5 per cent for the 1992 elections in order to punish small anti-reform, anti-federal parties but ended up eliminating tiny liberal, pro-federal parties as well. See Kopecký, *Parliaments in the Czech and Slovak Republics*, p. 59, and Milan Zemko, 'Politické strany a volebný systém na Slovensku v retrospektíve troch volieb do SNR a NR SR', in Soňa Szomolányi and Grigorij Mesežnikov (eds), *Slovensko: Vol'by 1994. Príčiny – dôsledky – perspektívy* (Bratislava: Interlingua, 1994), p. 47, 51.

17. Districts were not pre-assigned a number of mandates, but allocated them by Hare quota, also using the turnout figures. This practice of setting quotas on the basis of participation rather than population appears to date back to the 1920 law, when it was inserted to compel Slav voters to turn out in areas with large German or Hungarian minorities. See Digitální knihovna Národního shromáždění československého 1918–1920.125.schůze (27.února 1920), at <http://www.psp.cz/eknih/1918ns/ps/stenprot/125schuz/s125008.htm>.

18. Kopecký, *Parliaments in the Czech and Slovak Republics*, p. 58. The republic list could consist only of candidates who had already appeared on district lists, and the party leadership would have a free hand in deciding their ranking.

19. L'uboš Kubín and Marián Velšic, *Slovensko a jeho volebné pravidlá* (Bratislava: Veda, 1998), p. 32.

20. Jiří Kabele, 'Volební zákon', *Respekt*, no. 1, 6 January 1992, p. 3.

21. Drahoš Šmejc and Jiří Hudeček, *Predbižná zpráva o demoskopickém šetrení k problematice politického systému Národní fronty a volební soustavy v ČSSR* (Prague: unpublished typescript, 1968), pp. 144–7.
22. Václav Havel, *Letní přemítání* (Prague: Odeon, 1991), p. 40.
23. The bill is outlined and defended expertly in an accompanying justification report (*důvodová zpráva*), at <http://www.psp.cz/eknih/1990fs/tisky/t1125_02.htm>. The actual author of Havel's bill was Vladimír Klokočka, an émigré professor of law at Munich University, who later became a justice on the Czech constitutional court. See Vladimír Mlynár, 'Prezident contra parlament', *Respekt*, no. 50, 16 December 1991, p. 4. On the history of the supplementary (or contingent) vote, see Ben Reilly, 'The Plant Report and the Supplementary Vote: Not So Unique After All', *Representation*, vol. 34, no. 2 (1997), pp. 95–102. It should not be confused with Australia's alternative vote system, in which voters must rank all the candidates, or STV, which uses multi-member districts and usually encourages voters to register their opinion of more than two candidates.
24. This practice, inspired by Belgium and other European states, was seriously considered but then rejected in 1920. In its 1990 guise, it allowed voters to indicate their preference for up to four candidates on the district party list. Such indications would be taken into account only if at least 10 per cent of all of that party's supporters indicated preferences, and if a candidate's number was circled by at least half of them. Parliamentarian Václav Benda, present at the creation of the 1990 electoral law, later claimed that this possibility was inserted to give voters an illusion of choice while minimizing any real threat to parties' control of the ballot. See Digitální knihovna FS ČSFR 1990–1992. Společné schůze SL a SN. 20. schůze (28. ledna 1992), at <http://www.psp.cz/eknih/1990fs/slsn/stenprot/020schuz/s020046.htm>.
25. On the fear of imitating the experience of Poland after its 1991 election, see the speech by Otakar Motejl, president of the Supreme Court, sponsoring the bill before the Federal Assembly, in Digitální knihovna FS ČSFR 1990–1992. Společné schůze SL a SN. 20. schůze (28. ledna 1992), at <http://www.psp.cz/eknih/1990fs/slsn/stenprot/020schuz/s020040.htm>, and by deputy V. Ševčík on behalf of the party Civic Movement, at <http://www.psp.cz/eknih/1990fs/slsn/stenprot/020schuz/s020041.htm>.
26. The ODS position is outlined by deputy L. Voleník, in Digitální knihovna FS ČSFR 1990–1992. Společné schůze SL a SN. 20. schůze (28. ledna 1992), at <http://www.psp.cz/eknih/1990fs/slsn/stenprot/020schuz/s020042.htm>.
27. Vladimír Mlynár,' 'Vzestup a pád politických sekretariátů', *Respekt*, no. 3, 20 January 1992, p. 4.
28. The amendment retained the requirement that at least 10 per cent of voters for a party must exercise their right to indicate preferences, but now stipulated that a candidate would move to the top of the ballot in that district if just 3 per cent of that party's voters circled his or her number. So, if a hypothetical party received 10,000 votes and the required 1000 indicated preferences, a candidate would need the approval of only 300 voters under the new rules, compared to 500 under the previous. See Jiri Pehe, 'Czechoslovak Federal Assembly Adopts Electoral Law', *RFE/RL Research Report*, vol. 1, no. 7 (1992), p. 29.

29. For disporportionality rates in three dozen democracies from 1945 to 1996, see Arend Lijphart, *Patterns of Democracy: Government Forms and Performance in Thirty-Six Countries* (New Haven, CT: Yale University Press, 1999), p. 162. PR systems usually generate D rates between 1 and 5.

30. František Turnovec, 'Electoral Rules and the Fate of Nations: Czechoslovakia's Last Parliamentary Election', in Michael Kraus and Allison K. Stanger (eds), *Irreconcilable Differences? Explaining Czechoslovakia's Dissolution* (Lanham, MD: Rowman & Littlefield, 1999), pp. 107–25.

31. David Olson, 'Dissolution of the State: Political Parties and the 1992 Election in Czechoslovakia', *Communist and Post-Communist Studies*, vol. 26, no. 3 (1993), pp. 303–4, and Gordon Wightman, 'The Development of the Party System and the Break-Up of Czechoslovakia', in Gordon Wightman (ed.), *Party Formation in East-Central Europe: Post-communist Politics in Czechoslovakia, Hungary, Poland and Bulgaria* (Aldershot: Edward Elgar, 1994), pp. 59–78.

32. Bawn, 'The Logic of Institutional Preferences: German Electoral Law as a Social Choice Outcome', p. 976.

33. 'Speech of PM Vladimir Meciar [*sic*] at the Congress of HZDS, Zvolen, 23 March 1996', official HZDS translation (copy in author's possession). Although the reference to Italy reflects the good relations between HZDS and Berlusconi's Forza Italia, Mečiar may also have been emulating Boris Yeltsin's attempt in 1995 to polarize Russian party politics around two parties, one of which, Chernomyrdin's Our Home is Russia, also had a special relationship with HZDS.

34. According to an unauthorized recording of the congress, broadcast on Radio Free Europe's Slovak Service on 3 April 1996. I am grateful to Sharon Fisher for a transcript of that broadcast.

35. Darina Malová, 'Slovakia: From the Ambiguous Constitution to the Dominance of Informal Rules', in Jan Zielonka (ed.), *Democratic Consolidation in Eastern Europe. Volume 1: Institutional Engineering* (Oxford: Oxford University Press, 2001), pp. 347–77.

36. These infringements are enumerated in Peter Kresák, 'Budeme volit' podl'a protiústavného zákona?', *OS: Fórum občianskej spoločnosti*, no. 7 (July 1998), pp. 51–6, and Milan Galanda, 'Ústavnoprávne aspekty zákona o vol'bách do NR SR', in Martin Bútora, Grigorij Mesežnikov and Zora Bútorová (eds), *Slovenské vol'by '98: Kto? Prečo? Ako?* (Bratislava: Inštitút pre verejné otázky, 1999), pp. 89–91, and concern primarily the attempts to deprive citizens of their right to vote if they were in police custody or 48-hour detention; to impede scrutiny of the electoral rolls; and to increase the involvement of the interior ministry in the business of electoral commissions. As the NDI noted in its analysis, the law lacked explicit provision for monitoring of voting and counting and prohibited campaigning through private electronic media. See <http://chaos.partners-intl.net/NDI/library/1122_sk_amend.pdf>. The clause disenfranchising citizens in custody or detention was dropped before the bill was enacted.

37. Peter Lebovič, 'Zápas o udržanie demokracie: politické súvislosti novelizácie volebného zákona', in Bútora, Mesežnikov and Bútorová (eds), *Slovenské vol'by '98: Kto? Prečo? Ako?*, pp. 32–3.

38. Voters in Slovakia receive a bundle of individual party lists on arriving at the polling station and register their choice by inserting one party's ballot paper into a box; in the Czech Republic, voters receive the ballot papers through the post no later than the third day before the elections.

39. On the arduous formation of the SDK, see Lubomír Kopeček, 'Slovenská demokratická koalice – vznik, geneze and charakteristika', *Politologický časopis*, vol. 6, no. 3 (1999), pp. 248–67. The five parties were the Christian Democratic Movement, the Democratic Union, the Democratic Party, the Social Democratic Party of Slovakia and the Green Party.

40. The five parties of the SDK and three of the Hungarian alliance were joined in power by the ex-Communist Party of the Democratic Left and President Rudolf Schuster's Party of Civic Understanding.

41. The finding of the court was published in *Zbierka zákonov Slovenskej republiky*, part 29, no. 66 (3 April 1999), p. 522; the full opinion is available at <http://www.concourt.sk/A/a_index.htm>.

42. *Zbierka zákonov Slovenskej republiky*, part 95, no. 223 (4 September 1999), p. 1574.

43. See in particular the remarks by Ivan Šimko, one of the bill's sponsors, in Šiesty deň rokovania 17. schôdze Národnej rady Slovenskej republiky (7 July 1999), part two, at <http://www.nrsr.sk/Slovak/Schodze/Rozprava/17/Pl17z_23.htm> and especially in Desiaty deň rokovania 17. schôdze Národnej rady Slovenskej republiky (24. augusta 1999), part 2, at <http://www.nrsr.sk/Slovak/Schodze/Rozprava/17/Pl17z_42.htm>, in which he concedes that many of the features of the 1920 electoral system 'mechanically' adopted in 1990 were 'obsolete'.

44. The Slovak system of preference voting always differed from its federal counterpart: 10 per cent of votes had to indicate preferences and a candidate had to receive the preferences of 10 per cent of all of a party's voters. The 2001 bill would reduce the latter requirement to 3 per cent, in line with the 1992 federal amendment (see note 28). The text of the bill is available at <http://www.nrsr.sk/Slovak/Zakony/1citanie/981z.pdf>.

45. The text of Fico's bill can be found at <http://www.nrsr.sk/Slovak/Zakony/1citanie/887z.doc>. *Smer* remained committed to electoral reform, proposing a Russian-style parallel mixed system, with 60 deputies to be chosen by party list in a national electoral district (with an 8 per cent threshold) and 60 in single-member districts. See <http://www.strana-smer.sk/program/dokumenty/polit_reforma.html>.

46. *Lidové noviny*, 30 August 1995, p. 3.

47. Karen Henderson, 'Social Democracy Comes to Power: the 1998 Czech Elections', *Labour Focus on Eastern Europe*, no. 60 (1998), pp. 9–10, and author's correspondence from September 2001 with Jiří Pehe, a former advisor to President Havel and eyewitness to the failed coalition talks.

48. Pavel Šaradín, 'Nastala už doba pro zmìnu volebního zákona?', *Mladá fronta Dnes*, 28 July 1998, p. 10.

49. The text of the pact is printed in *Parlamentní zpravodaj*, vol. 4, no. 17 (1997–99), p. 550.

50. Václav Pavlíček and Jiří Hřebejček, *Ústava a ústavaní řád České republiky. Komentář. 1. díl: Ústavaní systém*, 2nd revised and enlarged edn (Prague: Linde, 1998), p. 126.

51. Martin Maňák, 'Lidovecký návrh senátorských voleb dává šanci slabším', *Lidové noviny*, 31 March 1995, p. 5, and Jiří Kunc, 'K přijatému volebnímu zákonu', *Parlamentní zpravodaj*, vol. 2, no. 2 (1995–6), pp. 105–7. Initially ODS was inclined to the alternative vote (AV), but then calculated that it would be better able to aggrandize its own seat share under the system used, *nota bene*, for French presidential, not legislative elections. Although the Christian Democrats complicated matters by suggesting three-member districts, AV would have been one of the best ways to satisfy the majority stipulation; see Clive Bean, 'Australia's Experience with the Alternative Vote', *Representation*, vol. 34, no. 2, (1997), p. 103., and Lijphart, *Patterns of Democracy*, p. 147.

52. Tomáš Chundela and Jan Pergler, 'ODS a ČSSD chtìjí mìnit ústavu, ale úplnì jasno ještì nemají, *Mladá fronta Dnes*, 9 July 1998, p. 3.

53. Michal Klíma, 'Volební reforma v České republice v letech 1998–2000', *Politologický časopis*, vol. 7, no. 3 (2000), p. 226.

54. Miroslav Kořecký, 'ČSSD a ODS již stojí před dohodou o zmìnách Ústavy ČR', *Lidové noviny*, 18 May 1999, p. 5. The student's work is summarized in Lebeda, 'Vládní stabilita v České republice a volební systém pomìrného zastoupení'. Lebeda updated his scenarios to take into account the 1998 election results, and issued similar recommendations for a reform that he felt would increase government stability. See Tomáš Lebeda, 'Vládní stabilita v České republice a volební systém pomìrného zastoupení II: Modelování výsledkù voleb do Poslanecké snìmovny z roku 1998', *Politologický časopis*, vol. 6, no. 2 (1999), pp. 153–6, 160. Lebeda's scenarios, however, worked from the assumption of 200 deputies and 38 districts, and when applied to the 1998 vote would have produced only two possible two-party majorities: the Social Democrats with the Communists, or the Social Democrats with the Christian Democrats.

55. *Mladá fronta Dnes*, 21 May 1999, p. 2.

56. Klíma, 'Volební reforma v České republice v letech 1998–2000', p. 227.

57. The other two parties were the extra-parliamentary Democratic Union (DEU) and the Civic Democratic Alliance (ODA), which in 1998 had six senators but failed to enter the Diet of Deputies.

58. The text of the 'patent of tolerance' can be found on the Social Democrats' website:<http://www.cssd.cz/vismo/index.asp?tz=6>.

59. Zdenìk Koudelka, 'Zmìna volebního systému', *Politologický časopis*, vol. 7, no. 1 (2000), p. 91.

60. Since 1992, the Czech electoral law had differed slightly from the federal and Slovak: it set up a scale of 5 per cent for single parties, 7 per cent for two-party alliances, 9 per cent for three-party and 11 per cent for four or more. The amendment was tabled by Jan Vidím. See Digitální knihovna PČR, PS 1998–. Stenoprotokoly. 25. schůze (19. května 2000), at <http://www.psp;cz/cgi-bin/lat2/eknih/1998ps/stenprot/025schuz/s025140.htm>.

61. Tomáš Lebeda, 'Přiblížení vybraných aspektù reformy volebního systemu', *Politologický časopis*, vol. 7, no. 3 (2000), p. 243, 250. On the possible effects of the combination of district magnitude, threshold and divisor, see Tomáš Kostelecký, 'Navrhované zmìny volebního zákona vzešlé z dodatků 'opozični smlouvy' v roce 2000 a jejich možne důsledky', *Sociologický časopis*, vol. 36, no. 3 (2000), pp. 301–5; Michal Klíma, 'Pomìrný 'nepomìrný'

volební systém po novelizaci zákona o volbách do Parlamentu ČR', *Politologický časopis*, vol. 7, no. 4 (2000), pp. 334–60; and Keith Crawford, 'A System of Disproportional Representation: The Proposed Electoral Law for the Czech Republic', *Representation*, vol. 38, no. 1 (2001), pp. 49–55.

62. The Spanish and Greek averages are from Lijphart, *Patterns of Democracy*, p. 163.

63. *Mladá fronta Dnes*, 24 June 2000, p. 1, and Adam Drda, 'Senátoři-rebelové nevydrželi zlý pohled domovníka', *Lidové noviny*, 26 June 2000, p. 10. Three Social Democrat senators and one independent affiliated to them did vote against the bill; the party's central executive committee chose not to carry out Zeman's threat of expulsion. See *Lidové noviny*, 26 June 2000, p. 3.

64. *Sbírka zákonů České republiky*, no. 204, part 63 (14 July 2000), pp. 3018–47.

65. Pavlíček and Hřebejček, *Ústava a ústavní řád České republiky*, pp. 127–32, and *Sbírka zákonů České republiky*, no. 64, part 24 (16 February 2001), pp. 2194–8.

66. *Sbírka zákonů České republiky*, no. 64, part 24 (16 February 2001), p. 2202.

67. Ibid., p. 2204.

68. Ibid., p. 2203.

69. The outcome of the court's deliberations was anticipated months before by law student Radek Policar in his article 'Jsou navrhované zmìny volebního zákona v souladu s ústavou?', *Politologický časopis*, vol. 7, no. 2 (2000), pp. 178–81, and by émigré political scientist Karel Vodička in ibid., no. 4 (pp. 365–9). The law was defended in ibid., no. 3 (pp. 282–4), by political scientist Michal Kubát, who then denounced the court's action in *Revue Proglas*, vol. 12, no. 2 (2001), pp. 13–15.

70. For the transcript of the third reading on 13 December 2001, see <http://www.psp.cz/eknih/1998ps/stenprot/043schuz/s043396.htm#r2>.

71. Takayuki Sakamoto, 'Explaining Electoral Reform: Japan versus Italy and New Zealand', *Party Politics*, vol. 5, no. 4 (1999), pp. 419–38; Patrick Dunleavy and Helen Margetts, 'Understanding the Dynamics of Electoral Reform', *International Political Science Review*, vol. 16, no. 1 (1995), pp. 9–29; Patrick Dunleavy and Helen Margetts, 'From Majoritarian to Pluralist Democracy? Electoral Reform in Britain since 1997', *Journal of Theoretical Politics*, vol. 13, no. 3 (2001), pp. 295–319; Andrej Auersperger Matic, 'Electoral Reform as a Constitutional Dilemma', *East European Constitutional Review*, vol. 9, no. 3 (2000), p. 77.

72. Kubín and Velšic, *Slovensko a jeho volebné pravidlá*, p. 42.

73. Zora Bútorová, 'Vývoj postojov verejnosti: od nespokojenosti k politickej zmene', in Bútora, Mesežnikov and Bútorová, *Slovenské voľby '98: Kto? Prečo? Ako?*, pp. 71–2. Polls also found, however, that a majority of respondents felt ill-informed about the electoral system and did not understand its potential effects.

74. *Mladá fronta Dnes*, 24 July 1998, p. 2.

75. The seminal articles are by Miroslav Novák: 'Malá politologická úvaha o vládní stabilitì', *Parlamentní zpravodaj*, vol. 2, no. 7 (1996), pp. 296–7, and 'Ještě jednou o vládní stabilitì, tentokrát po volbách', *Parlamentní zpravodaj*, vol. 3, nos. 1–2 (1996–97), pp. 15–17, which recommended a joint effort by the Social Democrats and Klaus's ODS to enact electoral reform. See also Miroslav Novák, 'Utváření stranického systému v českých zemích: Analýza dosavadních trendů a výhledy do budoucnu', *Politologický časopis*, vol. 6,

no. 2 (1999), pp. 141–3; and Tomáš Lebeda, 'Vládni stabilita v České republice a volebni systém pomirného zastoupeni', *Politologický časopis*, vol. 5, no. 2
(1998), pp. 115–36.

76. In this respect, post-communist states closely resemble those of Western
Europe. Of twelve countries tracked by Laver and Schofield, only three
(Belgium, Sweden and Denmark) exhibited a clear inverse relationship
between party system size and government duration. See Michael Laver and
Norman Schofield, *Multiparty Government: The Politics of Coalition in Europe*
(Oxford: Oxford University Press, 1990), pp. 148–9.

77. G. Bingham Powell, *Contemporary Democracies: Participation, Stability and
Violence* (Cambridge, MA: Harvard University Press, 1982), pp. 144–51; Carol
Skalnik Leff, 'Dysfunctional Democratization? Institutional Conflict in Post-
Communist Slovakia', *Problems of Post-Communism*, vol. 43, no. 5 (1996),
p. 42; Michal Kubát, 'Volby, fragmentace a polarizace stranického systému
a politická nestabilita v České republice', *Politologický časopis*, vol. 5, no. 3
(1998), pp. 231–43.

78. The Czech regional assemblies were elected under the same rules agreed by
ODS and the Social Democrats in 2000 for the Diet of Deputies; the Quad-
coalition came first in five of the 14 regions, second only (and narrowly) to
ODS in total seats won, while the Social Democrats trailed well behind the
Communists.

79. Sarah Birch, 'Electoral Systems and Party System Stability in Post-Communist
Europe', paper presented for the 97th annual meeting of the American
Political Science Association, San Francisco, 30 August–2 September 2001.

80. Stein Rokkan, *Citizens, Elections, Parties: Approaches to the Comparative Study
of the Processes of Development* (New York and Oslo: McKay, 1970), p. 158,
161; Matthew Soberg Shugart, 'Electoral Reform in Systems of Proportional
Representation', *European Journal of Political Research*, vol. 21 (1992),
pp. 220–1. At least eight major attempts to push electoral systems in win-
concentrating directions have been identified in Western Europe after
1945; see Alexander, 'Institutions, Path Dependence and Democratic
Consolidation', p. 263.

81. Bawn, 'The Logic of Institutional Preferences', pp. 986–8, and Richard
Gunther, 'Electoral Laws, Party Systems and Elites: The Case of Spain',
American Political Science Review, vol. 83, no. 3 (1989), pp. 837–8.

82. James Mahoney, 'Path Dependence in Historical Sociology', *Theory and
Society*, vol. 29, no. 4 (2000), pp. 521–3.

5   Romania: Stability without Consensus

1. See Marina Popescu, 'The 2000 Romanian Parliamentary and Presidential
Elections', *Electoral Studies* (forthcoming 2002).

2. Local Councils of the Front (CFSN) were organized at county and local levels. For more detail on the events of the period see Domniţa Ştefanescu, *Cinci
ani din istoria României* (Bucharest: Editura Maşina de Scris, 1995); also
Nestor Ratesh, *Romania: The Entangled Revolution* (Westport, CT: Praeger,
1991); Martyn Rady, *Romania in Turmoil* (London: I.B. Tauris, 1992).

3. Interwar Romania used several variants of proportional representation, including the notorious premium system to reward the largest party (see Chapter 1). For a summary see Keith Hitchins, *Rumania: 1866–1947* (New York: Oxford University Press, 1994); F. Costiniu and P. D. Şerban, *Aspecte ale evoluţiei sistemului electoral românesc* (Bucharest: Monitorul Oficial, 2000).

4. Chapter VIII of the Draft submitted to public debate: Decree Law of the CFSN on the election of parliament, the president of Romania and local councils, *Adevărul*, 1 February 1990; *România Liberă*, 1 February 1990.

5. Chapter II, Sections 1, 5, 6 and Chapter IV of the Draft.

6. Draft, Chapter VI.

7. A total of 251 supporting signatures were needed for independents, the same number as required to register a political party, according to the Law on Political Parties passed by the CFSN. That law also stated that one person/party list could run in one constituency only.

8. The decision of certain members of the Council of the Front to form the National Salvation Front and stand in elections triggered demonstrations of supporters of the historic parties, who felt that the FSN was both player and judge, while they were excluded from the ruling state bodies. The Council of the Front agreed to co-opt other political parties and the Provisional Council of National Unity (CPUN) was constituted on 16 February 1990. The constitutive principle was that half of its members were members of the former Council of the Front and half were representatives of registered political parties. For discussions of the composition of the Provisional Council and its internal rules see *Monitorul Oficial al României*, Anul 1, Second Part, No. 1.

9. *Monitorul Oficial*, Anul 1, Second Part, No. 8–9 (March 1990), pp. 36, 37. See Article 2 of Law 92/1990.

10. Many in local Councils of the National Salvation Front remained affiliated to the FSN, so it was the only body to have a presence at local level almost everywhere in the country; *Monitorul Oficial*, Anul 1, Part II, No. 12–13 (March 1990), p. 30.

11. A striking example was Senator Radu Timofte's comment that 'the Senate should be a chamber of the wise with less political intrusion'. See *Adevărul*, 15 March 1990.

12. For the debates see *Monitorul Oficial*, Anul 1, Part II, No. 12–13 (March 1990), pp. 29–32. See articles 71 and 72 of Decree-Law 92/1990. For a discussion of the intricacies of the reallocation of seats see A. Hylland, 'The Romanian Electoral Law of 1990: Discussion and Comments', Working Paper 9/1990 (Oslo: Handelshoyskolen BI Norwegian School of Management, 1990).

13. A representative of one party even proposed that foreign donations received by a party should be equally distributed to all registered parties; *Monitorul Oficial*, 12–13, p. 15.

14. On only one occasion were donations from other countries for minority organizations mentioned. Iosif Boda, *Monitorul Oficial*, 12–13, p. 14. For the rest of the debate see *Monitorul Oficial*, Anul 1, No. 8–9 (March 1990), p. 16.

15. See *Monitorul Oficial*, Anul 1, No. 8–9 (March 1990). In 1992 the legal threshold for political parties was raised, and from then on ethnic minority organizations had only to obtain 5 per cent of the quota for parties and more votes than any other list bearing the same ethnic label to receive a seat.

16. The historic parties shared enthusiasm for breaks and clear limits on duration because interwar Romanian legislation included such provisions. After
lengthy debate only the maximum length of a break (one hour) and of all
breaks (two hours) was set, but not exact times, with notification to be
placed at the entrance of the polling station at least one hour in advance.
They did not seem to consider that some voters might attend a closed
polling station.

17. For example, PNL-leader and former émigré Radu Câmpeanu managed to
shift majority opinion on the eligibility for public office of those not resident in Romania in the previous five years. He persuaded some by stressing
that many had left to escape political persecution, and others by drawing a
parallel between émigrés' right to run with that of the former communist
nomenklatura; see *Monitorul Oficial*, Anul 1, no. 8–9 (March 1990).

18. Iliescu was criticized for his rather authoritarian style of chairing the
debates, cutting short some interventions and deciding the time and topics
for casting a vote. But this method was effective not only in passing the law
but also in preventing extremist or anti-democratic opinions from gaining
momentum; see *Monitorul Oficial*, Anul 1, no. 8–13 (March 1990).

19. The Assembly of Deputies comprised 11 minority organizations (excluding
the Democratic Union of Hungarians), of which two gained representation without the help of the special provisions. In the Senate seven parties and one independent were elected. See election results at <http://
www.essex.ac.uk/elections>.

20. All groupings emanating from the FSN judged a unicameral parliament to be
more efficient and agreed that the sole argument for bicameralism was
Romanian tradition. They rejected the idea that unicameralism would be an
inheritance of the communist era and argued that many old and new
democracies had unicameral parliaments. See *Geneza Constituţiei României*
(Bucharest: Editura Monitorul Oficial, 1998) pp. 454–78.

21. A majority of 228 voted for such a system on 26 March 1991. See *Geneza ...*,
p. 480; *Monitorul Oficial*, Part II, no. 8 (28 March 1991).

22. Plenary sessions 15 October 1991 in *Geneza*, pp. 453–523, pp. 681–3, reproducing *Monitorul Oficial*, Part II, no. 30 (17 October 1991). For a list of
amendments proposed on this see *Geneza*, pp. 614–20.

23. 'Viaţa Parlamentară', *Adevărul*, 26 May 1992.

24. See, for instance, the parliamentary reports in *Adevărul* and *Cotidianul*, two
quality national dailies of distinct political orientations, March–June 1992.

25. See Ştefanescu, *Cinci ani ...*, also Michael Shafir, 'War of the Roses
in Romanian National Salvation Front', *RFE/RL Research Report*, vol. 1
(24 January 1992), pp. 15–22; Gabriel Topor, 'The National Salvation Front
in Crisis', *Report on Eastern Europe*, vol. 2 (16 August 1991), pp. 24–9. The
FSDN was renamed the Party of Social Democracy of Romania (PDSR) in July
1993 and Social Democratic Party (PSD) in 2001.

26. On the CDR see Steven Roper, 'From Opposition to Government Coalition:
Unity and Fragmentation within the Democratic Convention of Romania',
East European Quarterly, vol. XXXI, no. 4 (1998), pp. 519–42.

27. Although it was consistently employed, due to its cumbersome formulation
and lack of transparency it gave rise to potential risks of abuse and controversy. See also OSCE Office for Democratic and Human Rights, *Final Report*.

Romanian Parliamentary and Presidential Elections 3rd and 17th November 1996 (OSCE/ODIHR: Warsaw, n.d) and OSCE Office for Democratic and Human Rights, *Romania. Presidential and Parliamentary Elections 26 November and 10 December 2000. Final Report* (OSCE/ODIHR: Warsaw 15 January 2001); Popescu, 'The 2000 Romanian Parliamentary and Presidential Elections'; and Hylland, 'The Romanian Electoral Law of 1990...'

28. The PUNR proposed that the ballot should indicate whether party lists were joined, while the Liberals (PNL) opposed this.

29. Simona N. Popescu, 'Se vor amîna alegerile din cauza lipsei capsatoarelor?,' *Cotidianul*, 21 May 1992.

30. In 1996, the PDSR government used the same logic in another attempt to exclude the Hungarians (UDMR) from the party scene.

31. Understandably, the Democratic Convention was anxious to retain its name and symbol, and could do so by simply adding a circle to the previous symbol and changing its name from Democratic Convention of Romania to Romanian Democratic Convention. The pro-Iliescu splinters from the National Salvation Front ran in 1992 as the Democratic Front of National Salvation and used three roses as their symbol instead of the one in the FSN logo.

32. See <http://www.osce.org>.

33. Interviews conducted by Frances Millard and Marina Popescu with representatives of PDSR, PD, PNL, UDMR and PUNR in September 1999.

34. The new provisions allowed minority organizations to nominate the same list of candidates in several constituencies. The minority organizations advocated this in 1992 and included it in a 1999 legislative proposal of the Parliamentary Group of Minorities (this excludes the Hungarians), but it was never discussed in plenary sessions; Frances Millard and Marina Popescu, interview with Varujan Pambuccian, September 1999.

35. See Emergency Decrees Nos. 129, 140, and 165/2000.

36. It was indeed the case that at times the absence of a quorum prevented votes on legislation. Yet, as in most parliaments, most work is done in committees; and there was certainly improvement in the organization and functioning of the parliamentary groups.

37. Frances Millard and Marina Popescu, interview with Valeriu Stoica, (then Minister of Justice and Vice-President of PNL, after December 2000 president of PNL), September 1999.

38. In June 2001, the Romanian Party of Social Democracy (PDSR) merged with the historic Romanian Social Democratic Party (PSDR) and became the Social Democratic Party (PSD).

39. Frances Millard and Marina Popescu, interview with Victor Boştinaru (then chair of the International Relations Committee of the Chamber of Deputies and Vice-President of the PD), September 1999.

40. Frances Millard and Marina Popescu, interview with Béla Markó, president of the UDMR, September 1999.

41. See <http://www.gov.ro>.

42. Frances Millard and Marina Popescu, interviews with Senator Dan Mircea Popescu (former Minister of Social Protection in the PDSR government) and Ovidiu Muşetescu (then former deputy and head of the political analysis section of the PDSR, and government minister after the 2000 elections), September 1999.

43. Mayoral elections suggest that Hungarian candidates never received the support of any Romanian party.
44. Millard and Popescu, interview with Béla Markó.
45. See Lucian Gheorghiu, 'Se anunţă o vară fierbinte,' *Cotidianul*, 3 July 2001.
46. Andrew Reynolds 'Designing Electoral Systems', in Richard Rose (ed.), *International Encyclopedia of Elections* (Washington, DC and London: CQ Press and Macmillan, 2000) pp. 58–67.
47. For example, despite numerous provisions on the matter, no suspicion-free solution to the two problems behind these issues – ensuring that those who cannot go to the polling station but would like to vote are not disenfranchised, and ensuring that nobody votes twice – was found.

6   Bulgaria: Engineering Legitimacy through Electoral System Design

1. This is especially surprising in the light of the extensive debates and disputes that surrounded other aspects of constitutional design in post-1991 Bulgaria, especially regarding the separation of powers; see Albert P. Melone, 'Bulgaria's National Roundtable Talks and the Politics of Accommodation', *International Political Science Review*, vol. 15, no. 3 (1994), pp. 257–73; Albert P. Melone, *Creating Parliamentary Government: The Transition to Democracy in Bulgaria* (Columbus: Ohio State University Press, 1998); 'Constitution Watch: Bulgaria', *East European Constitutional Review*, various issues.
2. R. J. Crampton, *A Short History of Modern Bulgaria* (Cambridge: Cambridge University Press, 1987).
3. Mattei Dogan, 'Romania, 1919–1938', in Myron Weiner and Regun Ozbudun (eds), *Competitive Elections in Developing Countries* (Chapel Hill, NC: Duke University Press, 1987), pp. 369–89.
4. For a detailed account of electoral reform during this period, see Tatiana Kostadinova, *Bulgaria 1879–1946: The Challenge of Choice* (Boulder, CO: Columbia University Press, 1995).
5. Rumyana Kolarova and Dimitr Dimitrov, 'Bulgaria', *East European Constitutional Review*, vol. 3, no. 2 (1994), p. 50.
6. Maria Iordanova, 'Electoral Law and the Electoral System', in Georgi Karasimeonov (ed.), *The 1990 Election to the Bulgarian Grand National Assembly and the 1991 Election to the Bulgarian National Assembly: Analyses, Documents and Data* (Berlin: Sigma, 1997), p. 34.
7. Crampton, *A Short History of Modern Bulgaria*, p. 106.
8. Stephen Ashley, 'Bulgaria', *Electoral Studies*, vol. 9, no. 4 (1990), pp. 312–18; John D. Bell, 'Bulgaria', in Stephen White, Judy Batt and Paul Lewis (eds), *Developments in East European Politics* (Basingstoke: Macmillan, now Palgrave Macmillan, 1993), pp. 83–97.
9. For general discussions of the Round Table talks in Bulgaria, see Rada Nikolaev, 'Political Maneuvering Before the Round-table Talks', *Report on Eastern Europe*, vol. 1 (26 January 1990), pp. 5–7; Vera Gavrilov, 'Communist Party and Opposition Sign Key Political Agreements', *RFE/RL Report on Eastern Europe*, vol. 1 (6 April 1990), pp. 1–4; Melone, 'Bulgaria's National Roundtable Talks ...'; Melone, *Creating Parliamentary Government*; Rumyana Kolarova and Dimitr Dimitrov, 'The Roundtable Talks in Bulgaria', in

Jon Elster (ed.), *The Roundtable Talks and the Breakdown of Communism* (Chicago and London: University of Chicago Press, 1996), pp. 178–212.

10. *The Guardian*, 16 November 1990; *The Guardian*, 18 November, 1990.
11. Ashley, 'Bulgaria', p. 312.
12. Kolarova and Dimitrov, 'The Roundtable Talks in Bulgaria'; Georgi Karasimeonov, 'The Transition to Democracy', in Georgi Karasimeonov (ed.), *The 1990 Election to the Bulgarian Grand National Assembly and the 1991 Election to the Bulgarian National Assembly: Analyses, Documents and Data* (Berlin: Sigma, 1997), pp. 10–22. It is also alleged that the BCP leadership were as concerned to hang on to the party's economic resources and put themselves in a position to take advantage of marketization if they were to retain political power; Melone, *Creating Parliamentary Government*, pp. 54, 85, 103.
13. Nikolaev, 'Political Maneuvering Before the Round-table Talks', p. 6.
14. Melone, *Creating Parliamentary Government*, pp. 74–6.
15. This contrasts with the Round Table in Hungary, where the parliament subsequently altered the Round Table agreement on the electoral law; see Chapter 3 above.
16. The final decision on the name change was actually made by the party membership in a referendum on the issue in March.
17. Kolarova and Dimitrov, 'The Roundtable Talks in Bulgaria', p. 190.
18. *Kruglata Masa: Stenografski Protokoli (3 Yanuari – 15 Mai 1990)* (Sofia: Fondatsiya Dr. Zhelyu Zhelev, n.d.), p. 404.
19. *Kruglata Masa*, pp. 419–20.
20. Kolarova and Dimitrov, 'The Roundtable Talks in Bulgaria', p. 192.
21. Rada Nikolaev, 'Preparations for Free Elections of a Grand National Assembly', *Report on Eastern Europe*, 15 June 1990, pp. 6–14; Kolarova and Dimitrov, 'The Roundtable Talks in Bulgaria', p. 180.
22. Sarah Birch, interview with academic and Central Election Commission member Dimitr Dimitrov, Sofia, 19 September 2001.
23. Melone, *Creating Parliamentary Government*, p. 9.
24. Nikolaev, 'Preparations for Free Elections of a Grand National Assembly', pp. 6–14.
25. *Duma*, 25 April 1990.
26. Tatiana Kostatinova, 'Elite Negotiations, Uncertainty, and the Emergence of Mixed Systems during Democratic Transition', unpublished manuscript, n.d., p. 18.
27. Kolarova and Dimitrov, 'The Roundtable Talks in Bulgaria', p. 199.
28. Karasimeonov, 'The Transition to Democracy', p. 18; Duncan Perry, 'From Opposition to Government: Bulgaria's "Union of Democratic Forces"', in Wolfgan Hoepken (ed.), *Revolution auf Raten Bulgariens Weg zur Democratie* (Munich: R. Oldenbourg Verlag, 1996), p. 42.
29. Ashley, 'Bulgaria'; Perry, pp. 27–61; *The Guardian*, 2 June 1990.
30. 'Constitution Watch', *East European Constitutional Review*, vol. 2, no. 2 (1993), pp. 3–4.
31. Ashley, 'Bulgaria'.
32. Kolarova and Dimitrov, 'The Roundtable Talks in Bulgaria', pp. 194–7.
33. Kolarova and Dimitrov, 'The Roundtable Talks in Bulgaria', p. 185.
34. Kolarova and Dimitrov, 'The Roundtable Talks in Bulgaria'.

35. Iordanova, 'Electoral Law and the Electoral System', pp. 37–8.
36. Birch interview with Dimitr Dimitrov.
37. *Republika Bulgariya, Sedmo Veliko Narodno Subranie, Stenografski dnevnitsi 1990–1991*, vol. 57 (Sofia, 1992), p. 18 *et passim*.
38. 'Zakon za izbirane na narodin predstaviteli, obshchinski suvetnitsi i kmetove, Prilozhenie 5.II' (Art. 11), *Republika Bulgariya, Sedmo Veliko Narodno Subranie...*, vol. 57, p. 434.
39. See *Duma*, 26 April 1990; *Duma*, 5 May 1990.
40. 'Zakon za izbirane na narodin predstaviteli, obshchinski suvetnitsi i kmetove, Prilozhenie 5.I' (Art. 41), *Republika Bulgariya, Sedmo Veliko Narodno Subranie...*, vol. 57, p. 453.
41. *Republika Bulgariya, Sedmo Veliko Narodno Subranie...* vol. 57, pp. 128–37.
42. The ethnic Turkish-dominated DPS was denied the right to green ballots for the Grand National Assembly elections because it asserted broad aims to circumvent the ban on ethnic parties and could not then regain the right to the green ballot.
43. Duncan Perry, 'Bulgaria: A New Constitution and Free Elections', *RFE/RL Research Report* (3 January, 1992), pp. 78–82.
44. *East European Constitutional Review*, vol. 4, no. 1 (1995), p. 7.
45. *East European Constitutional Review*, vol. 4, no. 1 (1995), p. 8.
46. Organization for Security and Cooperation in Europe (OSCE), *Final Report: OSCE/ODIHR International Observer Mission: Bulgarian Parliamentary Elections*, 19 April 1997 (Warsaw, 1997), pp. 2–3.
47. OSCE, '*Final Report*'.
48. Sarah Birch, interview with Emil Koshlyukov, Sofia, 22 March 2002.
49. Sarah Birch, interview with Irina Bokova, Sofia, 20 March 2002.
50. See Kathleen Bawn, 'The Logic of Institutional Preferences: German Electoral Law as a Social Choice Outcome', *American Journal of Political Science*, vol. 37, no. 4 (1993), pp. 965–89.
51. Melone, *Creating Parliamentary Government*. This is perhaps all the more surprising given that one of the few references in the 1991 constitution to parliamentary elections is Article 66, which states that 'The legitimacy of an election may be contested before the Constitutional Court by a procedure established by law'.
52. Several rulings of minor importance included a rejection in May 2001 of an attempt to remove a clause guaranteeing candidates immunity from prosecution.
53. Birch, interview with Dimitr Dimitrov.

7 Russia: the Limits of Electoral Engineering

1. Brendan Kiernan, *The End of Soviet Politics: Elections, Legislatures, and the Demise of the Communist Party* (Boulder, CO: Westview, 1993), chapter 8; Kathleen Montgomery and Thomas F. Remington, 'Regime Transition and the 1990 Soviet Republican Elections', *Journal of Communist Studies and Transition Politics*, vol. 10, no. 1 (1994), p. 63.

214 *Notes*

2. A greater range of work collectives was allowed to put forward candidates, and the number of voters required for nomination was lowered from 500 in 1989 to 300 in 1990.
3. The survey findings reported in this paragraph are cited in Stephen White et al., *The Politics of Transition: Shaping a Post-Soviet Future* (Cambridge: Cambridge University Press, 1993), p. 30.
4. Stephen White, *After Gorbachev* (Cambridge: Cambridge University Press, 1993), p. 57.
5. The amendments were passed by the Supreme Soviet on 24 October and by the full Congress of People's Deputies on 20 December 1989.
6. Dawn Mann, 'The USSR Constitution: The Electoral System', *RFE/RL Report on the USSR*, vol. 2, no. 5 (1990), pp. 10–13.
7. Vera Tolz, 'The USSR this Week', *RFE/RL Report on the USSR*, vol. 1, no. 34 (1989), p. 37.
8. Iu. A. Novikov, *Izbiratel'naia sistema Rossii. 90 let istorii* (Moscow: Manuskript, 1996), pp. 316–19.
9. Kiernan, *The End of Soviet Politics*, p. 160.
10. White et al., *The Politics of Transition*, p. 34.
11. Kiernan, *The End of Soviet Politics*, p.174; Jerry F. Hough, *Democratization and Revolution in the USSR, 1985–1991* (Washington, DC: Brookings Institution, 1997), pp. 297–8; cf. A. V. Berezkin, V. A. Kolosov, M. E. Pavlovskaya, N. V. Petrov and L. V. Smirnyagin, *Vesna 1989: geografiia i anatomiia parlamentskikh vyborov* (Moscow: Progress, 1990).
12. Vera Tolz, 'Informal Political Groups Prepare for Elections in RSFSR', *RFE/RL Report on the USSR*, vol. 2, no. 8 (1990), pp. 23–8; Darrell Slider, 'The Soviet Union', *Electoral Studies*, vol. 9, no. 4 (1990), pp. 295–302; Conference on Security and Cooperation in Europe (CSCE), 'Report on the March 4, 1990 Congress of People's Deputies Elections in the Russian Republic', in *Elections in the Baltic States and the Soviet Republics: A Compendium of Reports on Parliamentary Elections Held in 1990* (Washington, DC, 1990).
13. Gavin Helf and Jeffrey W. Hahn, 'Old Dogs and New Tricks: Party Elites in the Russian Regional Elections of 1990', *Slavic Review*, vol. 51, no. 3 (1992), pp. 511–30; Hough, *Democratization and Revolution in the USSR*, pp. 278–9, 298.
14. Mann, 'The USSR Constitution ...'
15. Interview, the *Sunday Times*, 25 February 1990.
16. Mann, 'The USSR Constitution ...', p. 12.
17. Vladimir Gel'man, 'Institutional Design: Crafting the Electoral Law', in Vladimir Gel'man and Grigorii V. Golosov (eds), *Elections in Russia, 1993–1996: Analyses, Documents and Data* (Berlin: Sigma, 1999), p. 54; Vladimir Gel'man, 'Sozdavaiia pravila igry: Rossiiskoe izbiratel'noe zakonodatel'stvo perekhodnogo peroida', *Polis*, no. 4 (1997), pp. 129–34; E. M. Kozhokin and K. Kholodovskii, 'Kakim byt' rossiiskomu izbiratel'nomu zakonu?', *Mirovaia ekonomika i mezhdunarodnie otnosheniia*, no. 8 (1993), pp. 28–36; Viktor Sheinis [interviewed], 'Strane nuzhen izbiratel'nyi kodeks', *Obshchestvennye nauki i sovremennost'*, no. 1 (1995), pp. 7–9.
18. Michael McFaul, *Russia's Unfinished Revolution: Political Change from Gorbachev to Putin* (Ithaca, NY: Cornell University Press, 2001), pp. 217–18.
19. Gel'man, 'Institutional Design', pp. 51–2. He reached this conclusion after interviewing Sheinis in August 1994. Certainly there is no indication in

Sheinis's own contemporary description of the law that he was aware of the principal differences between the German linked system and the Russian parallel formula: B. A. Strashun and V. L. Sheinis, 'Politicheskaya situatsiia v Rossii i novyi izbiratel'nyi zakon', *Polis*, no. 3 (1993), p. 65; Viktor Sheinis [interviewed], 'Strane nuzhen izbiratel'nyi kodeks', p. 6.

20. Subsequent decrees augmented and clarified the law, but the result was considerable confusion on the part of contestants, electoral administrators and voters, as gaps were spotted, discrepancies noted and 'clarifying' decrees simply added to the problems they were designed to alleviate; National Institute for International Affairs (NDI). *NDI Pre-Election Report: The December 1993 Elections in the Russian Federation* (Washington, DC: 23 November 1993).

21. McFaul, *Russia's Unfinished Revolution*, p. 219; Laura Belin and Robert W. Orttung, *The Russian Parliamentary Elections of 1995: The Battle for the Duma* (Armonk, NY: M. E. Sharpe, 1997), p. 22.

22. Belin and Orttung, *The Russian Parliamentary Elections of 1995*, p. 19.

23. For example, districting began only on 6 October for elections to be held scarcely two months later; this resulted in considerable malapportionment, which was apparently largely unintentional. See Michael Urban, 'December 1993 as a Replication of Late-Soviet Electoral Practices', *Post-Soviet Affairs*, vol. 10, no. 2 (1994), p. 136.

24. Strashun and Sheinis, 'Politicheskaya situatsiia v Rossii ...', p. 66; Viktor Sheinis [interviewed], 'Strane nuzhen izbiratel'nyi kodeks', p. 7; McFaul, *Russia's Unfinished Revolution*, p. 219; Robert G. Moser and Frank C. Thames, Jr, 'Compromise Amidst Political Conflict: The Origins of Russia's Mixed-Member System', in Matthew Soberg Shugart and Martin P. Wattenberg, *Mixed-Member Electoral Systems: The Best of Both Worlds?* (Oxford: Oxford University Press, 2001), pp. 261–2; Gel'man, 'Institutional Design', p. 52.

25. Quoted in Stephen White, Richard Rose and Ian McAllister, *How Russia Votes* (Chatham, NJ: Chatham House, 1997), p. 109.

26. Strashun and Sheinis, 'Politicheskaya situatsiia v Rossii ...', p. 66.

27. Thomas F. Remington and Steven S. Smith, 'Political Goals, Institutional Context, and the Choice of an Electoral System: The Russian Parliamentary Election Law', *American Journal of Political Science*, vol. 40, no. 4 (1996), pp. 1259–60.

28. *Segodnia*, 9 October, p. 2.

29. NDI, *NDI Pre-Election Report*, p. 2.

30. Belin and Orttung, *The Russian Parliamentary Elections of 1995*, p. 18.

31. Thomas F. Remington and Steven S. Smith, 'Theories of Legislative Institutions and the Organization of the Russian Duma', *American Journal of Political Science*, vol. 42, no. 2 (1998) pp. 545–72; Moser and Thames, 'Compromise Amidst Political Conflict'; Stephen White and Ian McAllister, 'Reforming the Russian Electoral System', *Journal of Communist Studies and Transition Politics*, vol. 15, no. 4 (1999), pp. 17–40. Among those in the president's milieu with electoral ambitions were Sergei Filatov, the chief of staff, and Sergei Shakhrai, a Yeltsin adviser. See McFaul, *Russia's Unfinished Revolution*, p. 219.

32. Moser and Thames, 'Compromise Amidst Political Conflict', pp. 262–5.

33. Gel'man, 'Institutional Design', p. 55.

34. The Federation Council, the upper chamber of the bicameral Russian parliament, was directly elected in 1993 only; after that it was drawn from regional assemblies.
35. NDI, *NDI Pre-Election Report*.
36. See A. Sobianin, E. Gel'man and O. Kaiunov, 'The Political Climate of Russia's Regions: Voters and Deputies, 1991–93', *The Soviet and Post-Soviet Review*, vol. 21, no. 1 (1994), pp. 68–70 for a detailed analysis of the extent and nature of electoral irregularities.
37. Robert Moser, 'The Impact of the Electoral System on Post-Communist Party Development: the Case of the 1993 Russian Parliamentary Elections', *Electoral Studies*, vol. 14, no. 4 (1995), pp. 377–98; Robert Moser, *Unexpected Outcomes: Electoral Systems, Political Parties, and Representation in Russia* (Pittsburgh, PA: University of Pittsburgh Press, 2001).
38. McFaul, *Russia's Unfinished Revolution*, p. 219.
39. Remington and Smith, 'Theories of Legislative Institutions and the Organization of the Russian Duma', pp. 545–9.
40. Belin and Orttung, *The Russian Parliamentary Elections of 1995*, p. 21.
41. Urban, 'December 1993 ...'; Moser, *Unexpected Outcomes*; Moser and Thames, 'Compromise Amidst Political Conflict'.
42. White and McAllister, 'Reforming the Russian Electoral System', p. 18.
43. Belin and Orttung, *The Russian Parliamentary Elections of 1995*, pp. 23–4.
44. Remington and Smith, 'Political Goals, Institutional Context, and the Choice of an Electoral System', pp. 1271–3.
45. Belin and Orttung, *The Russian Parliamentary Elections of 1995*, pp. 25–9.
46. Gleb Cherkasov, 'Generaly gotoviatsia k proshloi voine', *Segodnia*, 19 May 1995, p. 3.
47. Belin and Orttung, *The Russian Parliamentary Elections of 1995*, pp. 111–28.
48. Belin and Orttung, *The Russian Parliamentary Elections of 1995*, pp. 61–4.
49. Dar'ia Korsunskaia, 'U prezidenta ravnye prava c grazhdanami Rossii', *Russkii telegraf*, 11 February 1998.
50. *Nezavisimaia gazeta*, 4 March 1998, on-line edition; Interfax, 2 April 1998; *Interfaks-AiF*, no. 18, 4–10 May 1998, p. 4.
51. For the full text of the 17 November 1998 ruling, see *Rossiiskaia Gazeta*, 8 December 1998, pp. 5–6.
52. For the details of the vote, see the Duma website at <http://www.akdi.ru/gd/PLEN_Z/l999/s02-06_u.htm>.
53. Laura Belin, 'How Did They Get on the Ballot?', *RFE/RL Russian Election Report*, no. 2 (12 November 1999).
54. Peter C. Ordeshook, 'Re-examining Russia: Institutions and Incentives', in Archie Brown (ed.), *Contemporary Russian Politics: A Reader* (Oxford: Oxford University Press, 2001), p. 26.
55. Laura Belin, 'Why Is the Ballot so Crowded?', *RFE/RL Russian Election Report*, no. 1 (5 November 1999).
56. Yitzhak M. Brudny, 'Continuity or Change in Russian Electoral Patterns? The December 1999 – March 2000 Election Cycle', in Brown (ed.), *Contemporary Russian Politics*, pp. 163–70. Brudny distinguishes between genuinely unaffiliated candidates (who were often put forward to represent a governor's interests) and the 29 registered as independents who in fact enjoyed a party's endorsement.

57. Moser, 'The Consequences of Russia's Mixed-Member Electoral System', pp. 514–15.
58. *RFE/RL Russian Political Weekly*, no. 31, 10 December 2001.
59. The term 'managed democracy' was used by Vitalii Tretiakov in *Nezavisimaia gazeta*, 23 March 2001; by Yevgeniya Albats in the *Guardian*, 11 May 2001; by Sergei Mitrokhin of the party Yabloko, in *Nezavismaia gazeta*, 23 June 2001; and by Oleg Liakhovich in *Obshchaia gazeta*, no. 35, 30 August 2001.
60. Urban, 'December 1993 …'
61. Moser and Thames, 'Compromise Amidst Political Conflict', p. 255.

8 Ukraine: the Struggle for Democratic Change

1. Valerii Hryshchuk, 'Antidemokraticheskomu zakonu o vyborakh', *Holos [Golos]*, 6 August 1989, p. 1; *Holos*, 20 August 1989, p. 1. See also Chapter 7 for a discussion of the CPD electoral institutions.
2. This survey was conducted by Valerii Khmel'ko and Volodymyr Paniotto and is reported in O. V. Haran, *Ubyty drakona: z istoriï Rukhu ta novykh partii Ukraïny* (Kiev: Lybid, 1993), p. 72.
3. Several prominent right-wing and centrist party leaders even claimed during parliamentary debates that they would be content with a leftist government, so long as it was a party-based government. Their left-wing critics quickly accused them of being disingenuous; *Vos'ma sesiya Verkhovnoï Rady Ukraïny dvanadtsyatoho sklykannya* (Kiev: Vydannya Verkhovnoï Rady Ukraïny, 1993) (East View Publications microfiche version), Bulletin No. 12, 7 October 1993, pp. 76–101.
4. For details of the alternative drafts, see Marina Stavniichuk, *Zakonodavstvo pro vybory Narodnykh Deputativ Ukraïny: aktual'nii problemy teoriï i praktyky* (Kiev: Fakt, 2001), pp. 68–9.
5. *Vos'ma sesiya Verkhovnoï Rady*, Bulletin No. 13, 7 October 1993, p. 3; Bulletin No. 14, 8 October 1993, p. 3; Bulletin No. 21, 9 October 1993, p. 50.
6. *Vos'ma sesiya Verkhovnoï Rady*, Bulletin No. 12, 7 October 1993, p. 60.
7. *Vos'ma sesiya Verkhovnoï Rady*, Bulletin No. 23, 10 November 1993, p. 6.
8. *Vos'ma sesiya Verkhovnoï Rady*, Bulletin No. 21, 9 November 1993, p. 107.
9. *Vos'ma sesiya Verkhovnoï Rady*, Bulletin No. 23, 10 November 1993, p. 4.
10. Dominique Arel and Andrew Wilson, 'The Ukrainian Parliamentary Elections', *RFE/RL Research Report*, vol. 3, no. 26 (1994), pp. 6–17; V. H. Kremen, Ye. H. Bazovkin, A. O. Bilous, M. D. Mishchenko, V. S. Nebozhenko, P. K. Sytnyk and Yu. V. Shylovetsev, *Vybory do Verkhovnoï Rady Ukraïny: Dosvid ta uroky* (Kiev: Natsionalnyi Institut Stratehichnykh Doslidzhen', 1994), p. 12. The parliamentary transcript is ambiguous on this point, but there is no indication that deputies realized they were adopting a provision different from that in force in the 1990 law (*Vos'ma sesiya Verkhovnoï Rady*, Bulletin No. 32, 18 November 1993).
11. Marko Bojcun, 'The Ukrainian Parliamentary Elections in March–April 1994', *Europe–Asia Studies*, vol. 47, no. 2 (1995), p. 232.
12. Cit. Myron Wasylyk, 'Ukraine Prepares for Parliamentary Elections', *RFE/RL Research Report*, vol. 3, no. 5 (1994), p. 13.
13. *Holos Ukraïny*, 23 February 1994, p. 2.

14. Database on Central and East European Elections at <www.essex.ac.uk/elections>.
15. Dominique Arel and Andrew Wilson, 'The Ukrainian Parliamentary Elections', pp. 9–10.
16. Sarah Birch, 'The Ukrainian Repeat Elections of 1995', *Electoral Studies*, vol. 15, no. 2 (1996), pp. 281–2; Verkhovna Rada law archive at <http://alpha.rada.kiev.ua>.
17. International Foundation for Electoral Systems, *Proposals Regarding the Parliamentary Election Law of Ukraine* (Kiev: International Foundation for Electoral Systems, 1994); Bohdan A. Futey, 'Analysis: The Vote for Parliament and Ukraine's Law on Elections', *Ukrainian Weekly*, 5 June 1994, pp. 8, 14.
18. See O. Berezyuk, 'Vybory Narodnykh Deputativ Ukraïny: Stan Zakonodavstva ta Shlyakhy Ioho Vdoskonalennya', *Pravo Ukraïny*, 5–6 (1995), p. 28.
19. For the views of leading members of Rukh, the Communists and the Socialists, respectively, see Oleksandr Lavrynovych, 'Electoral System Reform and the New Ukrainian Parliament', paper presented at the Conference on Electoral and Legislative Reform, School of Slavonic and East European Studies (13–14 December 1998); Valerii D. Mishura, 'Systema Vyborchoho zakonodavstva v Ukraïny: shlyakhy doskonalennya', in Tsentral'na Vyborcha Komisiya, *Ukraïna Vybory – 98: Dosvid. Problemy. Perspektyvy: Zbirnyk materialiv mizhnarodnoï naukovo-praktychnoï konferentsiï (dopovidi, vystupy, rekomendatsiï)* (Kiev, 1999), pp. 29–31; *Holos Ukraïny*, 20 November 1996, p. 2.
20. *Chetverta Sesiya Verkhovnoï Rady Ukraïny* (23rd/2nd Convocation), Bulletin No. 27, 17 October 1995.
21. For example, Borys Ol'khovs'kyi and Mark Tsvyk, 'Partii Skazhut: "Nado!", Izbirateli vynuzhdeny budut otvetyt' "Est"!', *Holos Ukraïny*, 25 October 1995, p. 11.
22. The draft was published in *Chas/Time*, 14 July 1995, pp. 3–4.
23. *Chetverta Sesiya Verkhovnoï Rady Ukraïny* (23rd/2nd Convocation), Bulletins No. 19, 23, and 27, 6, 12, 17 October 1995.
24. *Shosto Sesiya Verkhovnoï Rady Ukraïny* (23rd/2nd Convocation), Bulletins No. 43 and 44, 14 November 1996. Internet version Nos 14119606.43 and 14119606.44 at <www.rada.gov.ua>.
25. RFE/RL Newsline 1.97, Part II (18 August 1997).
26. A less contentious law on the Central Election Commission was also passed and signed by the president on 17 December. As laid out in the 1995 Lavrynovych draft, the CEC's 15 members were to be appointed by the Rada based on nominations presented by the president. It was established as an independent body whose members serve terms of six years.
27. See *Uryadovyi kur"yer*, 11 December 1997, p. 9; *Holos Ukraïny* 25 December 1997, p. 2; 21 January 1998, p. 4.
28. The ruling is published in *Holos Ukraïny*, 5 March 1998, pp. 3, 5–6. A second Constitutional Court ruling on 25 March, four days before the elections, required an alteration to the definition of precisely which figures constituted the results of the elections (*Holos Ukraïny*, 28 March 1998, p. 6).
29. Oleksyi Kordun, 'Konstitutsinii Sud Ukraïny i Vybory', *Nova Polityka*, 2 (1998), pp. 2–13.

30. Project on 'The Quality of Representative Democracy in Ukraine' conducted in March 1998 with funding from Economic and Social Research Council grant No. R000222380. Further details of the survey design are available from the authors upon request.
31. See Andrew Wilson and Sarah Birch, 'Voting Stability, Political Gridlock: Ukraine's 1998 Parliamentary Elections', *Europe–Asia Studies*, vol. 51, no. 6 (1999), pp. 1039–68.
32. See 'Verkhovna Rada: Zona, vil'na vid mazhorytarshchyny', *Ukraïns'ka Pravda*, 18 January 2001, <http://pravda.com.ua>.
33. See, for example, 'Kuchma maizhe tovaryshuye z Yushchenkom', *Ukraïns'ka Pravda*, 30 January 2001, <http://pravda.com.ua>; RFE/RL Newsline, 3 April 2001, Part II.
34. Interview with Sarah Birch, London, 13 December 1998.
35. Interview with Sarah Birch, Kiev, 13 November 1999.
36. See, for example, the criticisms voiced by M. Ryabets', chairman of the CEC; M. M. Ryabets', 'Vyborcha kampaniya 1998 roku po vyborakh narodnykh deputativ Ukraïny. Pidsumky. Problemy', in Tsentral'na Vyborcha Komisiya, *Ukraïna Vybory – 98: Dosvid. Problemy. Perspektyvy: Zbirnyk materialiv mizhnarodnoï naukovo-praktychnoï konferentsiï (dopovidi, vystupy, rekomendatsiï)* (Kiev, 1999), pp. 11–21.
37. Tsentral'na Vyborcha Komisiya, Proekt Zakon Ukraïny 'Pro Vnesennya Zmin do Zakony Ukraïny '"Pro Vybory Narodnykh Deputativ Ukraïny"' (Kiev: Tsentral'na Vyborcha Komisiya), 2000.
38. Leonid Kuchma, 'Propozitsii do Zakony Ukraïny "Pro vybory narodnykh deputativ Ukraïny"', Vykh. No. 1–14/192 (Kiev. Office of the President of Ukraine, 19 February 2001).
39. See, for example, 'New Election Law Vital', *Kyïv Post*, 24 May 2001, <www.kpnews.com>.
40. 'Election Update #17', Elections and Political Processes Project, Development Associates, Kiev, 17 August 2001.
41. The electoral law was again dogged by legal wrangling. But unlike its predecessor, it survived the March 2002 elections without a successful constitutional challenge.

9 Conclusion: Embodying Democracy

1. For a useful summary see Rein Taagepera, 'How Electoral Systems Matter for Democratization', *Democratization*, vol. 5, no. 3 (1998), pp. 71–4.
2. Jesse argues that the West German system acquired legitimacy, with PR coming to be seen as an 'established right', embedded in popular and party thinking, despite strong preferences within the CDU for a majoritarian system as late as 1966; see Eckhard Jesse, 'The West German Electoral System: The Case for Reform', *West European Politics*, vol. 10, no. 2 (1987), pp. 436–7.
3. By the time of the 1999 elections, the Russian political parties and movements had to have been established for at least a year in order to be allowed to compete in elections. A similar restriction was introduced in Ukraine in 2001.

4. See Sarah Birch, 'Electoral Systems and Party System Stability in Post-Communist Europe', paper presented for the 97th annual meeting of the American Political Science Association, San Francisco (30 August–2 September 2001) for an extended discussion of this finding. On district magnitude see Marina Popescu and Gábor Tóka, 'Districting and Redistricting in Eastern and Central Europe: Regulations and Practices', presented to the Conference, 'Redistricting from a Comparative Perspective', University of California at Irvine (6–8 December 2001).

5. One interesting aspect of the politics of electoral reform is that it is one of the few areas in which the natural fault lines are determined by party size, not by ideological position. This generates unholy alliances and strange bedfellows. It also increases the potential for horse-trading across issues.

Bibliography

Ágh, Attila, 'Defeat and Success as Promoters of Party Change', *Party Politics*, vol. 3, no. 3 (1997), pp. 427–44.

Ágh, Attila and Kurtán, Sándor, 'Parliamentary and Municipal Elections in 1998: A Comparative History of the Hungarian Elections in the Nineties', *Budapest Papers on Democratic Transition*, No. 235 (Budapest: Budapest University of Economics, 1999).

Alexander, Gerard, 'Institutions, Path Dependence and Democratic Consolidation', *Journal of Theoretical Politics*, vol. 13, no. 3 (2001), pp. 249–70.

Arel, Dominique and Wilson, Andrew, 'The Ukrainian Parliamentary Elections', *RFE/RL Research Report*, vol. 3, no. 26 (1994), pp. 6–17.

Ashley, Stephen, 'Bulgaria', *Electoral Studies*, vol. 9, no. 4 (1990), pp. 312–18.

Auersperger Matic, Andrej, 'Electoral Reform as a Constitutional Dilemma', *East European Constitutional Review*, vol. 9, no. 3 (2000), pp. 77–81.

Barany, Zoltan, 'Elections in Hungary', in Robert Furtak (ed.), *Elections in Socialist States* (New York: Harvester Wheatsheaf, 1990), pp. 71–97.

Bawn, Kathleen, 'The Logic of Institutional Preferences: German Electoral Law as a Social Choice Outcome', *American Journal of Political Science*, vol. 37, no. 4 (1993), pp. 965–89.

Bean, Clive, 'Australia's Experience with the Alternative Vote', *Representation*, vol. 34, no. 2 (1997), pp. 103–10.

Belin, Laura, 'Why Is the Ballot so Crowded?', *RFE/RL Russian Election Report*, no. 1 (5 November 1999).

Belin, Laura, 'How Did They Get on the Ballot?', *RFE/RL Russian Election Report*, no. 2 (12 November 1999).

Belin, Laura and Orttung, Robert W., *The Russian Parliamentary Elections of 1995: The Battle for the Duma* (Armonk, NY: M.E. Sharpe, 1997).

Bell, John D., 'Bulgaria', in Stephen White, Judy Batt and Paul Lewis (eds), *Developments in East European Politics* (Basingstoke: Macmillan, now Palgrave Macmillan, 1993), pp. 83–97.

Beneš, Václav, 'Democracy and its problems: 1918–1920', in Victor S. Mamatey and Radomír Luža (eds), *A History of the Czechoslovak Republic 1918–1948* (Princeton, NJ: Princeton University Press, 1973), pp. 39–98.

Benoit, Kenneth, 'Hungary's "Two-Vote" Electoral System', *Representation*, vol. 33, no. 4 (1996), pp. 162–70.

Benoit, Kenneth, 'A Theory of Electoral Systems', paper delivered at conference on Re-Thinking Democracy in the New Millennium (Houston, 16–19 February 2000).

Benoit, Kenneth, 'Two Steps Forward, One Step Back: Electoral Coordination in the Hungarian Election of 1998', paper presented to the 2000 Annual Meeting of the American Political Science Association, Mariott Wardman Park (31 August–3 September 2000).

Benoit, Kenneth, 'Evaluating Hungary's Mixed-Member Electoral System', in Matthew Soberg Shugart and Martin P. Wattenburg (eds), *Mixed-Member*

Electoral Systems. The Best of Both Worlds? (Oxford: Oxford University Press, 2001), pp. 476–93.

Benoit, Kenneth and Hayden, Jacqueline, 'Institutional Change and Persistence: The Origins and Evolution of Poland's Electoral System 1989–2001', paper presented at the ECPR general conference, Canterbury (6–8 September 2001), revised version of 15 October 2001.

Benoit, Kenneth and Schiemann, John, 'Institutional Choice in New Democracies. Bargaining over Hungary's 1989 Electoral Law', *Journal of Theoretical Politics*, vol. 13, no. 2 (2001), pp. 153–82.

Berezkin, A. V., Kolosov, V. A., Pavlovskaya, M. E., Petrov, N. V. and Smirnyagin, L. V., *Vesna 1989: geografiia i anatomiia parlamentskikh vyborov* (Moscow: Progress, 1990).

Berezyuk, O., 'Vybory Narodnykh Deputativ Ukraïny: Stan Zakonodavstva ta Shlyakhy Ioho Vdoskonalenyya', *Pravo Ukraïny*, 5–6 (1995).

Bernhard, Michael, 'Institutional Choice after Communism: A Critique of Theory-Building in an Empirical Wasteland', *East European Politics and Societies*, vol. 14, no. 2 (2000), pp. 316–47.

Birch, Sarah, 'The Ukrainian Repeat Elections of 1995', *Electoral Studies*, vol. 15, no. 2 (1996), pp. 281–2.

Birch, Sarah, 'Elections and Democratization in Contemporary Ukraine' (Basingstoke: Macmillan, now Palgrave Macmillan, 2000).

Birch, Sarah, 'Elections and Representation in Post-Communist Eastern Europe', in Hans-Dieter Klingemann, Ekkehard Mochmann and Kenneth Newton (eds), *Elections in Central and Eastern Europe: The First Wave* (Berlin: Sigma, 2000), pp. 13–35.

Birch, Sarah, *Electoral Systems and Party System Stability in Post-Communist Europe*, paper presented for the 97th annual meeting of the American Political Science Association, San Francisco (30 August–2 September 2001).

Blais, André and Massicotte, Louis, 'Electoral Formulas: A Macroscopic Perspective', *European Journal of Political Research*, vol. 32, no. 1 (1997), pp. 107–29.

Boix, Charles, 'Setting the Rules of the Game: The Choice of Electoral Systems in Advanced Democracies', *American Political Science Review*, vol. 93, no. 3 (1999), pp. 609–24.

Bojcun, Marko, 'The Ukrainian Parliamentary Elections in March–April 1994', *Europe–Asia Studies*, vol. 47, no. 2 (1995).

Bozóki, András, 'Political Transition and Constitutional Change', in András Bozóki, András Körösenyi and George Schöpflin (eds), *Post-Communist Transition. Emerging Pluralism in Hungary* (London: Pinter Publishers, 1992), pp. 60–71.

Bozóki, András, 'Hungary's Road to Systemic Change: The Opposition Roundtable', *East European Politics and Society*, vol. 7, no. 2 (1993), pp. 276–308.

Bozóki, András and Karácsony, Gergely, 'The Making of a Political Elite: Participants of the Hungarian Roundtable Talks in 1989', paper presented at the ECPR general conference, Canterbury, UK (6–8 September 2001).

Brady, Henry E. and Kaplan, Cynthia S., 'Eastern Europe and the Former Soviet Union', in David Butler and Austin Ranney (eds), *Referendums Around the World: The Growing Use of Direct Democracy* (Basingstoke: Macmillan, now Palgrave Macmillan, 1994), pp. 174–217.

Broklová, Eva, *Československá demokracie: Politický systém ČSR 1918–1938* (Prague: SLON, 1992).

Brudny, Yitzhak M., 'Continuity or Change in Russian Electoral Patterns? The December 1999–March 2000 Election Cycle', in Archie Brown (ed.), *Contemporary Russian Politics: A Reader* (Oxford: Oxford University Press, 2001), pp. 163–70.

Bútora, Martin, Mesežnikov, Grigorij and Bútorová, Zora (eds), *Slovenské voľby '98: Kto? Prečo? Ako?* (Bratislava: Inštitút pre verejné otázky, 1999).

Carey, John M. and Shugart, Matthew Soberg, 'Incentives to Cultivate a Personal Vote: A Rank Ordering of Electoral Formulas', *Electoral Studies*, vol. 14, no. 4 (1995), pp. 417–39.

Carstairs, Andrew McLaren, *A Short History of Electoral Systems in Western Europe* (London: George Allen & Unwin, 1980).

Chan, Kenneth Ka-Lok, 'Idealism versus Realism in Institutional Choice: Explaining Electoral Reform in Poland', *West European Politics*, vol. 24, no. 3 (2001), pp. 65–88.

Chiesa, Giulietto with Douglas Taylor Northrup, *Transition to Democracy: Political Change in the Soviet Union, 1987–1991* (Hanover, NH and London: University Press of New England, 1993).

Churchward, L. G., *Contemporary Soviet Government* (London: Routledge & Kegan Paul, 1968).

Colomer, Josep, 'Strategies and Outcomes in Eastern Europe', *Journal of Democracy*, vol. 6, no. 2 (1995), pp. 74–85.

Colomer, Josep, *Political Institutions: Democracy and Social Choice* (Oxford: Oxford University Press, 2001).

Costiniu, F. and Şerban, P. D., *Aspecte ale evoluţiei sistemului electoral românesc* (Bucharest: Monitorul Oficial, 2000).

Crampton, R. J., *A Short History of Modern Bulgaria* (Cambridge: Cambridge University Press, 1987).

Crawford, Keith, 'A System of Disproportional Representation: The Proposed Electoral Law for the Czech Republic', *Representation*, vol. 38, no. 1 (2001), pp. 46–58.

Dehnel-Szyc, Małgorzata and Stachura, Jadwiga, *Gry polityczne – Orientacje na dziś* (Warsaw: Volumen, 1991).

Dinka, Frank and Skidmore, Max J., 'The Functions of Communist One-Party Elections: The Case of Czechoslovakia, 1971', *Political Science Quarterly*, vol. 88, no. 3 (1973), pp. 395–422.

Dogan, Mattei, 'Romania, 1919–1938', in Myron Weiner and Regun Ozbudun (eds), *Competitive Elections in Developing Countries* (Chapel Hill, NC: Duke University Press, 1987), pp. 369–89.

Dunleavy, Patrick and Margetts, Helen, 'Understanding the Dynamics of Electoral Reform', *International Political Science Review*, vol. 16, no. 1 (1995), pp. 9–29.

Dunleavy, Patrick and Margetts, Helen, 'From Majoritarian to Pluralist Democracy? Electoral Reform in Britain since 1997', *Journal of Theoretical Politics*, vol. 13, no. 3 (2001), pp. 295–319.

Elster, Jon (ed.), *The Roundtable Talks and the Breakdown of Communism* (Chicago and London: University of Chicago Press, 1996).

Elster, Jon, Offe, Claus and Preuss, Ulrich, *Institutional Design in Post-communist Societies: Rebuilding the Ship at Sea* (Cambridge: Cambridge University Press, 1998).

Emmons, Terence, *The Formation of Political Parties in the First National Elections in Russia* (Cambridge, MA: Harvard University Press, 1983).

Enyedi, Zsolt, 'Organising a Subcultural Party in Eastern Europe: the Case of the Hungarian Christian Democrats', *Party Politics*, vol. 2, no. 3 (1996), pp. 377–96.

Farrell, David M., *Electoral Systems: A Comparative Introduction* (Basingstoke: Palgrave, now Palgrave Macmillan, 2001).

Friedgut, Theodore H., *Political Participation in the USSR* (Princeton, NJ: Princeton University Press, 1979).

Galanda, Milan, 'Ústavnoprávne aspekty zákona o vol'bach do NR SR', in Martin Bútora, Grigorij Mesežnikov and Zora Bútorová (eds), *Slovenské vol'by '98: Kto? Prečo? Ako?* (Bratislava: Inštitút pre verejné otázky, 1999), pp. 85–93.

Gallagher, Michael, 'Proportionality, Disproportionality and Electoral Systems', *Electoral Studies*, vol. 10, no. 1 (1991), pp. 34–51.

Garber, Larry and Bjornlund, Eric (eds), *The New Democratic Frontier: A Country by Country Report on Elections in Central and Eastern Europe* (Washington, DC: National Democratic Institute for International Affairs, 1992).

Gavrilov, Vera, 'Communist Party and Opposition Sign Key Political Agreements', *RFE/RL Report on Eastern Europe*, vol. 1 (6 April 1990), pp. 1–4.

Geddes, Barbara, 'A Comparative Perspective on the Leninist Legacy in Eastern Europe', *Comparative Political Studies*, vol. 28, no. 2 (1995), pp. 239–74.

Geddes, Barbara, 'Initiation of New Democratic Institutions in Eastern Europe and Latin America', in Arend Lijphart and Carlos H. Waisman (eds), *Institutional Design in New Democracies: Eastern Europe and Latin America* (Boulder, CO: Westview, 1996), pp. 15–42.

Gel'man, Vladimir, 'Sozdavaiia pravila igry: Rossiiskoe izbiratel'noe zakonodatel'stvo perekhodnogo peroida', *Polis*, no. 4 (1997), pp. 125–47.

Gel'man, Vladimir, 'Institutional Design: Crafting the Electoral Law', in Vladimir Gel'man and Grigorii V. Golosov (eds), *Elections in Russia, 1993–1996: Analyses, Documents and Data* (Berlin: Sigma, 1999).

Geneza Constitutiei Romaniei (Bucharest: Editura Monitorul Oficial, 1998).

Getty, J. Arch, 'State and Society under Stalin: Constitutions and Elections in the 1930s', *Slavic Review*, vol. 50, no. 1 (1991), pp. 18–35.

Gunther, Richard, 'Electoral Laws, Party Systems and Elites: The Case of Spain', *American Political Science Review*, vol. 83, no. 3 (1989), pp. 835–58.

Hahn, J., 'An Experiment in Competition: The 1987 Elections to the Local Soviets', *Slavic Review*, vol. 47, no. 3 (1988), pp. 434–47.

Hahn, Werner, 'Electoral "Choice" in the Soviet Bloc', *Problems of Communism*, vol. 36, no. 2 (1987), pp. 29–39.

Haran, O. V., *Ubyty drakona: z istorii Rukhu ta novykh partii Ukraïny* (Kiev: Lybid, 1993).

Havel, Václav, *Letní přemítání* (Prague: Odeon, 1991).

Heinrich, Hans-Georg, *Hungary, Politics and Economics* (London: Frances Pinter, 1986).

Helf, Gavin and Hahn, Jeffrey W., 'Old Dogs and New Tricks: Party Elites in the Russian Regional Elections of 1990', *Slavic Review*, vol. 51, no. 3 (1992), pp. 511–30.

Henderson, Karen, 'Social Democracy Comes to Power: the 1998 Czech Elections', *Labour Focus on Eastern Europe*, no. 60 (1998), pp. 5–25.

Hermet, Guy, Rose, Richard and Rouquié, Alain (eds), *Elections without Choice* (London: Macmillan, 1978).

Hibbing, John R. and Patterson, Samuel C., 'A Democratic Legislature in the Making. The Historic Hungarian Elections of 1990', *Comparative Political Studies*, vol. 24, no. 4 (1992), pp. 430–54.

Hill, Ronald J., 'Continuity and Change in USSR Supreme Soviet Elections', *British Journal of Political Science*, vol. 11, no. 1 (1972), pp. 47–62.

Hill, Ronald J., *Soviet Politics, Political Science, and Reform* (Oxford: Martin Robertson, 1980).

Hitchins, Keith, *Rumania: 1866–1947* (New York: Oxford University Press, 1994).

Hoensch, Jörg, *A History of Modern Hungary 1867–1994* (London: Longman, 1996).

Holmes, Stephen, 'Designing Electoral Regimes', *East European Constitutional Review*, vol. 3, no. 2 (spring 1994), pp. 39–41.

Hough, Jerry F., 'Democratization and Revolution in the USSR, 1985–1991' (Washington, DC: Brookings Institution, 1997).

Hylland, A., *The Romanian Electoral Law of 1990: Discussion and Comments*, Working Paper 9/1990 (Oslo: Handelshoyskolen BI Norwegian School of Management, 1990).

Ilonszki, Gabriella, 'Legislative Recruitment: Personnel and Institutional Development in Hungary, 1990–94', in Gábor Tóka (ed.), *The 1990 Election to the Hungarian National Assembly. Analyses, Documents and Data* (Berlin: Sigma, 1995), pp. 82–107.

Iordanova, Maria, 'Electoral Law and the Electoral System', in Georgi Karasimeonov (ed.), *The 1990 Election to the Bulgarian Grand National Assembly and the 1991 Election to the Bulgarian National Assembly: Analyses, Documents and Data* (Berlin: Sigma, 1997), pp. 34–43.

Ishiyama, John T., 'Electoral Systems Experimentation in the New Eastern Europe: The Single Transferable Vote and the Additional Member System in Estonia and Hungary', *East European Quarterly*, vol. XXIX, no. 4 (1996), pp. 487–507.

Ishiyama, John T., 'Transition Electoral Systems in Post-Communist Europe', *Political Science Quarterly*, vol. 112, no. 1 (1997), pp. 95–115.

Jasiewicz, Krzysztof, 'Elections and Voting Behaviour', in Stephen White, Judy Batt and Paul G. Lewis (eds), *Developments in Central and East European Politics* (Basingstoke: Macmillan, now Palgrave Macmillan, 1998), pp. 166–87.

Jesse, Eckhard, 'The West German Electoral System: The Case for Reform 1949–87', *West European Politics*, vol. 10, no. 2 (1987), pp. 434–48.

Karasimeonov, Georgi, 'The Transition to Democracy', in Georgi Karasimeonov (ed.), *The 1990 Election to the Bulgarian Grand National Assembly and the 1991 Election to the Bulgarian National Assembly: Analyses, Documents and Data* (Berlin: Sigma, 1997), pp. 10–22.

Kiernan, Brendan, *The End of Soviet Politics: Elections, Legislatures, and the Demise of the Communist Party* (Boulder, CO: Westview, 1993).

Kis, János, 'Between Reform and Revolution: Three Hypotheses about the Nature of the Regime Change', in Béla Király and András Bozóki (eds), *Lawful Revolution in Hungary, 1989–94* (Highland Lakes, NJ: Atlantic Research and Publications, 1995), pp. 33–60.

Kitschelt, Herbert, Mansfeldova, Zdenka, Markowski, Radoslaw and Tóka, Gabór, *Post-Communist Party Systems: Competition, Representation, and Inter-Party Competition* (Cambridge: Cambridge University Press, 1999).

Klíma, Michal, 'Volební reforma v České republice v letech 1998–2000', *Politologický časopis*, vol. 7, no. 3 (2000), pp. 223–241.

Klíma, Michal, 'Pomìrný "nepomìrný" volební systém po novelizaci zákona o volbách do Parlamentu ČR', *Politologický časopis*, vol. 7, no. 4 (2000), pp. 334–60.

Kolarova, Rumyana and Dimitrov, Dimitr, 'Electoral Law in Eastern Europe: Bulgaria', *East European Constitutional Review*, vol. 3, no. 2 (1994), pp. 50–5.

Kolarova, Rumyana and Dimitrov, Dimitr, 'The Roundtable Talks and the Breakdown of Communism in Bulgaria', in Jon Elster (ed.), *The Roundtable Talks and the Breakdown of Communism* (Chicago and London: University of Chicago Press, 1996), pp. 178–212.

Kopeček, Lubomír, 'Slovenská demokratická koalice – vznik, geneze and charakteristika', *Politologický časopis*, vol. 6, no. 3 (1999), pp. 248–67.

Kopecký, Petr, *Parliaments in the Czech and Slovak Republics: Party Competition and Parliamentary Institutionalization* (Aldershot: Ashgate, 2001).

Kordun, Oleksyi, 'Konstitutsinii Sud Ukraïny i Vybory', *Nova Polityka*, 2 (1998), pp. 2–13.

Körösényi, András, 'The Hungarian parliamentary elections, 1990', in András Bozóki, András Körösényi and George Schöpflin (eds), *Post-Communist Transition. Emerging Pluralism in Hungary* (London: Pinter, 1992), pp. 72–87.

Körösényi, András, *Government and Politics in Hungary* (Budapest: Central European University Press, 1999).

Kostadinova, Tatiana, *Bulgaria 1879–1946: The Challenge of Choice* (Boulder, CO: Columbia University Press, 1995).

Kostatinova, Tatiana, 'Elite Negotiations, Uncertainty, and the Emergence of Mixed Systems during Democratic Transition', unpublished manuscript, n.d.

Kostelecký, Tomáš, 'Navrhované zmìny volebního zákona vzešlé z dodatků "opoziční smlouvy" v roce 2000 a jejich možné důsledky', *Sociologický časopis*, vol. 36, no. 3 (2000), pp. 299–305.

Koudelka, Zdenìk, 'Zmìna volebního systému', *Politologický časopis*, vol. 7, no. 1 (2000), pp. 90–3.

Kovács, Zoltán and Dinsdale, Alan, 'Whither East European Democracies? The Geography of the 1994 Hungarian Parliamentary Election', *Political Geography*, vol. 17, no. 4 (1998), pp. 437–58.

Kovats, Martin, 'The Roma and Minority Self-Government in Hungary', *Immigrants and Minorities*, vol. 15, no. 1 (1996), pp. 42–58.

Kozakiewicz, Mikołaj, *Byłem Marszałkiem Kontraktowego* (Warsaw: BGW, c.1991).

Kozhokin, E. M. and Kholodovskii, K., 'Kakim byt' rossiiskomu izbiratel'nomu zakonu?', *Mirovaia ekonomika i mezhdunarodnie otnosheniia*, no. 8 (1993), pp. 28–36.

Kremen', V. H., Bazovkin, Ye. H., Bilous, A. O., Mishchenko, M. D., Nebozhenko, V. S., Sytnyk, P. K. and Shylovetsev, Yu. V., *Vybory do Verkhovnoï Rady Ukraïny: Dosvid ta uroky* (Kiev: Natsionalnyi Institut Stratehichnykh Doslidzhen', 1994).

Kubát, Michal, 'Volby, fragmentace a polarizace stranického systému a politická nestabilita v České republice', *Politologický časopis*, vol. 5, no. 3 (1998), pp. 231–43.

Kubín, L'uboš and Velšic, Marián, *Slovensko a jeho volebné pravidlá* (Bratislava: Veda, 1998).

Kukorelli, István, 'The Birth, Testing and Results of the 1989 Hungarian Electoral Law', *Soviet Studies*, vol. 43, no. 1 (1991), pp. 137–56.

Kunc, Jiří, 'K přijatému volebnímu zákonu', *Parlamentní zpravodaj*, vol. 2, no. 2 (1995–6), pp. 105–7.

Laver, Michael and Schofield, Norman, *Multiparty Government: The Politics of Coalition in Europe* (Oxford: Oxford University Press, 1990).

Lebeda, Tomáš, 'Vládní stabilita v České republice a volební systém pomìrného zastoupení', *Politologický časopis*, vol. 5, no. 2 (1998), pp. 115–36.

Lebeda, Tomáš, 'Vládní stabilita v České republice a volební systém pomìrného zastoupení II: Modelování výsledků voleb do Poslanecké snìmovny z roku 1998', *Politologický časopis*, vol. 6, no. 2 (1999), pp. 146–61.

Lebeda, Tomáš, 'Přiblížení vybraných aspektů reformy volebního systemu', *Politologický časopis*, vol. 7, no. 3 (2000), pp. 242–57.

Lengyel, László, 'The Character of Political Parties in Hungary (Autumn 1989)', in András Bozóki, András Körösenyi and George Schöpflin (eds), *Post-Communist Transition. Emerging Pluralism in Hungary* (London: Pinter, 1992), pp. 30–44.

Lentini, Peter, 'Reforming the Electoral System: The 1989 Elections to the USSR Congress of People's Deputies', *Journal of Communist Studies*, vol. 7, no. 1 (1991), pp. 69–94.

Lijphart, Arend, 'Democratization and Constitutional Choices', *Journal of Theoretical Politics*, vol. 4, no. 2 (1992), pp. 207–23.

Lijphart, Arend, *Electoral Systems and Party Systems. A Study of Twenty-Seven Democracies, 1945–1990* (Oxford: Oxford University Press, 1994).

Lijphart, Arend, *Patterns of Democracy: Government Forms and Performance in Thirty-Six Countries* (New Haven, CT: Yale University Press, 1999).

Loloci, Krenar, 'Electoral Law in Eastern Europe: Albania', *East European Constitutional Review*, vol. 3, no. 2 (1994), pp. 42–50.

Lomax, Bill, 'The 1998 Elections in Hungary: Third Time Lucky for the Young Democrats', *Journal of Communist Studies and Transition Politics*, vol. 15, no. 2 (1999), pp. 111–25.

McFaul, Michael, *Russia's Unfinished Revolution: Political Change from Gorbachev to Putin* (Ithaca, NY: Cornell University Press, 2001).

Mackenzie, W. J. M., 'The Export of Electoral Systems', *Political Studies*, vol. 5, no. 3 (1957), pp. 240–57.

Mahoney, James, 'Path Dependence in Historical Sociology', *Theory and Society*, vol. 29 (2000), pp. 17–26.

Malová, Darina, 'Slovakia: From the Ambiguous Constitution to the Dominance of Informal Rules', in Jan Zielonka (ed.), *Democratic Consolidation in Eastern Europe. Volume 1: Institutional Engineering* (Oxford: Oxford University Press, 2001), pp. 347–77.

Mann, Dawn, 'The USSR Constitution: The Electoral System', *Report on the USSR*, vol. 2, no. 5 (1990), pp. 10–13.

Mann, Dawn, 'The RSFSR Elections: Factory-Based Constituencies', *Report on the USSR*, vol. 2, no. 14 (1990), pp. 16–18.

Massicotte, Louis and Blais, André, 'Mixed Electoral Systems: A Conceptual and Empirical Survey', *Electoral Studies*, vol. 18, no. 3 (1999), pp. 341–66.

Melone, Albert P., 'Bulgaria's National Roundtable Talks and the Politics of Accommodation', *International Political Science Review*, vol. 15, no. 3 (1994), pp. 257–73.

Melone, Albert P., *Creating Parliamentary Government: The Transition to Democracy in Bulgaria* (Columbus: Ohio State University Press, 1998).

Merrill, Samuel III, *Making Multicandidate Elections More Democratic* (Princeton, NJ: Princeton University Press, 1988).

Mojak, Ryszard, *Instytucja prezydenta RP w okresie przekształceń ustrojowych* (Lublin: Uniwersytet Marii Curie-Skłodowskiej, 1995).

Montgomery, Kathleen and Remington, Thomas F., 'Regime Transition and the 1990 Soviet Republican Elections', *Journal of Communist Studies and Transition Politics*, vol. 10, no. 1 (1994), pp. 55–79.

Moser, Robert G., 'The Impact of the Electoral System on Post-Communist Party Development: the Case of the 1993 Russian Parliamentary Elections', *Electoral Studies*, vol. 14, no. 4 (1995), pp. 377–98.

Moser, Robert G., *Unexpected Outcomes: Electoral Systems, Political Parties, and Representation in Russia* (Pittsburgh, PA: University of Pittsburgh Press, 2001).

Moser, Robert G. and Thames, Frank C. Jr, 'Compromise Amidst Political Conflict: The Origins of Russia's Mixed-Member System', in Matthew Soberg Shugart and Martin P. Wattenberg, *Mixed-Member Electoral Systems: The Best of Both Worlds?* (Oxford: Oxford University Press, 2001), pp. 255–75.

Nagel, Jack H., 'Reform is the Error Term: Explaining Stability and Change in Electoral Systems', paper presented at the First Conference of the European Consortium for Political Research, University of Kent, Canterbury (6–8 September 2001).

National Democratic Institute for International Affairs (NDI), *NDI Pre-Election Report: The December 1993 Elections in the Russian Federation* (Washington, DC: 23 November 1993).

Nikolaev, Rada, 'Political Maneuvering Before the Round-table Talks', *Report on Eastern Europe*, vol. 1, no. 4 (26 January 1990), pp. 5–7.

Nikolaev, Rada, 'Preparations for Free Elections of a Grand National Assembly', *Report on Eastern Europe*, vol. 1, no. 24 (15 June 1990), pp. 6–14.

Nohlen, Dieter, *Wahlsysteme der Welt: Daten und Analysen* (Munich and Zurich: Piper, 1978).

Nohlen, Dieter, 'Changes and Choices in Electoral Systems', in Arend Lijphart and Bernard Grofman (eds), *Choosing an Electoral System: Issues and Alternatives* (New York: Praeger, 1994), pp. 217–29.

Nohlen, Dieter and Kasapovic, Mirjana, *Wahlsysteme und Systemwechsel in Osteuropa* (Opladen: Leske & Budrich, 1996).

Novák, Miroslav, 'Malá politologická úvaha o vládní stabilitì', *Parlamentní zpravodaj*, vol. 2, no. 7 (1996), pp. 296–7.

Novák, Miroslav, 'Ještě jednou o vládní stabilitì, tentokrát po volbách', *Parlamentní zpravodaj*, vol. 3, nos. 1–2 (1996–7), pp. 15–17.

Novák, Miroslav, 'Utváření stranického systému v českých zemích: Analýza dosavadních trendù a výhledy do budoucnu', *Politologický časopis*, vol. 6, no. 2 (1999), pp. 138–45.

Novikov, Iu. A., *Izbiratel'naia sistema Rossii. 90 let istorii* (Moscow: Manuskript, 1996).

Olson, David, 'Dissolution of the State: Political Parties and the 1992 Election in Czechoslovakia', *Communist and Post-Communist Studies*, vol. 26, no. 3 (1993), pp. 301–14.

Ordeshook, Peter C., 'Re-examining Russia: Institutions and Incentives', in Archie Brown (ed.), *Contemporary Russian Politics: A Reader* (Oxford: Oxford University Press, 2001), pp. 17–28.

Organization for Security and Cooperation in Europe (OSCE), *Final Report: OSCE/ODIHR International Observer Mission: Bulgarian Parliamentary Elections, 19 April 1997* (Warsaw, 1997).

OSCE Office for Democratic and Human Rights, *Final Report. Romanian Parliamentary and Presidential Elections 3rd and 17th November 1996* (Warsaw: OSCE/ODIHR, n.d.).

OSCE Office for Democratic and Human Rights, *Romania. Presidential and Parliamentary Elections 26 November and 10 December 2000. Final Report* (Warsaw: OSCE/ODIHR, 15 January 2001).

Pavlíček, Václav and Hřebejček, Jiří, *Ústava a ústavní řád České republiky. Komentář. 1. díl: Ústavní systém*, 2nd revised and enlarged edn (Prague: Linde, 1998).

Pehe, Jiri, 'Czechoslovak Federal Assembly Adopts Electoral Law', *RFE/RL Research Report*, vol. 1, no. 7 (1992), pp. 27–30.

Pérez-Liñan, Aníbal, 'Neoinstitutional Accounts of Voter Turnout: Moving beyond Industrial Democracies', *Electoral Studies*, vol. 20, no. 2 (2001), pp. 281–97.

Perry, Duncan, 'Bulgaria: A New Constitution and Free Elections', *RFE/RL Research Report*, vol. 1 (3 January 1992), pp. 78–82.

Perry, Duncan, 'From Opposition to Government: Bulgaria's "Union of Democratic Forces"', in Wolfgan Hoepken (ed.), *Revolution auf Raten Bulgariens Weg zur Democratie* (Munich: R. Oldenbourg Verlag, 1996), pp. 27–61.

Perzkowski, Stanisław (ed.), *Tajne dokumenty Biura Politycznego i Sekretariatu KC. Ostatni rok władzy 1988–1989* (London: Aneks, 1994).

Policar, Radek, 'Jsou navrhované změny volebního zákona v souladu s ústavou?', *Politologický časopis*, vol. 7, no. 2 (2000), pp. 178–82.

Polonsky, Antony, *Politics in Independent Poland 1921–1939. The Crisis of Constitutional Government* (Oxford: Clarendon Press, 1972).

Popescu, Marina, 'The 2000 Romanian Parliamentary and Presidential Elections', *Electoral Studies* (forthcoming 2002).

Popescu, Marina and Tóka, Gábor, 'Districting and Redistricting in Eastern and Central Europe: Regulations and Practices', paper prepared for the Conference, 'Redistricting from a Comparative Perspective', University of California at Irvine (6–8 December 2001).

Powell, G. Bingham, *Contemporary Democracies: Participation, Stability and Violence* (Cambridge, MA: Harvard University Press, 1982).

Pravda, Alex, 'Elections in Communist Party States', in Guy Hermet, Richard Rose and Alain Rouquié (eds), *Elections without Choice* (London: Macmillan, 1978).

Punnett, Malcolm and Ilonszki, Gabriella, 'Leading Democracy: The Emergence of Party Leaders and Their Roles in the Hungarian Parties', *Journal of Communist Studies and Transition Politics*, vol. 10, no. 3 (1994), pp. 101–19.

Raciborski, Jacek, 'Wzory zachowań wyborczych a dawne modele wyborców', in L. Kolarska-Bobińska, P. Łukasiewicz and Z. W. Rykowski (eds), *Wyniki badań – wyniki wyborów 4 czerwca 1989 r.* (Warsaw: PTS, 1990).

Raciborski, Jacek, *Polskie Wybory. Zachowanie wyborcze społeczeństwa polskiego 1989–1995* (Warsaw: Scholar, 1997).

Racz, Barnabas, 'Political Participation and Developed Socialism: the Hungarian Elections of 1985', *Soviet Studies*, vol. XXXIX, no. 1 (1987), pp. 40–62.

Racz, Barnabas, 'The Parliamentary Infrastructure and Political Reforms in Hungary', *Soviet Studies*, vol. XLI, no. 1 (1989), pp. 39–66.

Racz, Barnabas, 'Political Pluralisation in Hungary: the 1990 Elections', *Soviet Studies*, vol. 43, no. 1 (1991), pp. 107–36.

Radkey, Oliver H., *Russia Goes to the Polls: The Election to the All-Russian Constituent Assembly, 1917* (Ithaca, NY and London: Cornell University Press, 1990).

Rady, Martyn, *Romania in Turmoil* (London: I.B.Tauris, 1992).

Ratesh, Nestor, *Romania: The Entangled Revolution* (Westport, CT: Praeger, 1991).

Reed, Steven R. and Thies, Michael F., 'The Causes of Electoral Reform in Japan', in Matthew Soberg Shugart and Martin P. Wattenburg (eds), *Mixed-Member Electoral Systems. The Best of Both Worlds?* (Oxford: Oxford University Press, 2001), pp. 380–430.

Reilly, Ben, 'The Plant Report and the Supplementary Vote: Not So Unique After All', *Representation*, vol. 34, no. 2 (1997), pp. 95–102.

Remington, Thomas F. and Smith, Steven S., 'Political Goals, Institutional Context, and the Choice of an Electoral System: The Russian Parliamentary Election Law', *American Journal of Political Science*, vol. 40, no. 4 (1996), pp. 1253–79.

Remington, Thomas F. and Smith, Steven S., 'Theories of Legislative Institutions and the Organization of the Russian Duma', *American Journal of Political Science*, vol. 42, no. 2 (1998), pp. 545–72.

Reykowski, Janusz, 'Komentarz', *Studia Socjologiczne*, no. 2 (1997), pp. 40–5.

Reynolds, Andrew, 'Designing Electoral Systems', in Richard Rose (ed.), *International Encyclopedia of Elections* (Washington, DC and London: CQ Press and Macmillan, now Palgrave Macmillan, 2000), pp. 58–67.

Reynolds, Andrew and Reilly, Ben (eds), *The International IDEA Handbook of Electoral System Design* (Stockholm: International IDEA, 1997).

Roberts, Henry, *Rumania. Political Problems of an Agrarian State* (New Haven, CT: Yale University Press, 1951).

Robinson, William F., *The Pattern of Reform in Hungary: A Political, Economic and Cultural Analysis* (London: Praeger, 1973).

Roeder, Philip G., 'Electoral Avoidance in the Soviet Union', *Soviet Studies*, vol. 41, no. 3 (1989), pp. 462–83.

Rogowski, Ronald, 'Trade and the Variety of Democratic Institutions', *International Organization*, vol. 41 (1987), pp. 203–24.

Rokkan, Stein (with Angus Campbell, Per Torsvik and Henry Valen), *Citizens, Elections, Parties: Approaches to the Comparative Study of the Processes of Development* (New York and Oslo: McKay, 1970 and Oslo: Universitetsforlaget, 1970).

Roper, Steven, 'From Opposition to Government Coalition: Unity and Fragmentation within the Democratic Convention of Romania', *East European Quarterly*, vol. XXXI, no. 4 (1998), pp. 519–42.

Rothschild, Joseph, *East-Central Europe between the Two World Wars* (Seattle and London: University of Washington Press, 1974).

Sakamoto, Takayuki, 'Explaining Electoral Reform: Japan versus Italy and New Zealand', *Party Politics*, vol. 5, no. 4 (1999), pp. 419–38.

Schiemann, John W., 'Hedging against Uncertainty: Regime Change and the Origins of Hungary's Mixed-Member System', in Matthew Soberg Shugart and Martin P. Wattenburg (eds), *Mixed-Member Electoral Systems. The Best of Both Worlds?* (Oxford: Oxford University Press, 2001), pp. 231–54.

Schöpflin, George, 'Critical Currents in Hungary 1968–1978', in Rudolf Tőkés (ed.), *Opposition in Eastern Europe* (London: Macmillan, now Palgrave Macmillan, 1979), pp. 167–9.

Shafir, Michael, 'War of the Roses in Romanian National Salvation Front', *RFE/RL Research Report*, vol. 1 (24 January 1992), pp 15–22.

Shugart, Matthew Soberg, 'Electoral Reform in Systems of Proportional Representation', *European Journal of Political Research*, vol. 21 (1992), pp. 207–24.

Shugart, Matthew Soberg, *Efficiency and Reform: A Theory of Electoral System Change in the Context of Economic Liberalization*, paper prepared for delivery at the Annual Meeting of the American Political Science Association (Boston, 3–6 September 1998).

Shugart, Matthew Soberg, 'The Inverse Relationship Between Party Strength and Executive Strength: A Theory of Politicians' Constitutional Choices', *British Journal of Political Science*, vol. 28, no. 1 (1998), pp. 1–29.

Shugart, Matthew Soberg, 'Electoral "Efficiency" and the Move to Mixed-Member Systems', *Electoral Studies*, vol. 20, no. 2 (2001), pp. 173–93.

Skalnik Leff, Carol, 'Dysfunctional Democratization? Institutional Conflict in Post-Communist Slovakia', *Problems of Post-Communism*, vol. 43, no. 5 (1996), pp. 36–50.

Slider, Darrell, 'The Soviet Union', *Electoral Studies*, vol. 9, no. 4 (1990), pp. 295–302.

Sobianin, A., Gel'man, E. and Kaiunov, O., 'The Political Climate of Russia's Regions: Voters and Deputies, 1991–93', *Soviet and Post-Soviet Review*, vol. 21, no. 1 (1994), pp. 63–84.

Stanger, Allison K. (ed.), *Irreconcilable Differences? Explaining Czechoslovakia's Dissolution* (Lanham, MD: Rowman & Littlefield, 1999), pp. 107–25.

Stark, David and Bruszt, László, *Postsocialist Pathways. Transforming Politics and Property in East Central Europe* (Cambridge: Cambridge University Press, 1998).

Stavniichuk, Marina, *Zakonodavstvo pro vybory Narodnykh Deputativ Ukraïny: aktual'nii problemy teoriï i praktyky* (Kiev: Fakt, 2001).

Stefanescu, Domnita, *Cinci ani din istoria Romaniei* (Bucharest: Editura Masina de Scris, 1995).

Stengers, Jean, 'Histoire de la législation électorale en Belgique', in Serge Noiret (ed.), *Political Strategies and Electoral Reforms: Origins of Voting Systems in Europe in the 19th and 20th Centuries* (Baden-Baden: Nomos, 1990).

Strashun, B. A. and Sheinis, V. L., 'Politicheskaya situatsiia v Rossii i novyi izbiratel'nyi zakon', *Polis*, no. 3 (1993), pp. 65–9.

Suk, Jiří, *Občanské fórum. Listopad-prosinec 1989. 2. díl – Dokumenty* (Brno: Doplnìk, 1998), p. 220.

Szalai, Erzsébet, 'The Power Structure in Hungary after the Political Transition', in Christopher Bryant and Edmund Mokrzycki (eds), *The New Great Transformation?* (London: Routledge, 1994), pp. 120–43.

Taagepera, Rein and Shugart, Matthew Sobert, *Seats and Votes: The Effects and Determinants of Electoral Systems* (New Haven, CT and London: Yale University Press, 1989).

Taagepera, Rein, 'The Baltic States', *Electoral Studies*, vol. 9, no. 4 (1990), pp. 303–11.

Taagepera, Rein, 'How Electoral Systems Matter for Democratization', *Democratization*, vol. 5, no. 3 (1998), pp. 68–91.

Tóka, Gábor, 'Seats and Votes: Consequences of the Hungarian Electoral Law', in Gábor Tóka (ed.), *The 1990 Election to the Hungarian National Assembly. Analyses, Documents and Data* (Berlin: Sigma, 1995), pp. 41–66.

Tőkés, Rudolf, *Hungary's Negotiated Revolution. Economic Reform, Social Change and Political Succession* (Cambridge: Cambridge University Press, 1996).

Tolz, Vera, 'Informal Political Groups Prepare for Elections in RSFSR', *Report on the USSR*, vol. 2, no. 8 (1990), pp. 23–8.

Topor, Gabriel, 'The National Salvation Front in Crisis', *Report on Eastern Europe*, vol. 2 (16 August 1991), pp. 24–9.

Tsebelis, George, *Nested Games: Rational Choice in Comparative Politics* (Berkeley: University of California Press, 1990).

Tsentral'na Vyborcha Komisiya, *Ukraïna Vybory – 98: Dosvid. Problemy. Perspektyvy: Zbirnyk materialiv mizhnarodnoï naukovo-praktychnoï konferentsiï (dopovidi, vystupy, rekomendatsiï)* (Kiev, 1999).

Turnovec, František, 'Electoral Rules and the Fate of Nations: Czechoslovakia's Last Parliamentary Election', in Michael Kraus and Allison K. Stanger (eds), *Irreconcilable Differences? Explaining Czechoslovakia's Dissolution* (Lanham, MD: Rowman & Littlefield, 1999).

Urban, Michael, 'December 1993 as a Replication of Late-Soviet Electoral Practices', *Post-Soviet Affairs*, vol. 10, no. 2 (1994).

Urban, Michael, *More Power to the Soviets: The Democratic Revolution in the USSR* (Aldershot: Edward Elgar, 1990).

Wasylyk, Myron, 'Ukraine Prepares for Parliamentary Elections', *RFE/RL Research Report*, vol. 3, no. 5 (1994).

White, Stephen, 'Reforming the Electoral System', *Journal of Communist Studies*, vol. 4, no. 4 (1988), pp. 1–17.

White, Stephen, 'The Elections to the USSR Congress of People's Deputies March 1989', *Electoral Studies*, vol. 9, no. 1 (1990), pp. 59–66.

White, Stephen, *After Gorbachev* (Cambridge: Cambridge University Press, 1993).

White, Stephen and McAllister, Ian, 'Reforming the Russian Electoral System', *Journal of Communist Studies and Transition Politics*, vol. 15, no. 4 (1999), pp. 17–40.

White, Stephen, Gill, Graeme and Slider, Darrell, *The Politics of Transition: Shaping a Post-Soviet Future* (Cambridge: Cambridge University Press, 1993).

White, Stephen, Rose, Richard and McAllister, Ian, *How Russia Votes* (Chatham, NJ: Chatham House, 1997).

Wightman, Gordon, 'The Development of the Party System and the Break-Up of Czechoslovakia', in Gordon Wightman (ed.), *Party Formation in East-Central Europe: Post-communist Politics in Czechoslovakia, Hungary, Poland and Bulgaria* (Aldershot: Edward Elgar, 1994), pp. 59–78.

Wilson, Andrew and Birch, Sarah, 'Voting Stability, Political Gridlock: Ukraine's 1998 Parliamentary Elections', *Europe–Asia Studies*, vol. 51, no. 6 (1999), pp. 1039–68.

Wolff, Robert Lee, *The Balkans in Our Time* (Cambridge, MA: Harvard University Press, 1956).

Wynot, Edward D. Jr, *Polish Politics in Transition. The Camp of National Unity and the Struggle for Power 1935–1939* (Athens: University of Georgia Press, 1974).

Zaslavsky, Victor and Brym, Robert J., 'The Function of Elections in the USSR', *Soviet Studies*, vol. 30, no. 3 (1978), pp. 362–71.

Zemko, Milan, 'Politické strany a volebný systém na Slovensku v retrospektíve troch volieb do SNR a NR SR', in Soňa Szomolányi and Grigorij Mesežnikov (eds), *Slovensko: Vol'by 1994. Príčiny – dôsledky – perspektívy* (Bratislava: Interlingua, 1994), pp. 45–58.

Glossary

Alternative vote. A preferential majoritarian system in which voters rank all or some candidates in order of preference in single-member districts. Any candidate receiving over 50 per cent of first preference votes is elected. If no candidate achieves an absolute majority, votes are reallocated until one candidate gains an absolute majority of votes cast.

Apparentement. An arrangement in some PR-list systems that permits two or more party lists to be joined in the initial counting of votes and allocation of seats. The parties normally appear on the ballot as separate entities, but votes given for each are combined in the allocation of seats.

Ballot structure. Type and complexity of the choices that the voters can indicate on the ballot paper. Categorical ballots – typical under FPTP and in list PR – allow voters to choose just one party/candidate and thus reject all others, but semi-open list PR may also allow preference voting. Ordinal ballots – used under STV and implicitly employed in two-round systems where voters' choice may change from one round to the next – allow voters a more sophisticated ranking of the candidates.

Closed lists. A type of categorical ballot structure used in PR systems in which the voters cast just one vote and are restricted to voting for a party list only. In closed list systems the parties themselves control the order in which the candidates are placed on their lists.

Disproportionality of seat allocation. The extent to which the percentage distribution of parliamentary seats by party deviate from the percentage distribution of votes. The best-known measures of disproportionality are the Loosemore-Hanby and Gallagher indexes.

The *Loosemore-Hanby* index of disproportionality measures the disproportionality of seat allocation with the formula $D = \frac{1}{2}\Sigma|v_i - s_i|$ where v_i is each party's share of the vote and s_i each party's share of the seats.

The *Gallagher* index of disproportionality measures the disproportionality of seat allocation with the formula $LSq = \sqrt{[\frac{1}{2}\Sigma(v_i - s_i)^2]}$, where v_i and s_i are the proportions of votes and seats, respectively, won by party i.

District magnitude. The size of the electoral district in terms of seats, i.e. the number of members to be elected in each electoral district.

Effective number of parties. A formula devised by Marku Laasko and Rein Taagepera to measure the fragmentation of the party system. It is calculated as one divided by the sum of the squared proportion of popular votes (or legislative seats) won by each party.

Electoral formula. This refers to that element of the electoral system concerned with the translation of votes into seats.

First-past-the-post (FPTP) systems. A subtype of majoritarian electoral system, using a categorical ballot and candidate-centred voting. It is also known as the plurality system, in which the winning candidate secures more votes than any other, but not necessarily a majority. The FPTP system is widely used across the British Commonwealth and the USA, typically in single-member districts.

When the system is used in multi-member districts, as for the Polish Senate, it is known as the block vote, for voters have as many votes as there are seats to be filled.

Highest average methods of seat allocation. Highest average systems use a series of divisors (see d'Hondt and Sainte-Laguë below) to allocate *N* seats proportionally among the competing parties. At each stage the party with the highest average wins. The count continues with party total vote being divided by sequential divisors until all seats are filled.

d'Hondt formula. A highest average method that uses the divisors 1, 2, 3, 4, 5, ... It is more favourable for large parties than the Sainte-Laguë method.

Modified Sainte-Laguë formula. A highest average formula that replaces the first divisor (1) used in the Sainte-Laguë method with 1.4 but leaves the remaining divisors unchanged. It is slightly more favourable for larger parties than the Sainte-Laguë method.

Sainte-Laguë formula. A highest average formula that uses the divisors 1, 3, 5, 7, ..., *n*. It is more favourable for small parties than the d'Hondt method.

Largest remainder methods of seat allocation. Largest remainder systems use an electoral quota (see Hare, Droop, Hagenbach-Bischoff and Imperiali) to allocate *N* seats proportionally among the competing parties. First, parties are awarded seats in proportion to the number of quotas they fill. Second, the remaining votes are allocated in order of vote size.

Hare quota. A frequently used quota for seat allocation in largest remainder list systems. It is calculated as the total number of valid votes divided by the number of seats to be allocated. The seat allocation obtained with the Hare quota is *ceteris paribus* more favourable for small parties than those obtained with the Droop and Imperiali quotas.

Droop quota. A frequently used quota for seat allocation in largest remainder list systems. It is calculated as the total number of valid votes divided by the number of seats, then one is added to the product: [votes/(seats + 1)] + 1. The term '+ 1 vote' avoids a tie for the last seat.

Hagenbach-Bischoff quota. This is simply the number of total valid votes divided by the number of seats plus one (votes/(seats + 1)). It is often confused with Droop.

Imperiali quota. A quota that is infrequently used for seat allocation in largest remainder list systems. The quota is derived from the formula total seats divided by the number of seats plus two (seats/votes + 2). The seat allocation obtained with the Imperiali quota is *ceteris paribus* less favourable for small parties than those obtained with the Droop, Hare and Hagenbach-Bischoff quotas.

Majoritarian electoral systems. A system usually based on single-member districts in which a majority of votes is the criterion for allocating a seat. This may be a simple majority or plurality (the candidate/s receiving the highest number of votes in a constituency win/s the seat) or an absolute majority (50% + 1 vote), while the other candidates receive no seats. The most frequently mentioned advantages of majoritarian electoral systems are clear legislative majorities that facilitate enduring one-party governments, and closer ties between individual representatives and a geographically defined constituency.

Mixed electoral systems – also known as mixed member systems (MMS). Any electoral system comprising several segments, typically providing for a majoritarian element electing deputies in single-member districts and a PR-list element electing deputies in multi-member districts, and voters cast one vote in each element. Mixed systems may be *parallel*, with no formal relationship between the elements. Most states of the former USSR use mixed-parallel systems. Mixed systems are *linked* when the PR component is used to compensate for the disproportionality produced within the majoritarian component. The electoral systems of Germany, Hungary and currently New Zealand are examples of the second type, also known as mixed member systems. Germany, with its provision for a flexible number of deputies is also known as the additional member system.

Open lists. A type of ordinal ballot structure used in PR systems in which voters can express a preference for one or several candidates nominated on party lists. Voters may or must indicate a choice of candidate, and a vote for a candidate is also a vote for the candidate's party. Open list systems vary in the extent to which the voters can actually influence not only how many, but also which candidates are elected from a given list.

PR (proportional representation) systems. Any electoral system that primarily aims at at least a rough parity between the proportion of votes received and seats won by each party or other electoral contender. Proportional representation requires that deputies be elected in multi-member constituencies.

List-PR. This is the most common type of proportional representation, in which each party presents a list of candidates to the electorate, voters vote for a party and winning candidates are taken from the party list.

Preference voting. Any system that permits voters to rank candidates in order of preference. The alternative vote and STV are systems of this type. When used with PR preference voting is sometimes referred to as a semi-open list system.

Single transferable vote (STV). An electoral system that allows voters to rank all candidates who run in their multi-member constituency, thus promoting competition both between parties and between the candidates of the same party. To gain election candidates must reach or exceed a specified quota of first-preference votes. If there are fewer such winning candidates than seats to be allocated, the candidate with the lowest number of votes is eliminated, and his or her votes are transferred to the candidates who received the next highest preference of the given voter. The same happens with the surplus votes of the elected candidates, i.e. the number of votes they have above the electoral quota. This process continues until all seats for the constituency are filled.

Threshold. A minimum level of electoral support, usually defined as the percentage of the nationwide total of valid votes needed by a party in order to gain representation. Parties gaining less than the required percentage of votes are not included in the seat allocation procedures, and their votes are considered 'wasted'. The threshold value is one of the major determinants of how proportional the results are in a given PR electoral system.

Two-round electoral systems. A type of majoritarian electoral system in which a second round of voting is called if no candidate receives more than an absolute majority of the vote in the first round. Two-round systems vary in how many of the initial candidates may contest the second round, and whether the winner of the second round needs to win an absolute majority of the votes, as for a time in Ukraine, or just a plurality, as in French and Hungarian legislative elections, hence: majority–plurality and majority–majority two-round systems.

Index

Antall, József, 52, 55, 56, 63
Apparentement, 76–7, 96, 99

Benoit, Kenneth, 17
Blais, André, 10
Bulgaria, 11–12, 15, 109–27, 134, 142,
    164, 170, 171, 172, 173, 174, 178,
    179, 160, 181, 182, 183, 184, 185
  ballot papers, 122, 125
  candidature, 121–2
  Constitution, 110–11
  Constitutional Court, 126–7
  elections, 111, 112: of 1990,
      117–18; of 1991, 123; of 1994,
      124; of 1997, 124; of 2001, 125
  electoral history, 111–13
  electoral laws: of 1990, 110–11,
      114–17; of 1991, 119–23;
      summary of, 110
  finance, 123
  Grand National Assembly, 109, 110,
      114, 115, 117, 119, 120, 121,
      122, 125, 126
  political parties: Bulgarian Socialist
      Party (BSP), 109, 110, 114, 115,
      116, 117–18, 119, 120, 122,
      123, 124, 126, 167, 171, 184;
      Communist Party, 113;
      Movement for Rights and
      Freedoms (DPS), 114, 121, 124;
      National Movement for Simeon
      II (NDSV), 125, 172; Union of
      Democratic Forces (SDS),
      112–13, 114, 115, 117–18, 119,
      120, 121, 123, 124, 171, 173, 184
  Round Table, 109–10, 113–18, 120,
      123, 125, 167
  thresholds, 117, 122, 124
Buzek, Jerzy, 32

Chernomyrdin, Viktor, 137
Constitutional courts (see also under
    Bulgaria, Czech Republic, Russia,

Slovakia, Ukraine), 16, 177, 178,
    183
Corruption, 32, 111, 118, 126, 144,
    155–6, 172
Czechoslovakia, 12, 15, 67–75, 86,
    166, 168, 170, 171, 172, 173, 183
  Civic Forum, 68, 69, 70, 72, 88, 168,
      171, 176; 1946 law of, 70–1;
      1990 law of, 71–2
  disproportionality in, 74
  majoritarianism, support for, 71–2, 73
  political parties: Civic Democratic
      Party (ODS), 73, 74;
      Communist Party, 69
  preference voting, 74
  proportional representation, 68–70
  Public against Violence, 68, 69, 70,
      88, 168, 171, 183
  Round Table, 168
  supplementary vote, proposal for,
      72–3
Czech Republic, 79–89, 164, 165, 173,
    174, 176–7, 178, 179, 180, 181,
    183, 185, 186
  Constitution, 80–1
  Constitutional Court, 83–4, 177, 178
  disproportionality in, 81, 82, 83
  elections: of 1996, 80; of 1998, 80,
      82
  electoral laws, summary of, 85–6;
      law of 2002, 84–5, 177
  finance, 126
  political parties: Civic Democratic
      Party (ODS), 80, 81, 82, 83, 84,
      85, 88, 176, 186; Christian
      Democrats, 80, 81; Freedom
      Union, 80; Quad Coalition, 83,
      85; Republicans, 80; Social
      Democrats (CSSD), 80, 81, 82,
      83, 84, 85, 176
  proportional representation, nature
      of, 84–6
  Senate, 80, 81, 83, 85, 178

Democratization, xi, 1–2, 7

Elections (*see individual countries*)
Electoral systems (*see also individual
    countries*), 2–3
  changes in (*see also* electoral-system
    design, *individual countries*),
    20–2
  Communist, 3–7, 11, 20; reform of,
    5–7, 26, 49–51, 112, 128–32
  and party systems, 14, 23, 170
  majoritarian (*see also individual
    countries*), 4–5, 10, 14, 17
  proportional representation (*see also
    individual countries*), 10, 12,
    14
Electoral-system design, 1, 19, 106,
    109
  actors in, 2, 8–9, 16–18, 19, 20, 21,
    22, 23, 33–4, 45–7, 169–70
  decision-making fora, 8–9, 20, 21,
    35–6, 39, 42–3, 51–61, 166–9
  explanations of, 9–22, 45–7, 65–6,
    86–8, 105–8, 111, 125–6, 128,
    135–6, 178–88
  issues of (*see also individual
    countries*), 22, 170–2
  stability of, 1, 64–5, 67, 89, 106,
    125, 141–2, 163, 173–8
  stages of, xii, 1, 3, 9, 18, 20,
    166–72

Fejti, György, 54, 57, 186
Filatov, Sergei, 133, 134
Finance (*see* Bulgaria, Poland,
    Romania, Ukraine)
Franchise, 4, 7–8, 10, 91

Gebethner, Stanisław, 33, 35
Germany, 18, 22, 35, 49, 70, 75, 89,
    132, 182
Gorbachev, Mikhail, 2, 6, 129, 130

Habsburg Monarchy, 10, 70–1,
Havel, Václav, 72–3, 83–4, 85, 170
Hungary, 11–12, 15, 48–66, 116, 119,
    132, 134, 142, 164, 165, 166, 169,
    171, 172, 173, 174, 175–6, 178,
    179, 181, 182, 183

elections, 63–5
electoral law: under communism,
    49–51; of 1989, 60–1,
  amendments to, 61–2,
  incentives of, 64–5
  majoritarianism, support for, 55–6,
    59–60
  minorities, 62–3
  parliament, 58–60
  political parties, 50–3: Alliance of
    Free Democrats (SzDSz), 52, 53,
    54, 55, 58, 62, 63, 65, 171;
    Communist Party (MSzMP) of,
    48, 53, 54, 55, 56, 57, 66, 167,
    171, 172, 183; FIDESZ, 52, 53,
    55, 58, 62, 63, 65, 186;
    Hungarian Democratic Forum
    (MDF), 50, 51–2, 55, 63, 65,
    183; Hungarian Socialist Party
    (MSzP), 62, 63, 64; Smallholders
    (FKgP), 50, 53, 55, 65, 65;
    Justice and Life Party (MIEP),
    66
  Round Table, 48, 51–61, 167
  thresholds, 57, 58, 60, 61, 63, 64,
    66

Iliescu, Ion, 91, 93, 95, 97, 106, 167

Kitschelt, Herbert, 15
Klaus, Václav, 79, 80, 81, 84, 87, 176
Kravchuk, Leonid, 147, 168
Kuchma, Leonid , 154, 156, 158, 160,
    161, 178
Kwaśniewski, Aleksander, 32, 44, 45

Legitimacy, 46, 93, 106, 110, 118, 123,
    135, 172
Lijphart, Arend, 7–8, 26

Massicote, Louis, 10
Mazowiecki, Tadeusz, 5, 30, 34
Mečiar, Vladimír, 74, 75, 76, 77, 78,
    79, 82, 87, 176
Minorities, 12, 14, 28, 39, 45, 60,
    62–3, 91–2, 94, 95, 100
Mladenov, Petur, 113, 114, 173
Moroz, Oleksandr, 150, 154
Moser, Robert, 134, 141, 142

Olechowski, Andrzej, 25, 44
Olszewski, Jan, 30–1
Orbán, Viktor, 52

Pithart, Petr, 69
Plyushch, Ivan, 148, 149
Poland, 12, 15, 25–47, 57, 116, 119,
    132, 139, 143, 154, 155, 164, 165,
    166, 168, 169, 170, 172, 173, 174,
    177, 179, 180, 181, 182, 183, 186
    candidature, 26, 32, 40–1, 46
    constitution, 25, 26, 32, 36, 39, 41
    elections: of 1989, 28–30, 45; of
        1991, 30, 37; of 1993, 31, 46; of
        1997, 32; of 2001, 45
    electoral law: 27; of 1989, 28–9, 45;
        of 1991, 27, 34–38, 46; of 1993,
        38–41; of 2001, 41–5; changes,
        summary of, 27
    finance, 32, 43–4, 45
    majoritarianism, 26, 28–9, 33, 44,
        47
    minorities, 28, 39
    mixed system, proposals for, 35, 36,
        37, 38–9, 46
    open list, 26, 28, 36, 42, 177
    political parties, 30–4, 39–47;
        Alliance of the Democratic Left
        (SLD), 30, 31, 32, 33, 42, 44, 46;
        Christian National Union
        (ZChN), 38; Civic Platform
        (PO), 25, 44, 45; Communist
        Party (PZPR) of, 25, 28–30, 33,
        45; Democratic Union (UD), 30,
        31, 33, 34, 36, 37, 38, 39, 171;
        Freedom Union (UW), 32, 42,
        43, 45, 47; Labour Union (UP),
        31, 32; Polish Peasant Party
        (PSL), 31, 34, 35, 42, 46, 47,
        183; Self-Defence (SO), 45, 170;
        Social Democracy of the
        Republic of Poland (SdRP), 34,
        46, 183; Solidarity Election
        Action (AWS), 32, 33, 34, 42,
        44, 45, 47
    proportional repesentation, 26, 27,
        33, 35, 36, 37, 38, 39, 46
    quotas (women's), 42, 45
    Round Table, 25, 28, 167

Senate, 25, 26, 29, 30, 33, 37, 45,
    178
Solidarity, 25, 28–30, 34, 37, 38,
    45–6, 172, 185, 186
State Election Commission, 33
thresholds, 26, 27, 28, 31, 32, 33,
    35, 36, 38, 39–40, 42, 43, 45, 46
Pozsgay, Imre, 50, 54
Preference voting (*see* Czechoslovakia,
    Slovakia)
Presidents, 15
Proportional representation (*see*
    electoral system, proportional
    representation; *individual
    countries*)
Public opinion, 16, 38, 71, 108, 144,
    146, 151, 157, 177, 184
Putin, Vladimir, 140, 141

Representation, 3–5, 11, 14, 35, 38,
    43, 55, 59–60, 66, 102–3, 104,
    105, 131, 164
Rokkan, Stein, 17
Roman, Petre, 97, 107
Romania, 11, 12, 90–108, 164, 165,
    166, 167, 171, 172, 173, 174,
    175–6, 178, 179, 183, 185, 186
    Council of the National Salvation
        Front, 91, 92, 93, 94, 95, 106,
        107, 167
    elections: of 1990, 95; of 1996, 101;
        of 2000, 103
    electoral law: of 1990, 90–1; of
        1992, 96; Decree of 2000, 102;
        summary of changes, 90
    finance, 93–4, 99
    majoritarianism, support for, 90–2,
        102–5
    minorities, 91–2, 94, 95, 99–100
    political parties: Democratic
        Convention (CDR), 97, 98, 100,
        101, 103; Democratic Union of
        Hungarians in Romania
        (UDMR), 93, 97, 98, 99, 100,
        101, 103, 104, 105; Greater
        Romania Party, 99, 103, 107;
        Liberal Party (PNL), 92, 97, 98,
        99, 100, 101, 102–3; National
        Salvation Front (FSN, FDSN,

Romania – *continued*
  political parties – *continued*
    PDSR, PSD), 94, 95, 97, 98, 99,
      100, 101, 103, 104, 105, 106,
      107, 167, 171; Party of
      Romanian National Unity
      (PUNR), 97, 98, 99, 101; Peasant
      Party (PNŢCD), 92, 98, 99, 104
  Provisional Council of National
    Union, 92, 94, 95, 167
  Senate, 93, 95, 97, 103, 104, 178
  thresholds, 90, 98, 101, 102
Round Table (*see also* Bulgaria,
  Czechoslovakia, Hungary,
  Poland), 8–9, 15, 166–7
Russia, 7, 128–42, 143, 147, 153, 164,
  165, 166, 167, 169, 170, 173, 174,
  175, 178, 179, 180, 182, 183, 184,
  185
  candidature, 129, 136, 138, 140–1
  Central Election Commission, 139,
    141
  Constitutional Court, 139–40
  Federation Council, 138
  elections: of 1990, 128–31; of 1993,
    128, 132, 136–7, 147; of 1999,
    140
  electoral law: (decree) of 1993,
    132–37, 140, 141; of 1995,
    137–40; of 1999, 140
  political parties, 133, 134–5, 136,
    138, 140; Communist Party
    (KPRF), 134, 136, 137, 138, 139,
    140; Fatherland-All Russia
    Movement, 141; Liberal
    Democratic Party, 136, 137,
    138; Our Home is Russia, 137,
    139; Russia's Choice, 136, 137,
    138; Unity, 141
  Proportional representation,
    support for, 138
  thresholds, 135, 137, 138, 139, 140

Sheinis, Viktor, 132–33
Shugart, Matthew, 10, 19, 68
Slovakia, 70, 71, 75–9, 80, 87, 164,
  165, 166, 173, 174, 176, 178, 179,
  181, 183
  Constitutional Court, 77

disproportionality in, 77
electoral laws, summary of, 79
elections: of 1994, 75; of 1998, 77
majoritarianism, support for; 75
political parties in, 75, 76, 77:
  Association of Slovak Workers
  (ZRS), 75, 76; Movement for
  Democratic Slovakia (HZDS),
  74, 75, 76, 77, 78, 88, 176;
  Slovak Democratic Coalition
  (SDK), 77, 78, 83; Slovak
  National Party (SNS), 75
preference voting, 75, 76, 78
Stoyanov, Petur, 124
Suchocka, Hanna, 31, 41

Thames, Frank, 134, 142
Thresholds (*see also individual countries*),
  10, 12, 21, 22, 173, 174, 177
Tölgyessy, Péter, 54, 58

Ukraine, 7, 143–63, 164, 165, 166,
  167, 168, 169, 171, 172, 173, 174,
  175, 178, 180, 181, 182, 185, 186
  candidature, 144, 145, 149–50, 151,
    152, 155, 156
  Central Election Commission, 150,
    151, 154, 155, 156, 159
  Constitution, 152–3, 154, 155, 158,
    160
  Constitutional Court, 157, 159
  elections, 144; of 1990, 144, 146; of
    1994, 144, 146, 147, 151–2,
    153; of 1998, 153, 155, 157–8;
    of 2002, 160
  electoral laws: of 1990, 144, 146; of
    1993, 144, 148–52, 155, 156; of
    1997, 144, 153, 154–7, 159; of
    2001, 144, 158–62; summary of,
    144
  finance, 150, 155
  nomination, *see* candidature
  political parties, 143, 146–8, 151,
    153, 158–63; Communist Party,
    147, 148, 152, 153, 155, 159,
    161, 185; Party of Democratic
    Rebirth, 147, 148; *Rukh*, 146,
    147, 148, 152, 156; Socialist
    Party, 150, 152, 153, 156, 161

Ukraine – *continued*
  presidency (*see also* Leonid
    Kuchma, Leonid Kravchuk),
    158–61
  proportional representation,
    support for, 147–8, 153–4, 158,
    159–60
  thresholds, 156
  turnout requirement, 151
USSR, 2, 4, 6, 10, 11, 118, 128–31,
  144, 146, 147, 167
  Communist Party, 6, 7, 128–9, 131,
    162
  Congress of People's Deputies, 5, 6,
    128–9, 130, 131, 144, 146

Constituent Assembly, 1917, 4, 10
  elections in, 4, 6–7, 128–31, 167

Vavroušek, Josef, 68–9, 70

Wałęsa, Lech, 30, 32, 34, 36, 37–8, 46,
  169, 170

Yeltsin, Boris, 128, 131, 133, 134, 135,
  137, 138, 139, 141, 147, 168

Zeman, Miloš, 81, 83
Zhelev, Zhelyu, 119, 120, 122, 173
Zhirinovskii, Vladimir, 136, 137, 170
Zhivkov, Todor, 112–13